ELEMENTS OF

Literature

FOURTH COURSE

The Holt Reader: An Interactive WorkText

Instruction in Reading Literature and Informational Materials

Standardized Test Practice

HOLT, RINEHART AND WINSTON

A Harcourt Education Company

Austin • Orlando • Chicago • New York • Toronto • London • San Diego

CREDITS

Supervisory Editors: Juliana Koenig, Fannie Safier

Managing Editor: Mike Topp

Administrative Managing Editor: Michael Neibergall

Senior Product Manager: Don Wulbrecht

Editors: Terence J. Fitzgerald, Sari Wilson, Carroll Moulton

Copyediting Supervisor: Mary Malone

Copyeditors: Elizabeth Dickson, *Senior Copyeditor;* Christine Altgelt, Joel Bourgeois, Emily Force, Julie A. Hill, Julia Thomas Hu, Jennifer Kirkland, Millicent Ondras, Dennis Scharnberg

Project Administration: Elizabeth LaManna

Editorial Support: Bret Isaacs, Brian Kachmar, Mark Koenig, Erik Netcher

Editorial Permissions: Ann B. Farrar, Carrie Jones, David Smith

Design: Bruce Bond, *Design Director, Book Design*

Electronic Publishing: Nanda Patel, JoAnn Stringer, *Project Coordinators;* Sally Dewhirst, *Quality Control Team Leader;* Angela Priddy, Barry Bishop, Becky Golden-Harrell, Ellen Rees, *Quality Control;* Juan Baquera, *Electronic Publishing Technology Services Team Leader;* Christopher Lucas, *Team Leader;* Lana Kaupp, Kim Orne, Susan Savkov; *Senior Production Artists;* Ellen Kennedy, Patricia Zepeda, *Production Artists;* Heather Jernt, *Electronic Publishing Supervisor;* Robert Franklin, *Electronic Publishing Director*

Production/Manufacturing: Belinda Barbosa Lopez, Michael Roche, *Senior Production Coordinators;* Carol Trammel, *Production Manager;* Beth Prevelige, *Senior Production Manager*

Contents

PART 1 Reading Literature

PART 2 Reading Informational Materials

PART 3 Standardized Test Practice

Literature

Informational Materials

Skills Table of Contents

Literary Skills

Informational Reading Skills

Vocabulary Skills

To the Student

A Book for You

Imagine this: a book full of stories you want to read and informational articles that are really interesting. Make it a book that actually tells you to write in it, circling, underlining, jotting down responses. Fill it with graphic organizers that encourage you to think a different way. Make it a size that's easy to carry around. That's *The Holt Reader: An Interactive WorkText*—a book created especially for you.

The Holt Reader: An Interactive WorkText is designed to accompany *Elements of Literature*. Like *Elements of Literature,* it's designed to help you interact with the literature and informational materials you read. The chart below shows you what's in your book and how the book is organized.

PART 1 Reading Literature	PART 2 Reading Informational Materials	PART 3 Standardized Test Practice
Literary selections from *Elements of Literature*	Informational texts topically or thematically linked to literary selections	Standardized test practice in literature and informational reading

Learning to Read Literary and Informational Materials

When you read informational materials like a social studies textbook or a newspaper article, you usually read to get the facts. You read mainly to get information that is stated directly on the page. When you read literature, you need to go beyond understanding what the words mean and getting the facts straight. You need to read between the lines of a poem or story to discover the writer's meaning. No matter what kind of reading you do—literary or informational—*The Holt Reader: An Interactive WorkText* will help you practice the skills and strategies you need to become an active and successful reader.

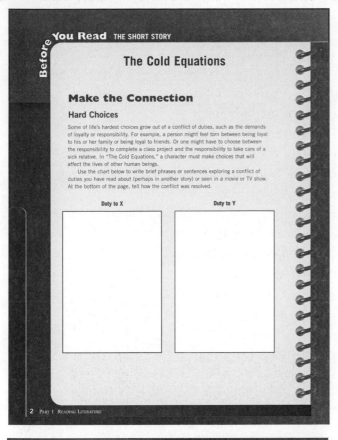

Setting the Stage: Before You Read

In Part 1, the Before-You-Read activity helps you make a personal connection with the selection you are about to read. It helps you sharpen your awareness of what you already know by asking you to think and write about a topic before you read. The more you know about the topic of a text, of course, the easier it is to understand the text. Sometimes this page will provide background information you need to know before you read the text.

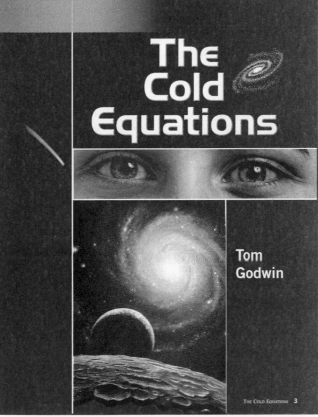

Interactive Selections from *Elements of Literature*

The literary selections in Part 1 are many of the same selections that appear in *Elements of Literature*, Fourth Course. The selections are reprinted in a single column and in larger type to give you the room you need to mark up the text.

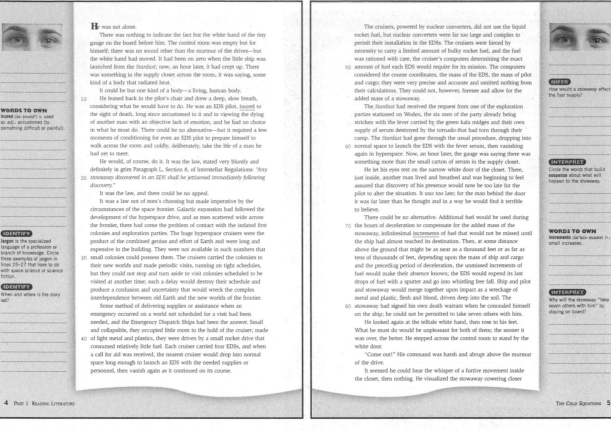

Strategies to Guide Your Reading: Side Notes

Notes in the side column accompany each selection. They guide your interaction with the text and help you unlock meaning. Many notes ask you to circle or underline in the text itself. Others provide lines on which you can write. Here are the kinds of notes you will work with as you read the selections: identify, retell, infer, predict, interpret, evaluate, visualize, and build fluency.

Identify asks you to find information (like the name of a character or a description of the setting) that is stated directly in the text. You will often be asked to circle or underline the information in the text.

Retell asks you to restate or explain in your own words something that appears in the text.

Infer asks you to make an **inference,** or an educated guess. You make inferences on the basis of clues writers give you and on experiences from your own life. When you make an inference, you read between the lines to figure out what the writer suggests but does not say directly.

Predict asks you to figure out what will happen next. Making predictions as you read helps you think about and understand what you are reading. To make predictions, look for clues that the writer gives you. Connect those clues with other things you've read, as well as your own experience. You'll probably find yourself adjusting predictions as you read.

Interpret asks you to explain the meaning of something. When you make an interpretation of a character, for example, you look at what the character says or does, and then you think about what the character's words and actions mean. You ask yourself why the character said those words and did those things. Your answer is the interpretation. Interpretations help you get at the main idea of a selection, the discovery about life you take away from it.

Evaluate asks you to form opinions about what you read. For example, you might see the following note at the end of a story: "How satisfying is the ending of this story? Give two reasons for your answer."

Visualize asks you to picture the characters, settings, and events being described in a selection. As you read, look for details that help you make a mental picture. Think of visualizing as making your own mental movie of a selection.

Build Fluency asks you to read aloud a poem or passages from a story. It lets you practice phrasing, expression, and reading in meaningful chunks. Sometimes hearing text read aloud makes the text easier to understand.

Words to Own lists words for you to learn and own. These words are underlined in the selection, letting you see the words in context. The words are defined for you right there in the side column.

The Cold Equations

Suspense

Suspense is a feeling of tension or anxious curiosity about what is going to happen next in a story. Writers may use several techniques to create suspense. These techniques include withholding information or using the setting or the dialogue to build a tense mood or atmosphere.

Explore suspense in "The Cold Equations" by completing the chart below. On the left are listed some passages from the story. Re-read each passage in context. Then use the right-hand column to indicate what questions each passage plants in the reader's mind.

Story Passages	Suspenseful Questions
1. There was something in the supply closet across the room, it was saying, some kind of a body that radiated heat. (page 4)	
2. "I know how you feel but I'm powerless to help you. You'll have to go through with it. I'll have you connected with Ship's Records." (page 9)	
3. "Gerry? He and two others went out in the helicopter this morning and aren't back yet. It's almost sundown, though, and he ought to be back right away—in less than an hour at the most." (page 17)	
4. She stepped into the air lock and turned to face him, only the pulse in her throat to betray the wild beating of her heart. (page 23)	

THE COLD EQUATIONS **25**

After You Read: Graphic Organizers

After each selection, **graphic organizers** give you a visual way to organize, interpret, and understand the reading or literary focus of the selection. You might be asked to chart the main events of the plot or complete a cause-and-effect chain.

In addition, you will find graphic organizers for use with different genres. These appear under the head **Graphic Organizers for Reading Strategies.**

The Cold Equations

Vocabulary: How to Own a Word

Word Maps

Create a word map for each Word to Own. Provide a synonym, an antonym, and the connotation for each word. Also provide the dictionary definition, and write a sentence using the word correctly. Be sure that the sentence you write reflects the connotation of the word. An example has been partially completed for you.

Word Bank
inured
increments
recoiled
paramount
annihilate
irrevocable
immutable
ponderous
apprehension
ineffably

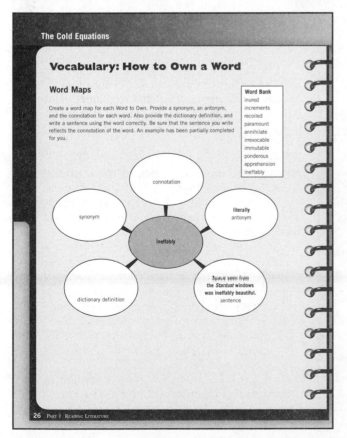

connotation

synonym

literally
antonym

ineffably

dictionary definition

Space seen from the *Stardust* windows was ineffably beautiful.
sentence

After You Read: Vocabulary: How to Own a Word

Vocabulary: How to Own a Word worksheets at the end of literary selections check your knowledge of the Words to Own and develop skills for vocabulary building.

A Walk Through) PART 2 Reading Informational Materials

Focus on Skills: Before You Read

The Before-You-Read page in Part 2 teaches skills and strategies you'll need to read informational materials like textbooks, newspaper and magazine articles, and instructional manuals. You'll learn how to recognize text structure, find the main idea, and determine an author's perspective or point of view on these Before-You-Read pages.

Interactive Informational Texts

The informational texts in Part 2 are linked by theme or by topic to the literature selections that appear in *Elements of Literature,* Fourth Course, and *The Holt Reader: An Interactive WorkText,* Fourth Course. The informational selections are printed in a single column and in larger type to give you the room you need to mark up the text.

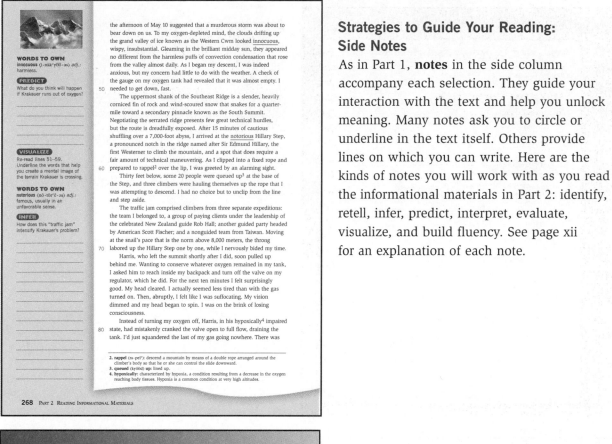

WORDS TO OWN
innocuous (ĭ-năk′yōō-əs) *adj.*: harmless.

PREDICT
What do you think will happen if Krakauer runs out of oxygen?

VISUALIZE
Re-read lines 51–59. Underline the words that help you create a mental image of the terrain Krakauer is crossing.

WORDS TO OWN
notorious (nō-tôr′ē-əs) *adj.*: famous, usually in an unfavorable sense.

INFER
How does this "traffic jam" intensify Krakauer's problem?

the afternoon of May 10 suggested that a murderous storm was about to bear down on us. To my oxygen-depleted mind, the clouds drifting up the grand valley of ice known as the Western Cwm looked innocuous, wispy, insubstantial. Gleaming in the brilliant midday sun, they appeared no different from the harmless puffs of convection condensation that rose from the valley almost daily. As I began my descent, I was indeed anxious, but my concern had little to do with the weather. A check of the gauge on my oxygen tank had revealed that it was almost empty. I needed to get down, fast.

The uppermost shank of the Southeast Ridge is a slender, heavily corniced fin of rock and wind-scoured snow that snakes for a quarter-mile toward a secondary pinnacle known as the South Summit. Negotiating the serrated ridge presents few great technical hurdles, but the route is dreadfully exposed. After 15 minutes of cautious shuffling over a 7,000-foot abyss, I arrived at the notorious Hillary Step, a pronounced notch in the ridge named after Sir Edmund Hillary, the first Westerner to climb the mountain, and a spot that does require a fair amount of technical maneuvering. As I clipped into a fixed rope and prepared to rappel[2] over the lip, I was greeted by an alarming sight.

Thirty feet below, some 20 people were queued up[3] at the base of the Step, and three climbers were hauling themselves up the rope that I was attempting to descend. I had no choice but to unclip from the line and step aside.

The traffic jam comprised climbers from three separate expeditions: the team I belonged to, a group of paying clients under the leadership of the celebrated New Zealand guide Rob Hall; another guided party headed by American Scott Fischer; and a nonguided team from Taiwan. Moving at the snail's pace that is the norm above 8,000 meters, the throng labored up the Hillary Step one by one, while I nervously bided my time.

Harris, who left the summit shortly after I did, soon pulled up behind me. Wanting to conserve whatever oxygen remained in my tank, I asked him to reach inside my backpack and turn off the valve on my regulator, which he did. For the next ten minutes I felt surprisingly good. My head cleared. I actually seemed less tired than with the gas turned on. Then, abruptly, I felt like I was suffocating. My vision dimmed and my head began to spin. I was on the brink of losing consciousness.

Instead of turning my oxygen off, Harris, in his hypoxically[4] impaired state, had mistakenly cranked the valve open to full flow, draining the tank. I'd just squandered the last of my gas going nowhere. There was

2. **rappel** (ră-pĕl′): descend a mountain by means of a double rope arranged around the climber's body so that he or she can control the slide downward.
3. **queued** (kyōōd) **up:** lined up.
4. **hypoxically:** characterized by hypoxia, a condition resulting from a decrease in the oxygen reaching body tissues. Hypoxia is a common condition at very high altitudes.

Strategies to Guide Your Reading: Side Notes

As in Part 1, **notes** in the side column accompany each selection. They guide your interaction with the text and help you unlock meaning. Many notes ask you to circle or underline in the text itself. Others provide lines on which you can write. Here are the kinds of notes you will work with as you read the informational materials in Part 2: identify, retell, infer, predict, interpret, evaluate, visualize, and build fluency. See page xii for an explanation of each note.

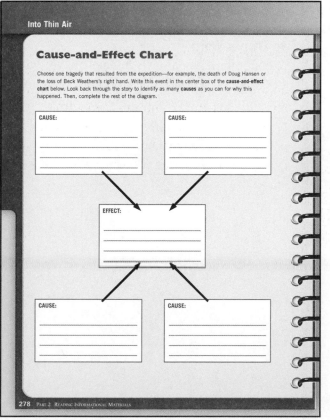

Into Thin Air

Cause-and-Effect Chart

Choose one tragedy that resulted from the expedition—for example, the death of Doug Hansen or the loss of Beck Weathers's right hand. Write this event in the center box of the **cause-and-effect chart** below. Look back through the story to identify as many **causes** as you can for why this happened. Then, complete the rest of the diagram.

CAUSE:

CAUSE:

EFFECT:

CAUSE:

CAUSE:

After You Read: Graphic Organizers

After each selection, a **graphic organizer** gives you a visual way to organize, interpret, and understand the selection. These organizers focus on the strategy introduced on the Before-You-Read page. You might be asked to collect supporting details that point to a main idea or to complete a comparison chart.

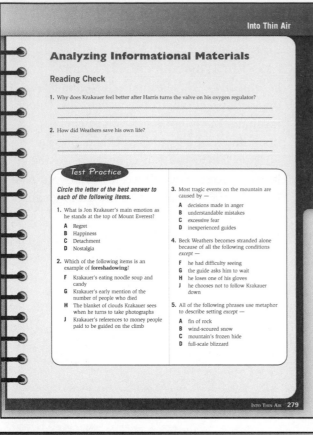

Into Thin Air

Analyzing Informational Materials

Reading Check

1. Why does Krakauer feel better after Harris turns the valve on his oxygen regulator?

_____

2. How did Weathers save his own life?

_____

Test Practice

Circle the letter of the best answer to each of the following items.

1. What is Jon Krakauer's main emotion as he stands at the top of Mount Everest?

   A Regret
   B Happiness
   C Detachment
   D Nostalgia

2. Which of the following items is an example of **foreshadowing**?

   F Krakauer's eating noodle soup and candy
   G Krakauer's early mention of the number of people who died
   H The blanket of clouds Krakauer sees when he turns to take photographs
   J Krakauer's references to money people paid to be guided on the climb

3. Most tragic events on the mountain are caused by —

   A decisions made in anger
   B understandable mistakes
   C excessive fear
   D inexperienced guides

4. Beck Weathers becomes stranded alone because of all the following conditions *except* —

   F he had difficulty seeing
   G the guide asks him to wait
   H he loses one of his gloves
   J he chooses not to follow Krakauer down

5. All of the following phrases use metaphor to describe setting *except* —

   A fin of rock
   B wind-scoured snow
   C mountain's frozen hide
   D full-scale blizzard

INTO THIN AIR 279

After You Read: Reading Check and Test Practice

Reading Check and **Test Practice** worksheets at the end of informational selections check your understanding of the selection with multiple-choice questions. The multiple-choice questions are similar to the ones you'll answer on state and national standardized tests.

Into Thin Air

Vocabulary: How to Own a Word

Analogies: Parallel Word Pairs

In an **analogy**, the words in one pair relate to each other in the same way as the words in a second pair. Fill in each blank below with the word from the Word Bank that best completes the analogy. (Two words on the list are synonyms and may be used interchangeably.)

Word Bank
deteriorate
innocuous
notorious
benign
apex
crucial
speculate
traverse
jeopardize
tenuous

1. base : bottom : : _____ : top.

2. safe : dangerous : : _____ : harmful.

3. mislead : deceive : : _____ : endanger.

4. trivial : minor : : _____ : important.

5. try : attempt : : _____ : guess.

6. minor : major : : _____ : malignant.

7. famous : star : : _____ : criminal.

8. weaken : strengthen : : _____ : improve.

9. climb : stairs : : _____ : bridge.

10. strong : powerful : : _____ : weak.

280 PART 2 READING INFORMATIONAL MATERIALS

After You Read: Vocabulary: How to Own a Word

When informational texts in Part 2 have Words to Own, you will practice your understanding of the words in exercises like the one shown here.

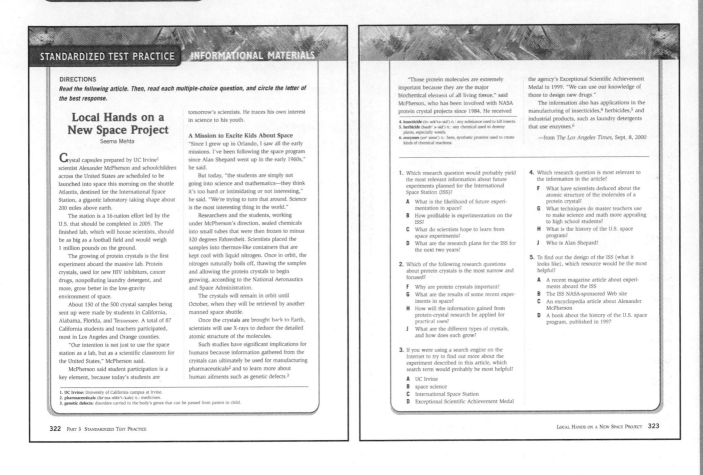

The last part of this book gives you practice in reading and responding to the kinds of literary and informational selections you read in Parts 1 and 2. The selections and multiple-choice questions are similar to the ones you'll see on state and national standardized tests.

PART 1 READING LITERATURE

The Cold Equations

Make the Connection

Hard Choices

Some of life's hardest choices grow out of a conflict of duties, such as the demands of loyalty or responsibility. For example, a person might feel torn between being loyal to his or her family or being loyal to friends. Or one might have to choose between the responsibility to complete a class project and the responsibility to take care of a sick relative. In "The Cold Equations," a character must make choices that will affect the lives of other human beings.

Use the chart below to write brief phrases or sentences exploring a conflict of duties you have read about (perhaps in another story) or seen in a movie or TV show. At the bottom of the page, tell how the conflict was resolved.

Duty to X	Duty to Y

The Cold Equations

Tom
Godwin

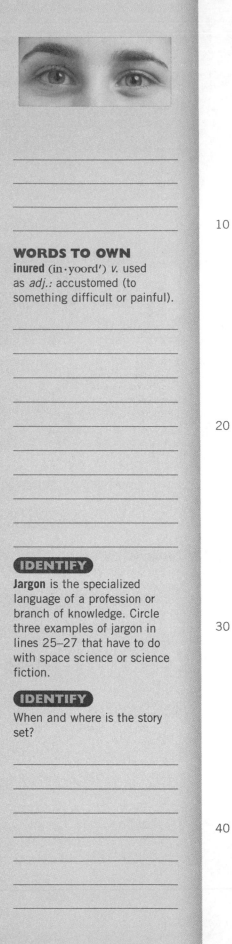

IDENTIFY

Jargon is the specialized
language of a profession or
branch of knowledge. Circle
three examples of jargon in
lines 25–27 that have to do
with space science or science
fiction.

IDENTIFY

When and where is the story
set?

He was not alone.

There was nothing to indicate the fact but the white hand of the tiny gauge on the board before him. The control room was empty but for himself; there was no sound other than the murmur of the drives—but the white hand had moved. It had been on zero when the little ship was launched from the *Stardust*; now, an hour later, it had crept up. There was something in the supply closet across the room, it was saying, some kind of a body that radiated heat.

It could be but one kind of a body—a living, human body.

10   He leaned back in the pilot's chair and drew a deep, slow breath, considering what he would have to do. He was an EDS pilot, <u>inured</u> to the sight of death, long since accustomed to it and to viewing the dying of another man with an objective lack of emotion, and he had no choice in what he must do. There could be no alternative—but it required a few moments of conditioning for even an EDS pilot to prepare himself to walk across the room and coldly, deliberately, take the life of a man he had yet to meet.

He would, of course, do it. It was the law, stated very bluntly and definitely in grim Paragraph L, Section 8, of Interstellar Regulations: *"Any*
20   *stowaway discovered in an EDS shall be jettisoned immediately following discovery."*

It was the law, and there could be no appeal.

It was a law not of men's choosing but made imperative by the circumstances of the space frontier. Galactic expansion had followed the development of the hyperspace drive, and as men scattered wide across the frontier, there had come the problem of contact with the isolated first colonies and exploration parties. The huge hyperspace cruisers were the product of the combined genius and effort of Earth and were long and expensive in the building. They were not available in such numbers that
30   small colonies could possess them. The cruisers carried the colonists to their new worlds and made periodic visits, running on tight schedules, but they could not stop and turn aside to visit colonies scheduled to be visited at another time; such a delay would destroy their schedule and produce a confusion and uncertainty that would wreck the complex interdependence between old Earth and the new worlds of the frontier.

Some method of delivering supplies or assistance when an emergency occurred on a world not scheduled for a visit had been needed, and the Emergency Dispatch Ships had been the answer. Small and collapsible, they occupied little room in the hold of the cruiser; made
40   of light metal and plastics, they were driven by a small rocket drive that consumed relatively little fuel. Each cruiser carried four EDSs, and when a call for aid was received, the nearest cruiser would drop into normal space long enough to launch an EDS with the needed supplies or personnel, then vanish again as it continued on its course.

The cruisers, powered by nuclear converters, did not use the liquid rocket fuel, but nuclear converters were far too large and complex to permit their installation in the EDSs. The cruisers were forced by necessity to carry a limited amount of bulky rocket fuel, and the fuel was rationed with care, the cruiser's computers determining the exact amount of fuel each EDS would require for its mission. The computers considered the course coordinates, the mass of the EDS, the mass of pilot and cargo; they were very precise and accurate and omitted nothing from their calculations. They could not, however, foresee and allow for the added mass of a stowaway.

The *Stardust* had received the request from one of the exploration parties stationed on Woden, the six men of the party already being stricken with the fever carried by the green kala midges and their own supply of serum destroyed by the tornado that had torn through their camp. The *Stardust* had gone through the usual procedure, dropping into normal space to launch the EDS with the fever serum, then vanishing again in hyperspace. Now, an hour later, the gauge was saying there was something more than the small carton of serum in the supply closet.

He let his eyes rest on the narrow white door of the closet. There, just inside, another man lived and breathed and was beginning to feel assured that discovery of his presence would now be too late for the pilot to alter the situation. It *was* too late; for the man behind the door it was far later than he thought and in a way he would find it terrible to believe.

There could be no alternative. Additional fuel would be used during the hours of deceleration to compensate for the added mass of the stowaway, infinitesimal <u>increments</u> of fuel that would not be missed until the ship had almost reached its destination. Then, at some distance above the ground that might be as near as a thousand feet or as far as tens of thousands of feet, depending upon the mass of ship and cargo and the preceding period of deceleration, the unmissed increments of fuel would make their absence known; the EDS would expend its last drops of fuel with a sputter and go into whistling free fall. Ship and pilot and stowaway would merge together upon impact as a wreckage of metal and plastic, flesh and blood, driven deep into the soil. The stowaway had signed his own death warrant when he concealed himself on the ship; he could not be permitted to take seven others with him.

He looked again at the telltale white hand, then rose to his feet. What he must do would be unpleasant for both of them; the sooner it was over, the better. He stepped across the control room to stand by the white door.

"Come out!" His command was harsh and abrupt above the murmur of the drive.

It seemed he could hear the whisper of a furtive movement inside the closet, then nothing. He visualized the stowaway cowering closer

INFER
How would a stowaway affect the fuel supply?

INTERPRET
Circle the words that build **suspense** about what will happen to the stowaway.

WORDS TO OWN
increments (in′krə·mənts) *n.*: small increases.

INTERPRET
Why will the stowaway "take seven others with him" by staying on board?

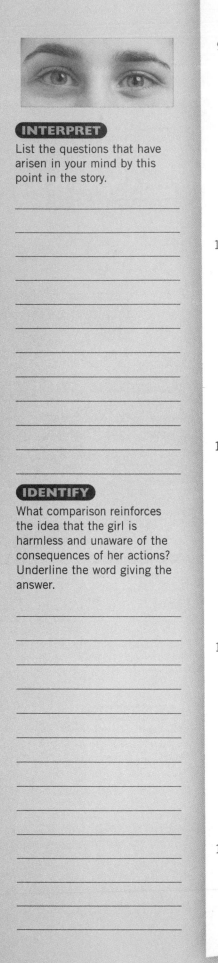

INTERPRET

List the questions that have arisen in your mind by this point in the story.

_____

_____

_____

_____

_____

_____

_____

_____

_____

_____

IDENTIFY

What comparison reinforces the idea that the girl is harmless and unaware of the consequences of her actions? Underline the word giving the answer.

_____

_____

_____

_____

_____

_____

_____

_____

_____

_____

_____

_____

90 into one corner, suddenly worried by the possible consequences of his act, his self-assurance evaporating.

"I said *out!*"

He heard the stowaway move to obey, and he waited with his eyes alert on the door and his hand near the blaster at his side.

The door opened and the stowaway stepped through it, smiling. "All right—I give up. Now what?"

It was a girl.

He stared without speaking, his hand dropping away from the blaster, and acceptance of what he saw coming like a heavy and

100 unexpected physical blow. The stowaway was not a man—she was a girl in her teens, standing before him in little white gypsy sandals, with the top of her brown, curly head hardly higher than his shoulder, with a faint, sweet scent of perfume coming from her, and her smiling face tilted up so her eyes could look unknowing and unafraid into his as she waited for his answer.

Now what? Had it been asked in the deep, defiant voice of a man, he would have answered it with action, quick and efficient. He would have taken the stowaway's identification disk and ordered him into the air lock. Had the stowaway refused to obey, he would have used the blaster.

110 It would not have taken long; within a minute the body would have been ejected into space—had the stowaway been a man.

He returned to the pilot's chair and motioned her to seat herself on the boxlike bulk of the drive-control units that were set against the wall beside him. She obeyed, his silence making the smile fade into the meek and guilty expression of a pup that has been caught in mischief and knows it must be punished.

"You still haven't told me," she said. "I'm guilty, so what happens to me now? Do I pay a fine, or what?"

"What are you doing here?" he asked. "Why did you stow away on

120 this EDS?"

"I wanted to see my brother. He's with the government survey crew on Woden and I haven't seen him for ten years, not since he left Earth to go into government survey work."

"What was your destination on the *Stardust*?"

"Mimir. I have a position waiting for me there. My brother has been sending money home all the time to us—my father and mother and me— and he paid for a special course in linguistics I was taking. I graduated sooner than expected and I was offered this job in Mimir. I knew it would be almost a year before Gerry's job was done on Woden so he could come

130 on to Mimir, and that's why I hid in the closet there. There was plenty of room for me and I was willing to pay the fine. There were only the two of us kids—Gerry and I—and I haven't seen him for so long, and I didn't want to wait another year when I could see him now, even though I knew I would be breaking some kind of a regulation when I did it."

I knew I would be breaking some kind of a regulation. In a way, she could not be blamed for her ignorance of the law; she was of Earth and had not realized that the laws of the space frontier must, of necessity, be as hard and relentless as the environment that gave them birth. Yet, to protect such as her from the results of their own ignorance of the
140 frontier, there had been a sign over the door that led to the section of the *Stardust* that housed the EDSs, a sign that was plain for all to see and heed: UNAUTHORIZED PERSONNEL KEEP OUT!

"Does your brother know that you took passage on the *Stardust* for Mimir?"

"Oh, yes. I sent him a spacegram telling him about my graduation and about going to Mimir on the *Stardust* a month before I left Earth. I already knew Mimir was where he would be stationed in a little over a year. He gets a promotion then, and he'll be based on Mimir and not have to stay out a year at a time on field trips, like he does now."

150 There were two different survey groups on Woden, and he asked, "What is his name?"

"Cross—Gerry Cross. He's in Group Two—that was the way his address read. Do you know him?"

Group One had requested the serum: Group Two was eight thousand miles away, across the Western Sea.

"No, I've never met him," he said, then turned to the control board and cut the deceleration to a fraction of a gravity, knowing as he did so that it could not avert the ultimate end, yet doing the only thing he could do to prolong that ultimate end. The sensation was like that of the ship
160 suddenly dropping, and the girl's involuntary movement of surprise half lifted her from her seat.

"We're going faster now, aren't we?" she asked. "Why are we doing that?"

He told her the truth. "To save fuel for a little while."

"You mean we don't have very much?"

He delayed the answer he must give her so soon to ask, "How did you manage to stow away?"

"I just sort of walked in when no one was looking my way," she said. "I was practicing my Gelanese on the native girl who does the
170 cleaning in the Ship's Supply office when someone came in with an order for supplies for the survey crew on Woden. I slipped into the closet there after the ship was ready to go just before you came in. It was an impulse of the moment to stow away, so I could get to see Gerry—and from the way you keep looking at me so grim, I'm not sure it was a very wise impulse. But I'll be a model criminal—or do I mean prisoner?" She smiled at him again. "I intended to pay for my keep on top of paying the fine. I can cook and I can patch clothes for everyone and I know how to do all kinds of useful things, even a little bit about nursing."

INFER

Why is the girl ignorant of the penalty for stowing away?

_____

_____

_____

_____

_____

_____

_____

_____

_____

_____

_____

_____

_____

_____

_____

_____

_____

_____

BUILD FLUENCY

Imagine that you are the stowaway. Read lines 168–178, using an appropriate tone, volume, rate, and emphasis.

_____

_____

_____

INTERPRET

What **conflict** is posed now for the EDS pilot?

There was one more question to ask:

180 "Did you know what the supplies were that the survey crew ordered?"

"Why, no. Equipment they needed in their work, I supposed."

Why couldn't she have been a man with some ulterior motive? A fugitive from justice hoping to lose himself on a raw new world; an opportunist seeking transportation to the new colonies where he might find golden fleece for the taking; a crackpot with a mission. Perhaps once in his lifetime an EDS pilot would find such a stowaway on his ship—warped men, mean and selfish men, brutal and dangerous men— but never before a smiling, blue-eyed girl who was willing to pay her

190 fine and work for her keep that she might see her brother.

He turned to the board and turned the switch that would signal the *Stardust*. The call would be futile, but he could not, until he had exhausted that one vain hope, seize her and thrust her into the air lock as he would an animal—or a man. The delay, in the meantime, would not be dangerous with the EDS decelerating at fractional gravity.

A voice spoke from the communicator. "*Stardust*. Identify yourself and proceed."

"Barton, EDS 34GII. Emergency. Give me Commander Delhart."

There was a faint confusion of noises as the request went through

200 the proper channels. The girl was watching him, no longer smiling.

"Are you going to order them to come back after me?" she asked.

The communicator clicked and there was the sound of a distant voice saying, "Commander, the EDS requests . . ."

"Are they coming back after me?" she asked again. "Won't I get to see my brother after all?"

"Barton?" The blunt, gruff voice of Commander Delhart came from the communicator. "What's this about an emergency?"

"A stowaway," he answered.

"A stowaway?" There was a slight surprise to the question. "That's

210 rather unusual—but why the 'emergency' call? You discovered him in time, so there should be no appreciable danger, and I presume you've informed Ship's Records so his nearest relatives can be notified."

"That's why I had to call you, first. The stowaway is still aboard and the circumstances are so different—"

"Different?" the commander interrupted, impatience in his voice. "How can they be different? You know you have a limited supply of fuel; you also know the law as well as I do: 'Any stowaway discovered in an EDS shall be jettisoned immediately following discovery.'"

There was the sound of a sharply indrawn breath from the girl.

220 *"What does he mean?"*

"The stowaway is a girl."

"What?"

"She wanted to see her brother. She's only a kid and she didn't know what she was really doing."

"I see." All the curtness was gone from the commander's voice. "So you called me in the hope I could do something?" Without waiting for an answer he went on, "I'm sorry—I can do nothing. This cruiser must maintain its schedule; the life of not one person but the lives of many depend on it. I know how you feel but I'm powerless to help you. You'll have to go through with it. I'll have you connected with Ship's Records."

The communicator faded to a faint rustle of sound, and he turned back to the girl. She was leaning forward on the bench, almost rigid, her eyes fixed wide and frightened.

> "What did he mean, to go through with it? To jettison me . . . to go through with it—what did he mean? Not the way it sounded . . . he couldn't have. What did he mean—what did he really mean?"
>
> Her time was too short for the comfort of a lie to be more than a cruelly fleeting delusion.
>
> "He meant it the way it sounded."
>
> *"No!"* She <u>recoiled</u> from him as though he had struck her, one hand half raised as though to fend him off and stark unwillingness to believe in her eyes.
>
> "It will have to be."
>
> "No! You're joking—you're insane! You can't mean it!"
>
> "I'm sorry." He spoke slowly to her, gently. "I should have told you before—I should have, but I had to do what I could first; I had to call the *Stardust.* You heard what the commander said."
>
> "But you can't—if you make me leave the ship, I'll *die.*"
>
> "I know."

She searched his face, and the unwillingness to believe left her eyes, giving way slowly to a look of dazed horror.

"You know?" She spoke the words far apart, numbly and wonderingly.

"I know. It has to be like that."

"You mean it—you really mean it." She sagged back against the wall, small and limp like a little rag doll, and all the protesting and disbelief gone. "You're going to do it—you're going to make me die?"

"I'm sorry," he said again. "You'll never know how sorry I am. It has to be that way and no human in the universe can change it."

"You're going to make me die and I didn't do anything to die for—I didn't *do* anything———"

He sighed, deep and weary. "I know you didn't, child. I know you didn't."

"EDS." The communicator rapped brisk and metallic. "This is Ship's Records. Give us all information on subject's identification disk."

EVALUATE

Are you surprised by how quickly the commander decides to jettison the stowaway? Should he have taken time to brainstorm possible ways to save her life?

WORDS TO OWN

recoiled (ri·koild´) *v.:* drew back in fear, surprise, or disgust.

BUILD FLUENCY

Read lines 234–249 aloud, using an appropriate tone for each character in the dialogue.

IDENTIFY/INTERPRET

In lines 255–268, what two comparisons does the author use to describe the girl's appearance? Underline the words giving the answer. What impressions do these **similes** convey?

He got out of his chair to stand over her. She clutched the edge of the seat, her upturned face white under the brown hair and the lipstick standing out like a blood-red cupid's bow.

"*Now?*"

270 "I want your identification disk," he said.

She released the edge of the seat and fumbled at the chain that suspended the plastic disk from her neck with fingers that were trembling and awkward. He reached down and unfastened the clasp for her, then returned with the disk to his chair.

"Here's your data, Records: Identification Number T837——"

"One moment," Records interrupted. "This is to be filed on the gray card, of course?"

"Yes."

"And the time of execution?"

280 "I'll tell you later."

"Later? This is highly irregular; the time of the subject's death is required before——"

He kept the thickness out of his voice with an effort. "Then we'll do it in a highly irregular manner—you'll hear the disk read first. The subject is a girl and she's listening to everything that's said. Are you capable of understanding that?"

There was a brief, almost shocked silence; then Records said meekly, "Sorry. Go ahead."

He began to read the disk, reading it slowly to delay the inevitable
290 for as long as possible, trying to help her by giving her what little time he could to recover from her first horror and let it resolve into the calm of acceptance and resignation.

"Number T8374 dash Y54. Name, Marilyn Lee Cross. Sex, female. Born July 7, 2160." *She was only eighteen.* "Height, five-three. Weight, a hundred and ten." *Such a slight weight, yet enough to add fatally to the mass of the shell-thin bubble that was an EDS.* "Hair, brown. Eyes, blue. Complexion, light. Blood type O." *Irrelevant data.* "Destination, Port City, Mimir." *Invalid data.*

He finished and said, "I'll call you later," then turned once again to
300 the girl. She was huddled back against the wall, watching him with a look of numb and wondering fascination.

"They're waiting for you to kill me, aren't they? They want me dead, don't they? You and everybody on the cruiser want me dead, don't you?" Then the numbness broke and her voice was that of a frightened and bewildered child. "Everybody wants me dead and I didn't *do* anything. I didn't hurt anyone—I only wanted to see my brother."

"It's not the way you think—it isn't that way at all," he said. "Nobody wants it this way; nobody would ever let it be this way if it was humanly possible to change it."

INTERPRET

In lines 294–298, why does the author use italics?

310 "Then why is it? I don't understand. Why is it?"

"This ship is carrying kala fever serum to Group One on Woden. Their own supply was destroyed by a tornado. Group Two—the crew your brother is in—is eight thousand miles away across the Western Sea, and their helicopters can't cross it to help Group One. The fever is invariably fatal unless the serum can be had in time, and the six men in Group One will die unless this ship reaches them on schedule. These little ships are always given barely enough fuel to reach their destination, and if you stay aboard, your added weight will cause it to use up all its fuel before it reaches the ground. It will crash then, and you and I will
320 die and so will the six men waiting for the fever serum."

It was a full minute before she spoke, and as she considered his words, the expression of numbness left her eyes.

"Is that it?" she asked at last. "Just that the ship doesn't have enough fuel?"

"Yes."

"I can go alone or I can take seven others with me—is that the way it is?"

"That's the way it is."

"And nobody wants me to have to die?"
330 "Nobody."

"Then maybe——— Are you sure nothing can be done about it? Wouldn't people help me if they could?"

"Everyone would like to help you, but there is nothing anyone can do. I did the only thing I could do when I called the *Stardust*."

"And it won't come back—but there might be other cruisers, mightn't there? Isn't there any hope at all that there might be someone, somewhere, who could do something to help me?"

She was leaning forward a little in her eagerness as she waited for his answer.
340 "No."

The word was like the drop of a cold stone and she again leaned back against the wall, the hope and eagerness leaving her face. "You're sure—you *know* you're sure?"

"I'm sure. There are no other cruisers within forty light-years; there is nothing and no one to change things."

She dropped her gaze to her lap and began twisting a pleat of her skirt between her fingers, saying no more as her mind began to adapt itself to the grim knowledge.

It was better so; with the going of all hope would go the fear; with
350 the going of all hope would come resignation. She needed time and she could have so little of it. How much?

The EDSs were not equipped with hull-cooling units; their speed had to be reduced to a moderate level before they entered the atmosphere.

PREDICT

Pause after line 310. What do you think will happen, and why?

_____

_____

_____

_____

_____

_____

_____

_____

_____

_____

_____

_____

_____

IDENTIFY

What word from the story's title is echoed in this comparison? Circle the word.

_____

_____

_____

_____

_____

_____

WORDS TO OWN
paramount (par′ə·mount′) *adj.:*
supreme; dominant.

IDENTIFY

What kind of time measurement
is represented by *seventeen
fifty?*

They were decelerating at .10 gravity, approaching their destination at a far higher speed than the computers had calculated on. The *Stardust* had been quite near Woden when she launched the EDS; their present velocity was putting them nearer by the second. There would be a critical point, soon to be reached, when he would have to resume deceleration. When he did so, the girl's weight would be multiplied
360 by the gravities of deceleration, would become, suddenly, a factor of <u>paramount</u> importance, the factor the computers had been ignorant of when they determined the amount of fuel the EDS should have. She would have to go when deceleration began; it could be no other way. When would that be—how long could he let her stay?

"How long can I stay?"

He winced involuntarily from the words that were so like an echo of his own thoughts. How long? He didn't know; he would have to ask the ship's computers. Each EDS was given a meager surplus of fuel to compensate for unfavorable conditions within the atmosphere, and
370 relatively little fuel was being consumed for the time being. The memory banks of the computers would still contain all data pertaining to the course set for the EDS; such data would not be erased until the EDS reached its destination. He had only to give the computers the new data—the girl's weight and the exact time at which he had reduced the deceleration to .10.

"Barton." Commander Delhart's voice came abruptly from the communicator as he opened his mouth to call the *Stardust*. "A check with Records shows me you haven't completed your report. Did you reduce the deceleration?"

So the commander knew what he was trying to do.

380 "I'm decelerating at point ten," he answered. "I cut the deceleration at seventeen fifty and the weight is a hundred and ten. I would like to stay at point ten as long as the computers say I can. Will you give them the question?"

It was contrary to regulations for an EDS pilot to make any changes in the course or degree of deceleration the computers had set for him, but the commander made no mention of the violation. Neither did he ask the reason for it. It was not necessary for him to ask; he had not become commander of an interstellar cruiser without both intelligence and an understanding of human nature. He said only, "I'll have that
390 given to the computers."

The communicator fell silent and he and the girl waited, neither of them speaking. They would not have to wait long; the computers would give the answer within moments of the asking. The new factors would be fed into the steel maw[1] of the first bank, and the electrical impulses would go through the complex circuits. Here and there a relay might click, a tiny cog turn over, but it would be essentially the electrical impulses

---

1. **maw:** huge, all-consuming mouth.

that found the answer; formless, mindless, invisible, determining with utter precision how long the pale girl beside him might live. Then five little segments of metal in the second bank would trip in rapid
400 succession against an inked ribbon and a second steel maw would spit out the slip of paper that bore the answer.

The chronometer on the instrument board read 18:10 when the commander spoke again.

"You will resume deceleration at nineteen ten."

She looked toward the chronometer, then quickly away from it. "Is that when . . . when I go?" she asked. He nodded and she dropped her eyes to her lap again.

"I'll have the course correction given to you," the commander said. "Ordinarily I would never permit anything like this, but I understand
410 your position. There is nothing I can do, other than what I've just done, and you will not deviate from these new instructions. You will complete your report at nineteen ten. Now—here are the course corrections."

The voice of some unknown technician read them to him, and he wrote them down on the pad clipped to the edge of the control board. There would, he saw, be periods of deceleration when he neared the atmosphere when the deceleration would be five gravities—and at five gravities, one hundred ten pounds would become five hundred fifty pounds.

The technician finished and he terminated the contact with a brief
420 acknowledgment. Then, hesitating a moment, he reached out and shut off the communicator. It was 18:13 and he would have nothing to report until 19:10. In the meantime, it somehow seemed indecent to permit others to hear what she might say in her last hour.

He began to check the instrument readings, going over them with unnecessary slowness. She would have to accept the circumstances, and there was nothing he could do to help her into acceptance; words of sympathy would only delay it.

It was 18:20 when she stirred from her motionlessness and spoke.

"So that's the way it has to be with me?"

430 He swung around to face her. "You understand now, don't you? No one would ever let it be like this if it could be changed."

"I understand," she said. Some of the color had returned to her face and the lipstick no longer stood out so vividly red. "There isn't enough fuel for me to stay. When I hid on this ship, I got into something I didn't know anything about and now I have to pay for it."

She had violated a man-made law that said KEEP OUT, but the penalty was not for men's making or desire and it was a penalty men could not revoke. A physical law had decreed: *h amount of fuel will power an EDS with a mass of m safely to its destination*; and a second physical law had
440 decreed: *h amount of fuel will not power an EDS with a mass of m plus x safely to its destination*.

INTERPRET

What view of technology is conveyed by lines 392–401? List your impressions.

_____

_____

_____

_____

_____

_____

_____

_____

_____

IDENTIFY

What will happen at 19:10?

_____

_____

_____

_____

INTERPRET

How do you think the mathematical formulas in lines 438–441 are related to the title of the story?

_____

_____

_____

_____

_____

_____

_____

EDSs obeyed only physical laws, and no amount of human sympathy for her could alter the second law.

"But I'm afraid. I don't want to die—not now. I want to live, and nobody is doing anything to help me; everybody is letting me go ahead and acting just like nothing was going to happen to me. I'm going to die and nobody *cares*."

"We all do," he said. "I do and the commander does and the clerk in Ship's Records; we all care and each of us did what little he could to 450 help you. It wasn't enough—it was almost nothing—but it was all we could do."

"Not enough fuel—I can understand that," she said, as though she had not heard his own words. "But to have to die for it. *Me* alone . . ."

How hard it must be for her to accept the fact. She had never known danger of death, had never known the environments where the lives of men could be as fragile and fleeting as sea foam tossed against a rocky shore. She belonged on gentle Earth, in that secure and peaceful society where she could be young and gay and laughing with the others of her kind, where life was precious and well guarded and there was always the 460 assurance that tomorrow would come. She belonged in that world of soft winds and a warm sun, music and moonlight and gracious manners, and not on the hard, bleak frontier.

"How did it happen to me so terribly quickly? An hour ago I was on the *Stardust*, going to Mimir. Now the *Stardust* is going on without me and I'm going to die and I'll never see Gerry and Mama and Daddy again—I'll never see anything again."

He hesitated, wondering how he could explain it to her so she would really understand and not feel she had somehow been the victim of a reasonlessly cruel injustice. She did not know what the frontier was like; 470 she thought in terms of safe, secure Earth. Pretty girls were not jettisoned on Earth; there was a law against it. On Earth her plight would have filled the newscasts and a fast black patrol ship would have been racing to her rescue. Everyone, everywhere, would have known of Marilyn Lee Cross, and no effort would have been spared to save her life. But this was not Earth and there were no patrol ships; only the *Stardust*, leaving them behind at many times the speed of light. There was no one to help her; there would be no Marilyn Lee Cross smiling from the newscasts tomorrow. Marilyn Lee Cross would be but a poignant memory for an EDS pilot and a name on a gray card in Ship's Records.

480 "It's different here; it's not like back on Earth," he said. "It isn't that no one cares; it's that no one can do anything to help. The frontier is big, and here along its rim the colonies and exploration parties are scattered so thin and far between. On Woden, for example, there are only sixteen men—sixteen men on an entire world. The exploration parties, the survey crews, the little first colonies—they're all fighting alien environments, trying to make a way for those who will follow after. The

RETELL

Briefly summarize the ideas expressed in lines 473–479.

environments fight back, and those who go first usually make mistakes only once. There is no margin of safety along the rim of the frontier; there can't be until the way is made for the others who will come later, until the new worlds are tamed and settled. Until then men will have to pay the penalty for making mistakes, with no one to help them, because there is no one *to* help them."

"I was going to Mimir," she said. "I didn't know about the frontier; I was only going to Mimir and *it's* safe."

"Mimir is safe, but you left the cruiser that was taking you there."

She was silent for a little while. "It was all so wonderful at first; there was plenty of room for me on this ship and I would be seeing Gerry so soon. I didn't know about the fuel, didn't know what would happen to me. . . ."

Her words trailed away, and he turned his attention to the viewscreen, not wanting to stare at her as she fought her way through the black horror of fear toward the calm gray of acceptance.

Woden was a ball, enshrouded in the blue haze of its atmosphere, swimming in space against the background of star-sprinkled dead blackness. The great mass of Manning's Continent sprawled like a gigantic hourglass in the Eastern Sea, with the western half of the Eastern Continent still visible. There was a thin line of shadow along the right-hand edge of the globe, and the Eastern Continent was disappearing into it as the planet turned on its axis. An hour before, the entire continent had been in view; now a thousand miles of it had gone into the thin edge of shadow and around to the night that lay on the other side of the world. The dark blue spot that was Lotus Lake was approaching the shadow. It was somewhere near the southern edge of the lake that Group Two had their camp. It would be night there soon, and quick behind the coming of night the rotation of Woden on its axis would put Group Two beyond the reach of the ship's radio.

He would have to tell her before it was too late for her to talk to her brother. In a way, it would be better for both of them should they not do so, but it was not for him to decide. To each of them the last words would be something to hold and cherish, something that would cut like the blade of a knife yet would be infinitely precious to remember, she for her own brief moments to live and he for the rest of his life.

He held down the button that would flash the grid lines on the viewscreen and used the known diameter of the planet to estimate the distance the southern tip of Lotus Lake had yet to go until it passed beyond radio range. It was approximately five hundred miles. Five hundred miles; thirty minutes—and the chronometer read 18:30. Allowing for error in estimating, it would not be later than 19:05 that the turning of Woden would cut off her brother's voice.

INTERPRET
List some parallels between frontier life in space and frontier life during the westward expansion of the United States.

_____

_____

_____

_____

_____

_____

VISUALIZE
What does an hourglass look like? Visualize the scene on Woden that Barton observes.

_____

_____

_____

_____

_____

_____

_____

IDENTIFY
What new uncertainties provide **suspense** at this point in the story?

_____

_____

_____

_____

_____

_____

_____

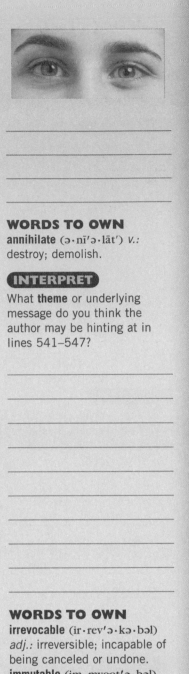

WORDS TO OWN
annihilate (ə·nī′ə·lāt′) *v.:*
destroy; demolish.

INTERPRET

What **theme** or underlying message do you think the author may be hinting at in lines 541–547?

_____

_____

_____

_____

_____

_____

_____

_____

WORDS TO OWN
irrevocable (ir·rev′ə·kə·bəl)
adj.: irreversible; incapable of
being canceled or undone.
immutable (im·myoot′ə·bəl)
adj.: unchangeable; never
changing or varying.
ponderous (pän′dər·əs) *adj.:*
heavy and slow-moving.

_____

_____

_____

_____

_____

530   The first border of the Western continent was already in sight along the left side of the world. Four thousand miles across it lay the shore of the Western Sea and the camp of Group One. It had been in the Western Sea that the tornado had originated, to strike with such fury at the camp and destroy half their prefabricated buildings, including the one that housed the medical supplies. Two days before, the tornado had not existed; it had been no more than great gentle masses of air over the calm Western Sea. Group One had gone about their routine survey work, unaware of the meeting of air masses out at sea, unaware of the force the union was spawning. It had struck their camp without warning—

540   a thundering, roaring destruction that sought to <u>annihilate</u> all that lay before it. It had passed on, leaving the wreckage in its wake. It had destroyed the labor of months and had doomed six men to die and then, as though its task was accomplished, it once more began to resolve into gentle masses of air. But, for all its deadliness, it had destroyed with neither malice nor intent. It had been a blind and mindless force, obeying the laws of nature, and it would have followed the same course with the same fury had men never existed.

Existence required order, and there was order; the laws of nature, <u>irrevocable</u> and <u>immutable</u>. Men could learn to use them, but men could

550   not change them. The circumference of a circle was always pi times the diameter, and no science of man would ever make it otherwise. The combination of chemical A with chemical B under condition C invariably produced reaction D. The law of gravitation was a rigid equation, and it made no distinction between the fall of a leaf and the <u>ponderous</u> circling of a binary star system. The nuclear conversion process powered the cruisers that carried men to the stars; the same process in the form of a nova would destroy a world with equal efficiency. The laws *were*, and the universe moved in obedience to them. Along the frontier were arrayed all the forces of nature, and sometimes they destroyed those who were

560   fighting their way outward from Earth. The men of the frontier had long ago learned the bitter futility of cursing the forces that would destroy them, for the forces were blind and deaf; the futility of looking to the heavens for mercy, for the stars of the galaxy swung in their long, long sweep of two hundred million years, as inexorably controlled as they by the laws that knew neither hatred nor compassion. The men of the frontier knew—but how was a girl from Earth to fully understand? *h amount of fuel will not power an EDS with a mass of m plus x safely to its destination.* To him and her brother and parents she was a sweet-faced girl in her teens; to the laws of nature she was *x*, the unwanted factor in a cold equation.

570   **S**he stirred again on the seat. "Could I write a letter? I want to write to Mama and Daddy. And I'd like to talk to Gerry. Could you let me talk to him over your radio there?"

"I'll try to get him," he said.

He switched on the normal-space transmitter and pressed the signal button. Someone answered the buzzer almost immediately.

"Hello. How's it going with you fellows now—is the EDS on its way?"

"This isn't Group One; this is the EDS," he said. "Is Gerry Cross there?"

580 "Gerry? He and two others went out in the helicopter this morning and aren't back yet. It's almost sundown, though, and he ought to be back right away—in less than an hour at the most."

"Can you connect me through to the radio in his copter?"

"Huh-uh. It's been out of commission for two months—some printed circuits went haywire and we can't get any more until the next cruiser stops by. Is it something important—bad news for him, or something?"

"Yes—it's very important. When he comes in, get him to the transmitter as soon as you possibly can."

"I'll do that; I'll have one of the boys waiting at the field with a
590 truck. Is there anything else I can do?"

"No, I guess that's all. Get him there as soon as you can and signal me."

He turned the volume to an inaudible minimum, an act that would not affect the functioning of the signal buzzer, and unclipped the pad of paper from the control board. He tore off the sheet containing his flight instructions and handed the pad to her, together with pencil.

"I'd better write to Gerry too," she said as she took them. "He might not get back to camp in time."

She began to write, her fingers still clumsy and uncertain in the way
600 they handled the pencil, and the top of it trembling a little as she poised it between words. He turned back to the viewscreen, to stare at it without seeing it.

She was a lonely little child trying to say her last goodbye, and she would lay out her heart to them. She would tell them how much she loved them and she would tell them to not feel bad about it, that it was only something that must happen eventually to everyone and she was not afraid. The last would be a lie and it would be there to read between the sprawling, uneven lines: a valiant little lie that would make the hurt all the greater for them.

610 Her brother was of the frontier and he would understand. He would not hate the EDS pilot for doing nothing to prevent her going; he would know there had been nothing the pilot could do. He would understand, though the understanding would not soften the shock and pain when he learned his sister was gone. But the others, her father and mother—they would not understand. They were of Earth and they would think in the manner of those who had never lived where the safety margin of life was a thin, thin line—and sometimes nothing at all. What would they think of the faceless, unknown pilot who had sent her to her death?

INTERPRET

How does the author draw out the **suspense** at this point in the story?

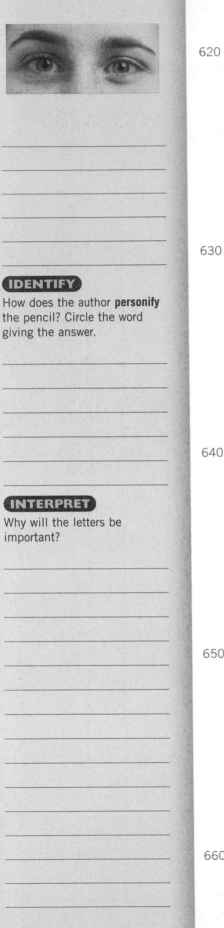

IDENTIFY

How does the author **personify** the pencil? Circle the word giving the answer.

INTERPRET

Why will the letters be important?

They would hate him with cold and terrible intensity, but it really
620 didn't matter. He would never see them, never know them. He would
have only the memories to remind him; only the nights of fear, when
a blue-eyed girl in gypsy sandals would come in his dreams to die
again. . . .

He scowled at the viewscreen and tried to force his thoughts into less
emotional channels. There was nothing he could do to help her. She had
unknowingly subjected herself to the penalty of a law that recognized
neither innocence nor youth nor beauty, that was incapable of sympathy
or leniency. Regret was illogical—and yet, could knowing it to be illogical
ever keep it away?

630 She stopped occasionally, as though trying to find the right words to
tell them what she wanted them to know; then the pencil would resume
its whispering to the paper. It was 18:37 when she folded the letter in a
square and wrote a name on it. She began writing another, twice looking
up at the chronometer, as though she feared the black hand might reach
its rendezvous before she had finished. It was 18:45 when she folded it
as she had done the first letter and wrote a name and address on it.

She held the letters out to him. "Will you take care of these and see
that they're enveloped and mailed?"

"Of course." He took them from her hand and placed them in a
640 pocket of his gray uniform shirt.

"These can't be sent off until the next cruiser stops by, and the
Stardust will have long since told them about me, won't it?" she asked.
He nodded and she went on: "That makes the letters not important in
one way, but in another way they're very important—to me, and to
them."

"I know. I understand, and I'll take care of them."

She glanced at the chronometer, then back to him. "It seems to move
faster all the time, doesn't it?"

He said nothing, unable to think of anything to say, and she asked,
650 "Do you think Gerry will come back to camp in time?"

"I think so. They said he should be in right away."

She began to roll the pencil back and forth between her palms. "I
hope he does. I feel sick and scared and I want to hear his voice again
and maybe I won't feel so alone. I'm a coward and I can't help it."

"No," he said, "you're not a coward. You're afraid, but you're not a
coward."

"Is there a difference?"

He nodded. "A lot of difference."

"I feel so alone. I never did feel like this before; like I was all by
660 myself and there was nobody to care what happened to me. Always,
before, there were Mama and Daddy there and my friends around me. I
had lots of friends, and they had a going-away party for me the night
before I left."

Friends and music and laughter for her to remember—and on the viewscreen Lotus Lake was going into the shadow.

"Is it the same with Gerry?" she asked. "I mean, if he should make a mistake, would he have to die for it, all alone and with no one to help him?"

"It's the same with all, along the frontier; it will always be like that so long as there is a frontier."
670

"Gerry didn't tell us. He said the pay was good, and he sent money home all the time because Daddy's little shop just brought in a bare living, but he didn't tell us it was like this."

"He didn't tell you his work was dangerous?"

"Well—yes. He mentioned that, but we didn't understand. I always thought danger along the frontier was something that was a lot of fun; an exciting adventure, like in the three-D shows." A wan smile touched her face for a moment. "Only it's not, is it? It's not the same at all, because when it's real you can't go home after the show is over."
680

"No," he said. "No, you can't."

Her glance flicked from the chronometer to the door of the air lock, then down to the pad and pencil she still held. She shifted her position slightly to lay them on the bench beside her, moving one foot out a little. For the first time he saw that she was not wearing Vegan gypsy sandals, but only cheap imitations; the expensive Vegan leather was some kind of grained plastic, the silver buckle was gilded iron, the jewels were colored glass. *Daddy's little shop just brought in a bare living. . . .* She must have left college in her second year, to take the course in linguistics that would enable her to make her own way and help her brother provide for
690 her parents, earning what she could by part-time work after classes were over. Her personal possessions on the *Stardust* would be taken back to her parents—they would neither be of much value nor occupy much storage space on the return voyage.

"Isn't it———" She stopped, and he looked at her questioningly. "Isn't it cold in here?" she asked, almost apologetically. "Doesn't it seem cold to you?"

"Why, yes," he said. He saw by the main temperature gauge that the room was at precisely normal temperature. "Yes, it's colder than it should be."
700

"I wish Gerry would get back before it's too late. Do you really think he will, and you didn't just say so to make me feel better?"

"I think he will—they said he would be in pretty soon." On the viewscreen Lotus Lake had gone into the shadow but for the thin blue line of its western edge, and it was apparent he had overestimated the time she would have in which to talk to her brother. Reluctantly, he said to her, "His camp will be out of radio range in a few minutes; he's on that part of Woden that's in the shadow"—he indicated the viewscreen— "and the turning of Woden will put him beyond contact. There may not

INTERPRET

Why do you think the narrator mentions this detail about Lotus Lake?

_____
_____
_____
_____
_____
_____
_____
_____
_____

INTERPRET

What does Barton's observation of these details add to our understanding of Marilyn?

_____
_____
_____
_____
_____
_____
_____
_____
_____
_____
_____
_____
_____

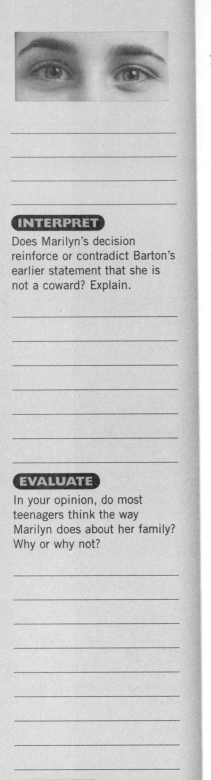

INTERPRET

Does Marilyn's decision reinforce or contradict Barton's earlier statement that she is not a coward? Explain.

EVALUATE

In your opinion, do most teenagers think the way Marilyn does about her family? Why or why not?

EVALUATE

Do you agree with Barton's statement in line 747? Why or why not?

be much time left when he comes in—not much time to talk to him
710 before he fades out. I wish I could do something about it—I would call
him right now if I could."

"Not even as much time as I will have to stay?"

"I'm afraid not."

"Then———" She straightened and looked toward the air lock with
pale resolution. "Then I'll go when Gerry passes beyond range. I won't
wait any longer after that—I won't have anything to wait for."

Again there was nothing he could say.

"Maybe I shouldn't wait at all. Maybe I'm selfish—maybe it would
be better for Gerry if you just told him about it afterward."

720 There was an unconscious pleading for denial in the way she spoke
and he said, "He wouldn't want you to do that, to not wait for him."

"It's already coming dark where he is, isn't it? There will be all the
long night before him, and Mama and Daddy don't know yet that I won't
ever be coming back like I promised them I would. I've caused everyone
I love to be hurt, haven't I? I didn't want to—I didn't intend to."

"It wasn't your fault," he said. "It wasn't your fault at all. They'll
know that. They'll understand."

"At first I was so afraid to die that I was a coward and thought only
of myself. Now I see how selfish I was. The terrible thing about dying
730 like this is not that I'll be gone but that I'll never see them again; never
be able to tell them that I didn't take them for granted; never be able to
tell them I knew of the sacrifices they made to make my life happier, that
I knew all the things they did for me and that I loved them so much
more than I ever told them. I've never told them any of those things. You
don't tell them such things when you're young and your life is all before
you—you're so afraid of sounding sentimental and silly. But it's so
different when you have to die—you wish you had told them while you
could, and you wish you could tell them you're sorry for all the little
mean things you ever did or said to them. You wish you could tell them
740 that you didn't really mean to ever hurt their feelings and for them to
only remember that you always loved them far more than you ever let
them know."

"You don't have to tell them that," he said. "They will know—
they've always known it."

"Are you sure?" she asked. "How can you be sure? My people are
strangers to you."

"Wherever you go, human nature and human hearts are the same."

"And they will know what I want them to know—that I love them?"

"They've always known it, in a way far better than you could ever
750 put in words for them."

"I keep remembering the things they did for me, and it's the little
things they did that seem to be the most important to me, now. Like
Gerry—he sent me a bracelet of fire rubies on my sixteenth birthday. It

was beautiful—it must have cost him a month's pay. Yet I remember him more for what he did the night my kitten got run over in the street. I was only six years old and he held me in his arms and wiped away my tears and told me not to cry, that Flossy was gone for just a little while, for just long enough to get herself a new fur coat, and she would be on the foot of my bed the very next morning. I believed him and quit crying

760 and went to sleep dreaming about my kitten coming back. When I woke up the next morning, there was Flossy on the foot of my bed in a brand-new white fur coat, just like he had said she would be. It wasn't until a long time later that Mama told me Gerry had got the pet-shop owner out of bed at four in the morning and, when the man got mad about it, Gerry told him he was either going to go down and sell him the white kitten right then or he'd break his neck."

"It's always the little things you remember people by, all the little things they did because they wanted to do them for you. You've done the same for Gerry and your father and mother; all kinds of things that

770 you've forgotten about, but that they will never forget."

"I hope I have. I would like for them to remember me like that."

"They will."

"I wish———" She swallowed. "The way I'll die—I wish they wouldn't ever think of that. I've read how people look who die in space—their insides all ruptured and exploded and their lungs out between their teeth and then, a few seconds later, they're all dry and shapeless and horribly ugly. I don't want them to ever think of me as something dead and horrible like that."

"You're their own, their child and their sister. They could never think

780 of you other than the way you would want them to, the way you looked the last time they saw you."

"I'm still afraid," she said. "I can't help it, but I don't want Gerry to know it. If he gets back in time, I'm going to act like I'm not afraid at all and———"

The signal buzzer interrupted her, quick and imperative.

"Gerry!" She came to her feet. "It's Gerry now!"

He spun the volume control knob and asked, "Gerry Cross?"

"Yes," her brother answered, an undertone of tenseness to his reply. "The bad news—what is it?"

790 She answered for him, standing close behind him and leaning down a little toward the communicator, her hand resting small and cold on his shoulder.

"Hello, Gerry." There was only a faint quaver to betray the careful casualness of her voice. "I wanted to see you———"

"Marilyn!" There was sudden and terrible <u>apprehension</u> in the way he spoke her name. "What are you doing on that EDS?"

"I wanted to see you," she said again. "I wanted to see you, so I hid on this ship———"

INFER

What remains unknown in the story, now that it is clear that Marilyn will get a chance to speak with Gerry?

WORDS TO OWN

apprehension (ap′rē·hen′shən) *n.:* dread; fear of a future event.

INFER

Why do you think that Gerry says that everything is all right?

EVALUATE

Do you wonder why Marilyn defends Barton, the man who is about to kill her? Do you find her attitude surprising? Tell why or why not.

"You *hid* on it?"

800   "I'm a stowaway. . . . I didn't know what it would mean———"

"*Marilyn!*" It was the cry of a man who calls, hopeless and desperate, to someone already and forever gone from him. "What have you done?"

"I . . . it's not———" Then her own composure broke and the cold little hand gripped his shoulder convulsively. "Don't, Gerry—I only wanted to see you; I didn't intend to hurt you. Please, Gerry, don't feel like that———"

Something warm and wet splashed on his wrist, and he slid out of the chair to help her into it and swing the microphone down to her level.

810   "Don't feel like that. Don't let me go knowing you feel like that———"

The sob she had tried to hold back choked in her throat, and her brother spoke to her. "Don't cry, Marilyn." His voice was suddenly deep and infinitely gentle, with all the pain held out of it. "Don't cry, Sis—you mustn't do that. It's all right, honey—everything is all right."

"I———" Her lower lip quivered and she bit into it. "I didn't want you to feel that way—I just wanted us to say goodbye, because I have to go in a minute."

"Sure—sure. That's the way it'll be, Sis. I didn't mean to sound the way I did." Then his voice changed to a tone of quick and urgent

820   demand. "EDS—have you called the *Stardust*? Did you check with the computers?"

"I called the *Stardust* almost an hour ago. It can't turn back; there are no other cruisers within forty light-years, and there isn't enough fuel."

"Are you sure that the computers had the correct data—sure of everything?"

"Yes—do you think I could ever let it happen if I wasn't sure? I did everything I could do. If there was anything at all I could do now, I would do it."

830   "He tried to help me, Gerry." Her lower lip was no longer trembling and the short sleeves of her blouse were wet where she had dried her tears. "No one can help me and I'm not going to cry anymore and everything will be all right with you and Daddy and Mama, won't it?"

"Sure—sure it will. We'll make out fine."

Her brother's words were beginning to come in more faintly, and he turned the volume control to maximum. "He's going out of range," he said to her. "He'll be gone within another minute."

"You're fading out, Gerry," she said. "You're going out of range. I wanted to tell you—but I can't now. We must say goodbye so soon—but

840   maybe I'll see you again. Maybe I'll come to you in your dreams with my hair in braids and crying because the kitten in my arms is dead; maybe I'll be the touch of a breeze that whispers to you as it goes by; maybe I'll be one of those gold-winged larks you told me about, singing

my silly head off to you; maybe, at times, I'll be nothing you can see, but you will know I'm there beside you. Think of me like that, Gerry; always like that and not—the other way."

Dimmed to a whisper by the turning of Woden, the answer came back:

"Always like that, Marilyn—always like that and never any other way."

850

"Our time is up, Gerry—I have to go now. Good———" Her voice broke in midword and her mouth tried to twist into crying. She pressed her hand hard against it and when she spoke again the words came clear and true:

"Goodbye, Gerry."

Faint and ineffably poignant and tender, the last words came from the cold metal of the communicator:

"Goodbye, little sister . . ."

She sat motionless in the hush that followed, as though listening to

860

the shadow-echoes of the words as they died away; then she turned away from the communicator, toward the air lock, and he pulled down the black lever beside him. The inner door of the air lock slid swiftly open to reveal the bare little cell that was waiting for her, and she walked to it.

She walked with her head up and the brown curls brushing her shoulders, with the white sandals stepping as sure and steady as the fractional gravity would permit and the gilded buckles twinkling with little lights of blue and red and crystal. He let her walk alone and made no move to help her, knowing she would not want it that way. She

870

stepped into the air lock and turned to face him, only the pulse in her throat to betray the wild beating of her heart.

"I'm ready," she said.

He pushed the lever up and the door slid its quick barrier between them, enclosing her in black and utter darkness for her last moments of life. It clicked as it locked in place and he jerked down the red lever. There was a slight waver of the ship as the air gushed from the lock, a vibration to the wall as though something had bumped the outer door in passing; then there was nothing and the ship was dropping true and steady again. He shoved the red lever back to close the door on the

880

empty air lock and turned away, to walk to the pilot's chair with the slow steps of a man old and weary.

Back in the pilot's chair he pressed the signal button of the normal-space transmitter. There was no response; he had expected none. Her brother would have to wait through the night until the turning of Woden permitted contact through Group One.

It was not yet time to resume deceleration, and he waited while the ship dropped endlessly downward with him and the drives purred softly.

INTERPRET

What is your response to Marilyn's final words to her brother?

_____

_____

_____

_____

_____

_____

_____

WORDS TO OWN

ineffably (in·ef′ə·blē) *adv.:* indescribably; inexpressibly.

PREDICT

Pause here. Do you think Barton will have a change of heart as Marilyn turns toward the air lock? Why or why not?

_____

_____

_____

_____

_____

_____

_____

_____

_____

_____

_____

_____

INTERPRET

Do you wonder what the "something shapeless and ugly" is? What do you think the author is describing?

_____

_____

_____

_____

_____

_____

_____

EVALUATE

In your opinion, is this a good way to end this story? Why or why not?

_____

_____

_____

_____

_____

_____

_____

_____

_____

_____

_____

_____

_____

_____

_____

_____

He saw that the white hand of the supply-closet temperature gauge was on zero. A cold equation had been balanced and he was alone on the 890 ship. Something shapeless and ugly was hurrying ahead of him, going to Woden, where her brother was waiting through the night, but the empty ship still lived for a little while with the presence of the girl who had not known about the forces that killed with neither hatred nor malice. It seemed, almost, that she still sat, small and bewildered and frightened, on the metal box beside him, her words echoing hauntingly clear in the void she had left behind her:

I didn't do anything to die for. . . . I didn't do anything. . . .

Suspense

Suspense is a feeling of tension or anxious curiosity about what is going to happen next in a story. Writers may use several techniques to create suspense. These techniques include withholding information or using the setting or the dialogue to build a tense mood or atmosphere.

Explore suspense in "The Cold Equations" by completing the chart below. On the left are listed some passages from the story. Re-read each passage in context. Then use the right-hand column to indicate what questions each passage plants in the reader's mind.

Story Passages	Suspenseful Questions
1. There was something in the supply closet across the room, it was saying, some kind of a body that radiated heat. (page 4)	
2. "I know how you feel but I'm powerless to help you. You'll have to go through with it. I'll have you connected with Ship's Records." (page 9)	
3. "Gerry? He and two others went out in the helicopter this morning and aren't back yet. It's almost sundown, though, and he ought to be back right away—in less than an hour at the most." (page 17)	
4. She stepped into the air lock and turned to face him, only the pulse in her throat to betray the wild beating of her heart. (page 23)	

Vocabulary: How to Own a Word

Word Maps

Create a word map for each Word to Own. Provide a synonym, an antonym, and the connotation for each word. Also provide the dictionary definition, and write a sentence using the word correctly. Be sure that the sentence you write reflects the connotation of the word. An example has been partially completed for you.

Word Bank
inured
increments
recoiled
paramount
annihilate
irrevocable
immutable
ponderous
apprehension
ineffably

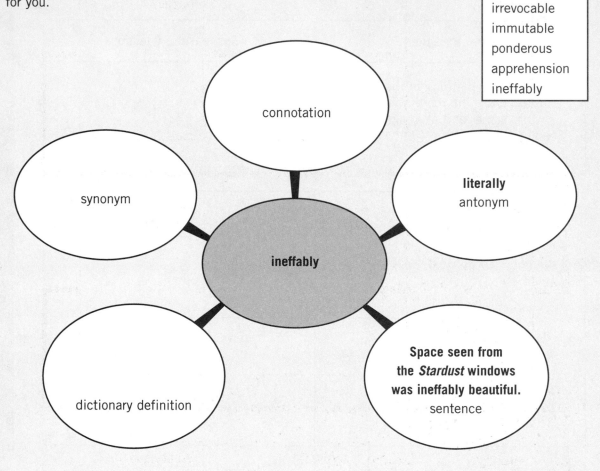

connotation

synonym

literally
antonym

ineffably

dictionary definition

Space seen from the *Stardust* windows was ineffably beautiful.
sentence

Selection: _____

Plot

Record the title of the story you are analyzing. Then, list the events of the plot in the order they occur. Note: You may need to combine events (or add boxes) or leave some boxes blank.

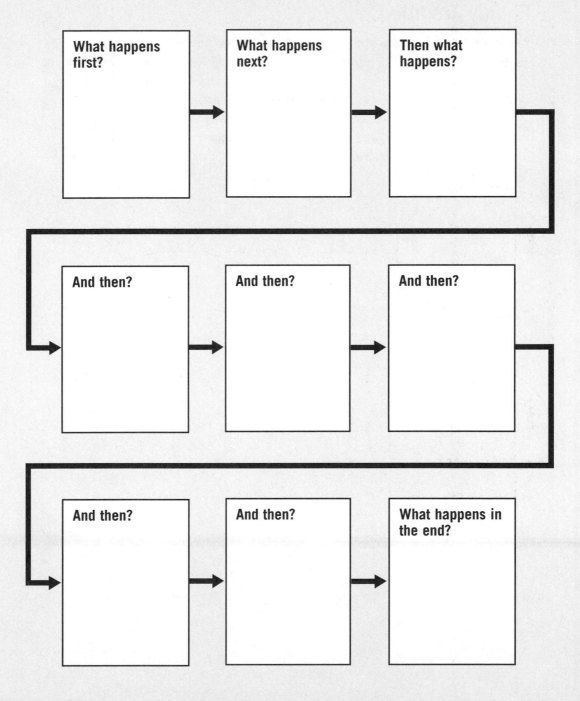

Everyday Use

Make the Connection

Family Traditions

Many families cherish traditions or heirlooms that are passed down from one generation to the next. "Everyday Use" focuses on the role such traditions play in a family. In Alice Walker's story, there is a clash between generations, as well as a strong difference of opinion about family heritage.

Consider the values of your generation and those of the older generation. What values are different and what values are the same? Fill in the Venn diagram. In the spaces where the circles overlap, write the values that you think both generations share.

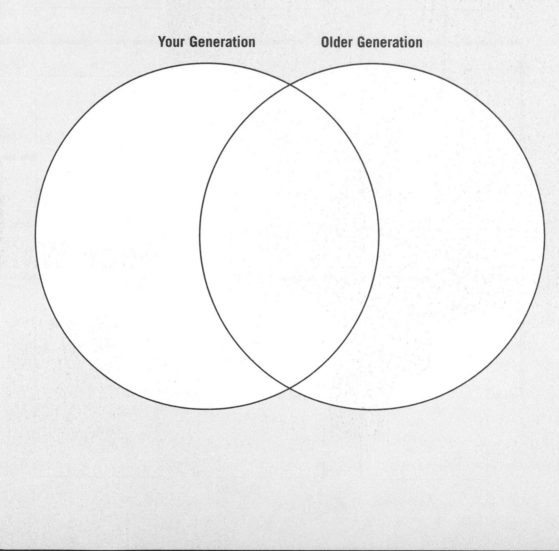

Your Generation   **Older Generation**

Everyday Use

For Your Grandmama

Alice Walker

What differences between the sisters are clear from the beginning of the story?

_____

_____

_____

_____

_____

_____

_____

_____

_____

_____

_____

_____

_____

_____

_____

_____

_____

_____

_____

_____

_____

_____

_____

_____

_____

_____

_____

I will wait for her in the yard that Maggie and I made so clean and wavy yesterday afternoon. A yard like this is more comfortable than most people know. It is not just a yard. It is like an extended living room. When the hard clay is swept clean as a floor and the fine sand around the edges lined with tiny, irregular grooves, anyone can come and sit and look up into the elm tree and wait for the breezes that never come inside the house.

Maggie will be nervous until after her sister goes: She will stand hopelessly in corners, homely and ashamed of the burn scars down her
10 arms and legs, eyeing her sister with a mixture of envy and awe. She thinks her sister had held life always in the palm of one hand, that "no" is a word the world never learned to say to her.

You've no doubt seen those TV shows where the child who has "made it" is confronted, as a surprise, by her own mother and father, tottering in weakly from backstage. (A pleasant surprise, of course: What would they do if parent and child came on the show only to curse out and insult each other?) On TV mother and child embrace and smile into each other's faces. Sometimes the mother and father weep; the child wraps them in her arms and leans across the table to tell how she would not
20 have made it without their help. I have seen these programs.

Sometimes I dream a dream in which Dee and I are suddenly brought together on a TV program of this sort. Out of a dark and soft-seated limousine I am ushered into a bright room filled with many people. There I meet a smiling, gray, sporty man like Johnny Carson who shakes my hand and tells me what a fine girl I have. Then we are on the stage, and Dee is embracing me with tears in her eyes. She pins on my dress a large orchid, even though she had told me once that she thinks orchids are tacky flowers.

In real life I am a large, big-boned woman with rough, man-working
30 hands. In the winter I wear flannel nightgowns to bed and overalls during the day. I can kill and clean a hog as mercilessly as a man. My fat keeps me hot in zero weather. I can work outside all day, breaking ice to get water for washing; I can eat pork liver cooked over the open fire minutes after it comes steaming from the hog. One winter I knocked a bull calf straight in the brain between the eyes with a sledgehammer and had the meat hung up to chill before nightfall. But of course all this does not show on television. I am the way my daughter would want me to be: a hundred pounds lighter, my skin like an uncooked barley pancake. My hair glistens in the hot bright lights. Johnny Carson has much to do to
40 keep up with my quick and witty tongue.

But that is a mistake. I know even before I wake up. Who ever knew a Johnson with a quick tongue? Who can even imagine me looking a strange white man in the eye? It seems to me I have talked to them always with one foot raised in flight, with my head turned in whichever way is farthest from them. Dee, though. She would always look anyone in the eye. Hesitation was no part of her nature.

"How do I look, Mama?" Maggie says, showing just enough of her thin body enveloped in pink skirt and red blouse for me to know she's there, almost hidden by the door.

50   "Come out into the yard," I say.

Have you ever seen a lame animal, perhaps a dog run over by some careless person rich enough to own a car, sidle up to someone who is ignorant enough to be kind to him? That is the way my Maggie walks. She has been like this, chin on chest, eyes on ground, feet in shuffle, ever since the fire that burned the other house to the ground.

Dee is lighter than Maggie, with nicer hair and a fuller figure. She's a woman now, though sometimes I forget. How long ago was it that the other house burned? Ten, twelve years? Sometimes I can still hear the flames and feel Maggie's arms sticking to me, her hair smoking and
60   her dress falling off her in little black papery flakes. Her eyes seemed stretched open, blazed open by the flames reflected in them. And Dee. I see her standing off under the sweet gum tree she used to dig gum out of, a look of concentration on her face as she watched the last dingy gray board of the house fall in toward the red-hot brick chimney. Why don't you do a dance around the ashes? I'd wanted to ask her. She had hated the house that much.

I used to think she hated Maggie, too. But that was before we raised the money, the church and me, to send her to Augusta to school. She used to read to us without pity, forcing words, lies, other folks' habits,
70   whole lives upon us two, sitting trapped and ignorant underneath her voice. She washed us in a river of make-believe, burned us with a lot of knowledge we didn't necessarily need to know. Pressed us to her with the serious ways she read, to shove us away at just the moment, like dimwits, we seemed about to understand.

Dee wanted nice things. A yellow organdy dress to wear to her graduation from high school; black pumps to match a green suit she'd made from an old suit somebody gave me. She was determined to stare down any disaster in her efforts. Her eyelids would not flicker for minutes at a time. Often I fought off the temptation to shake her. At
80   sixteen she had a style of her own: and knew what style was.

I never had an education myself. After second grade the school closed down. Don't ask me why: In 1927 colored asked fewer questions than they do now. Sometimes Maggie reads to me. She stumbles along good-naturedly but can't see well. She knows she is not bright. Like good looks and money, quickness passed her by. She will marry John Thomas

WORDS TO OWN
sidle (sīd'ʼl) v.: move sideways, especially in a shy or sneaky manner.

BUILD FLUENCY
Read this paragraph aloud, using an appropriate, expressive tone.

INTERPRET
Why does Mama resent Dee's reading to her and Maggie?

EVALUATE
How do you feel about Dee? Explain.

WORDS TO OWN

furtive (fur'tiv) *adj.*: acting as
if trying not to be seen. *Furtive*
also means "done secretly."

RETELL

Summarize what you have
learned about Dee's
relationship with her family
before she arrives.

(who has mossy teeth in an earnest face), and then I'll be free to sit here
and I guess just sing church songs to myself. Although I never was a
good singer. Never could carry a tune. I was always better at a man's
job. I used to love to milk till I was hooked in the side in '49. Cows are
90 soothing and slow and don't bother you, unless you try to milk them the
wrong way.

I have deliberately turned my back on the house. It is three rooms,
just like the one that burned, except the roof is tin; they don't make
shingle roofs anymore. There are no real windows, just some holes cut
in the sides, like the portholes in a ship, but not round and not square,
with rawhide holding the shutters up on the outside. This house is in a
pasture, too, like the other one. No doubt when Dee sees it she will want
to tear it down. She wrote me once that no matter where we "choose"
to live, she will manage to come see us. But she will never bring her
100 friends. Maggie and I thought about this and Maggie asked me, "Mama,
when did Dee ever *have* any friends?"

She had a few. Furtive boys in pink shirts hanging about on washday
after school. Nervous girls who never laughed. Impressed with her, they
worshiped the well-turned phrase, the cute shape, the scalding humor
that erupted like bubbles in lye. She read to them.

When she was courting Jimmy T, she didn't have much time to pay
to us but turned all her faultfinding power on him. He *flew* to marry a
cheap city girl from a family of ignorant, flashy people. She hardly had
time to recompose herself.

110 When she comes, I will meet—but there they are!

Maggie attempts to make a dash for the house, in her shuffling way,
but I stay her with my hand. "Come back here," I say. And she stops and
tries to dig a well in the sand with her toe.

It is hard to see them clearly through the strong sun. But even the
first glimpse of leg out of the car tells me it is Dee. Her feet were always
neat looking, as if God himself shaped them with a certain style. From
the other side of the car comes a short, stocky man. Hair is all over his
head a foot long and hanging from his chin like a kinky mule tail. I hear
Maggie suck in her breath. "Uhnnnh" is what it sounds like. Like when
120 you see the wriggling end of a snake just in front of your foot on the
road. "Uhnnnh."

Dee next. A dress down to the ground, in this hot weather. A dress
so loud it hurts my eyes. There are yellows and oranges enough to throw
back the light of the sun. I feel my whole face warming from the heat
waves it throws out. Earrings gold, too, and hanging down to her
shoulders. Bracelets dangling and making noises when she moves her
arm up to shake the folds of the dress out of her armpits. The dress
is loose and flows, and as she walks closer, I like it. I hear Maggie go

"Uhnnnh" again. It is her sister's hair. It stands straight up like the wool
130 on a sheep. It is black as night and around the edges are two long
pigtails that rope about like small lizards disappearing behind her ears.

"Wa-su-zo-Tean-o!" she says, coming on in that gliding way the dress
makes her move. The short, stocky fellow with the hair to his navel is
all grinning, and he follows up with "Asalamalakim,[1] my mother and
sister!" He moves to hug Maggie but she falls back, right up against the
back of my chair. I feel her trembling there, and when I look up I see the
perspiration falling off her chin.

"Don't get up," says Dee. Since I am stout, it takes something of a
push. You can see me trying to move a second or two before I make it.
140 She turns, showing white heels through her sandals, and goes back to
the car. Out she peeks next with a Polaroid. She stoops down quickly
and lines up picture after picture of me sitting there in front of the house
with Maggie <u>cowering</u> behind me. She never takes a shot without
making sure the house is included. When a cow comes nibbling around
in the edge of the yard, she snaps it and me and Maggie and the house.
Then she puts the Polaroid in the back seat of the car and comes up and
kisses me on the forehead.

Meanwhile, Asalamalakim is going through motions with Maggie's
hand. Maggie's hand is as limp as a fish, and probably as cold, despite
150 the sweat, and she keeps trying to pull it back. It looks like Asalamalakim
wants to shake hands but wants to do it fancy. Or maybe he don't know
how people shake hands. Anyhow, he soon gives up on Maggie.

"Well," I say. "Dee."

"No, Mama," she says. "Not 'Dee,' Wangero Leewanika Kemanjo!"

"What happened to 'Dee'?" I wanted to know.

"She's dead," Wangero said. "I couldn't bear it any longer, being
named after the people who oppress me."

"You know as well as me you was named after your aunt Dicie," I
said. Dicie is my sister. She named Dee. We called her "Big Dee" after
160 Dee was born.

"But who was *she* named after?" asked Wangero.

"I guess after Grandma Dee," I said.

"And who was she named after?" asked Wangero.

"Her mother," I said, and saw Wangero was getting tired. "That's
about as far back as I can trace it," I said. Though, in fact, I probably
could have carried it back beyond the Civil War through the branches.

"Well," said Asalamalakim, "there you are."

"Uhnnnh," I heard Maggie say.

"There I was not," I said, "before 'Dicie' cropped up in our family, so
170 why should I try to trace it that far back?"

---

1. **Asalamalakim:** Asalaam aleikum (ä·sə·läm′ ä·lā′koom′), greeting used by Muslims
   meaning "peace to you."

WORDS TO OWN
cowering (kou′ər·iŋ) *v.* used as
adj.: drawing back or huddling
in fear.

EVALUATE
Which name do you think
better reflects Dee's heritage,
and why?

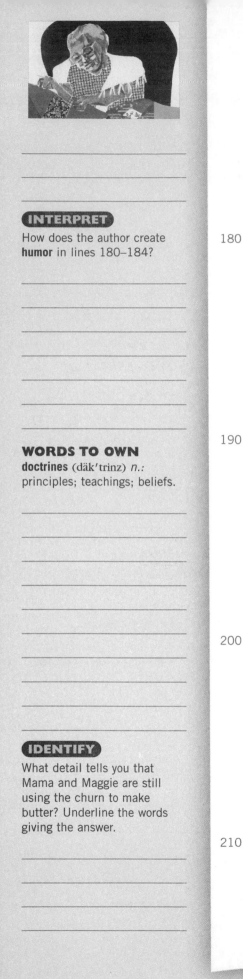

INTERPRET

How does the author create **humor** in lines 180–184?

WORDS TO OWN
doctrines (däk′trinz) *n.*:
principles; teachings; beliefs.

IDENTIFY

What detail tells you that Mama and Maggie are still using the churn to make butter? Underline the words giving the answer.

He just stood there grinning, looking down on me like somebody inspecting a Model A car. Every once in a while he and Wangero sent eye signals over my head.

"How do you pronounce this name?" I asked.

"You don't have to call me by it if you don't want to," said Wangero.

"Why shouldn't I?" I asked. "If that's what you want us to call you, we'll call you."

"I know it might sound awkward at first," said Wangero.

"I'll get used to it," I said. "Ream it out again."

180   Well, soon we got the name out of the way. Asalamalakim had a name twice as long and three times as hard. After I tripped over it two or three times, he told me to just call him Hakim-a-barber. I wanted to ask him was he a barber, but I didn't really think he was, so I didn't ask.

"You must belong to those beef-cattle peoples down the road," I said. They said "Asalamalakim" when they met you, too, but they didn't shake hands. Always too busy: feeding the cattle, fixing the fences, putting up salt-lick shelters, throwing down hay. When the white folks poisoned some of the herd, the men stayed up all night with rifles in
190   their hands. I walked a mile and a half just to see the sight.

Hakim-a-barber said, "I accept some of their doctrines, but farming and raising cattle is not my style." (They didn't tell me, and I didn't ask, whether Wangero—Dee—had really gone and married him.)

We sat down to eat and right away he said he didn't eat collards, and pork was unclean. Wangero, though, went on through the chitlins and corn bread, the greens, and everything else. She talked a blue streak over the sweet potatoes. Everything delighted her. Even the fact that we still used the benches her daddy made for the table when we couldn't afford to buy chairs.

200   "Oh, Mama!" she cried. Then turned to Hakim-a-barber. "I never knew how lovely these benches are. You can feel the rump prints," she said, running her hands underneath her and along the bench. Then she gave a sigh, and her hand closed over Grandma Dee's butter dish. "That's it!" she said. "I knew there was something I wanted to ask you if I could have." She jumped up from the table and went over in the corner where the churn stood, the milk in it clabber[2] by now. She looked at the churn and looked at it.

"This churn top is what I need," she said. "Didn't Uncle Buddy whittle it out of a tree you all used to have?"

210   "Yes," I said.

"Uh huh," she said happily. "And I want the dasher,[3] too."

"Uncle Buddy whittle that, too?" asked the barber.

---

2. **clabber:** thickly curdled sour milk.
3. **dasher:** pole that stirs the milk in a churn.

Dee (Wangero) looked up at me.

"Aunt Dee's first husband whittled the dash," said Maggie so low you almost couldn't hear her. "His name was Henry, but they called him Stash."

"Maggie's brain is like an elephant's," Wangero said, laughing. "I can use the churn top as a centerpiece for the alcove table," she said, sliding a plate over the churn, "and I'll think of something artistic to do with the
220 dasher."

When she finished wrapping the dasher, the handle stuck out. I took it for a moment in my hands. You didn't even have to look close to see where hands pushing the dasher up and down to make butter had left a kind of sink in the wood. In fact, there were a lot of small sinks; you could see where thumbs and fingers had sunk into the wood. It was beautiful light-yellow wood, from a tree that grew in the yard where Big Dee and Stash had lived.

After dinner Dee (Wangero) went to the trunk at the foot of my bed and started <u>rifling</u> through it. Maggie hung back in the kitchen over the
230 dishpan. Out came Wangero with two quilts. They had been pieced by Grandma Dee, and then Big Dee and me had hung them on the quilt frames on the front porch and quilted them. One was in the Lone Star pattern. The other was Walk Around the Mountain. In both of them were scraps of dresses Grandma Dee had worn fifty and more years ago. Bits and pieces of Grandpa Jarrell's paisley shirts. And one teeny faded blue piece, about the size of a penny matchbox, that was from Great Grandpa Ezra's uniform that he wore in the Civil War.

"Mama," Wangero said sweet as a bird. "Can I have these old quilts?"
240 I heard something fall in the kitchen, and a minute later the kitchen door slammed.

"Why don't you take one or two of the others?" I asked. "These old things was just done by me and Big Dee from some tops your grandma pieced before she died."

"No," said Wangero. "I don't want those. They are stitched around the borders by machine."

"That'll make them last better," I said.

"That's not the point," said Wangero. "These are all pieces of dresses Grandma used to wear. She did all this stitching by hand. Imagine!" She
250 held the quilts securely in her arms, stroking them.

"Some of the pieces, like those lavender ones, come from old clothes her mother handed down to her," I said, moving up to touch the quilts. Dee (Wangero) moved back just enough so that I couldn't reach the quilts. They already belonged to her.

"Imagine!" she breathed again, clutching them closely to her bosom.

WORDS TO OWN
rifling (rī′fliŋ) *v.* used as *n.:* searching thoroughly or in a rough manner.

INFER
Why does Maggie slam the door when she hears Dee ask for the quilts?

IDENTIFY

Circle the words in this passage that are used for the story's title.

_____

_____

_____

_____

_____

INTERPRET

Besides the question of who is entitled to the quilts, what other issue surrounds the quilts?

_____

_____

_____

_____

_____

_____

_____

_____

_____

_____

_____

_____

_____

_____

_____

_____

_____

_____

_____

"The truth is," I said, "I promised to give them quilts to Maggie, for when she marries John Thomas."

She gasped like a bee had stung her.

"Maggie can't appreciate these quilts!" she said. "She'd probably be
260   backward enough to put them to everyday use."

"I reckon she would," I said. "God knows I been saving 'em for long enough with nobody using 'em. I hope she will!" I didn't want to bring up how I had offered Dee (Wangero) a quilt when she went away to college. Then she had told me they were old-fashioned, out of style.

"But they're _priceless_!" she was saying now, furiously; for she has a temper. "Maggie would put them on the bed and in five years they'd be in rags. Less than that!"

"She can always make some more," I said. "Maggie knows how to quilt."

270   Dee (Wangero) looked at me with hatred. "You just will not understand. The point is _these_ quilts, these quilts!"

"Well," I said, stumped. "What would _you_ do with them?"

"Hang them," she said. As if that was the only thing you _could_ do with quilts.

Maggie by now was standing in the door. I could almost hear the sound her feet made as they scraped over each other.

"She can have them, Mama," she said, like somebody used to never winning anything or having anything reserved for her. "I can 'member Grandma Dee without the quilts."

280   I looked at her hard. She had filled her bottom lip with checkerberry snuff, and it gave her face a kind of dopey, hangdog look. It was Grandma Dee and Big Dee who taught her how to quilt herself. She stood there with her scarred hands hidden in the folds of her skirt. She looked at her sister with something like fear, but she wasn't mad at her. This was Maggie's portion. This was the way she knew God to work.

When I looked at her like that, something hit me in the top of my head and ran down to the soles of my feet. Just like when I'm in church and the spirit of God touches me and I get happy and shout. I did something I never had done before: hugged Maggie to me, then dragged
290   her on into the room, snatched the quilts out of Miss Wangero's hands, and dumped them into Maggie's lap. Maggie just sat there on my bed with her mouth open.

"Take one or two of the others," I said to Dee.

But she turned without a word and went out to Hakim-a-barber.

"You just don't understand," she said, as Maggie and I came out to the car.

"What don't I understand?" I wanted to know.

"Your heritage," she said. And then she turned to Maggie, kissed her, and said, "You ought to try to make something of yourself, too, Maggie.

300 It's really a new day for us. But from the way you and Mama still live, you'd never know it."

   She put on some sunglasses that hid everything above the tip of her nose and her chin.

   Maggie smiled, maybe at the sunglasses. But a real smile, not scared. After we watched the car dust settle, I asked Maggie to bring me a dip of snuff. And then the two of us sat there just enjoying, until it was time to go in the house and go to bed.

INTERPRET

How does the author create **irony** in lines 298–301?

_____

_____

_____

_____

_____

_____

_____

_____

_____

_____

_____

_____

_____

_____

_____

_____

_____

_____

_____

_____

_____

Conflict Analysis

Conflict is a struggle that usually occurs when the desires of the main character in a work are blocked in some way. In an **external conflict,** a character is pitted against another character, society as a whole, or a force of nature. In an **internal conflict,** the blocking of a character's needs or desires causes a clash of forces within the person.

What do you think is the principal source of the conflicts in "Everyday Use"? Consider the following questions. Then, write a brief analysis of the conflict on the lines provided below.

- Which character sets the action in motion?
- Which of her desires are blocked?
- Who or what is blocking them?
- Is the battle **external** or **internal** or both?

_____

_____

_____

_____

_____

_____

_____

_____

_____

_____

_____

_____

_____

_____

Vocabulary: How to Own a Word

Question and Answer

Each of the following questions has an italicized Word to Own. Answer the question and then explain your answer on the lines provided.

Word Bank
sidle
furtive
cowering
doctrines
rifling

EXAMPLE: Asalamalakim is described as stocky. Does that mean he is a good businessman? _____No_____.

Explanation: __It means that he is heavily built, sturdy, and short.__

1. Does Dee *sidle* up to people as Maggie does? _____

   Explanation: _____

   _____

2. Suppose that Dee behaves in a sneaky manner and that Maggie behaves in an open, honest manner. Which one would be *furtive*? _____

   Explanation: _____

   _____

3. Can you picture yourself *cowering* before the narrator? _____

   Explanation: _____

   _____

4. The narrator believes in the practical application of heritage. Would that be considered one of her personal *doctrines*? _____

   Explanation: _____

   _____

5. When Dee finished *rifling* through the trunk, would the trunk's contents likely be straightened up or messed up? _____

   Explanation: _____

   _____

Two Kinds

Make the Connection

What Might the Future Hold?

Sometimes our biggest conflicts are with the people we love the most. In "Two Kinds," Amy Tan focuses on a conflict between a girl and her mother. The parent and child have differing views on how the child should live her life and what her goals should be.

What would you like to be doing in ten years? What do you think your parents and older relatives would want you to be doing? Explore your thoughts by filling out the chart below. You needn't show your writing to anyone.

Ten Years from Now	
What I'd like to be doing	**What others might expect**

Two Kinds

Amy Tan

EVALUATE

The opening paragraph reveals the beliefs of the narrator's mother. Do you agree with these beliefs? Why or why not?

I don't because in America you have to get an education and then try pursue your career.

WORDS TO OWN

prodigy (präd′ə·jē) *n.:* child of highly unusual talent or genius.

INTERPRET

An **allusion** is a reference to a work of literature or to a well-known historical event, person, or place. What does the allusion to Shirley Temple reveal about the mother's expectations?

She wants her to be famous and rich.

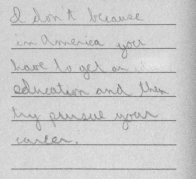

My mother believed you could be anything you wanted to be in America. You could open a restaurant. You could work for the government and get good retirement. You could buy a house with almost no money down. You could become rich. You could become instantly famous.

"Of course you can be <u>prodigy</u>, too," my mother told me when I was nine. "You can be best anything. What does Auntie Lindo know? Her daughter, she is only best tricky."

America was where all my mother's hopes lay. She had come here in 1949 after losing everything in China: her mother and father, her family home, her first husband, and two daughters, twin baby girls. But she never looked back with regret. There were so many ways for things to get better.

We didn't immediately pick the right kind of prodigy. At first my mother thought I could be a Chinese Shirley Temple.[1] We'd watch Shirley's old movies on TV as though they were training films. My mother would poke my arm and say, "Ni kan"—You watch. And I would see Shirley tapping her feet, or singing a sailor song, or pursing her lips into a very round O while saying, "Oh my goodness."

"Ni kan," said my mother as Shirley's eyes flooded with tears. "You already know how. Don't need talent for crying!"

Soon after my mother got this idea about Shirley Temple, she took me to a beauty training school in the Mission district and put me in the hands of a student who could barely hold the scissors without shaking. Instead of getting big fat curls, I emerged with an uneven mass of crinkly black fuzz. My mother dragged me off to the bathroom and tried to wet down my hair.

"You look like Negro Chinese," she lamented, as if I had done this on purpose.

The instructor of the beauty training school had to lop off these soggy clumps to make my hair even again. "Peter Pan is very popular these days," the instructor assured my mother. I now had hair the length of a boy's, with straight-across bangs that hung at a slant two inches above my eyebrows. I liked the haircut and it made me actually look forward to my future fame.

In fact, in the beginning, I was just as excited as my mother, maybe even more so. I pictured this prodigy part of me as many different images, trying each one on for size. I was a dainty ballerina girl standing by the curtains, waiting to hear the right music that would send me floating on my tiptoes. I was like the Christ child lifted out of the straw

---

1. **Shirley Temple** (1928–): child movie star who was popular during the 1930s. Mothers all across the United States tried to set their daughters' hair to look like Shirley Temple's sausage curls.

manger, crying with holy indignity. I was Cinderella stepping from her pumpkin carriage with sparkly cartoon music filling the air.

In all of my imaginings, I was filled with a sense that I would soon become *perfect*. My mother and father would adore me. I would be beyond reproach. I would never feel the need to sulk for anything.

But sometimes the prodigy in me became impatient. "If you don't hurry up and get me out of here, I'm disappearing for good," it warned. "And then you'll always be nothing."

Every night after dinner, my mother and I would sit at the Formica
50 kitchen table. She would present new tests, taking her examples from stories of amazing children she had read in *Ripley's Believe It or Not*, or *Good Housekeeping, Reader's Digest*, and a dozen other magazines she kept in a pile in our bathroom. My mother got these magazines from people whose houses she cleaned. And since she cleaned many houses each week, we had a great assortment. She would look through them all, searching for stories about remarkable children.

The first night she brought out a story about a three-year-old boy who knew the capitals of all the states and even most of the European countries. A teacher was quoted as saying the little boy could also
60 pronounce the names of the foreign cities correctly.

"What's the capital of Finland?" my mother asked me, looking at the magazine story.

All I knew was the capital of California, because Sacramento was the name of the street we lived on in Chinatown. "Nairobi!"[2] I guessed, saying the most foreign word I could think of. She checked to see if that was possibly one way to pronounce "Helsinki" before showing me the answer.

The tests got harder—multiplying numbers in my head, finding the queen of hearts in a deck of cards, trying to stand on my head without
70 using my hands, predicting the daily temperatures in Los Angeles, New York, and London.

One night I had to look at a page from the Bible for three minutes and then report everything I could remember. "Now Jehoshaphat had riches and honor in abundance and . . . that's all I remember, Ma," I said.

And after seeing my mother's disappointed face once again, something inside of me began to die. I hated the tests, the raised hopes and failed expectations. Before going to bed that night, I looked in the mirror above the bathroom sink and when I saw only my face staring
80 back—and that it would always be this ordinary face—I began to cry. Such a sad, ugly girl! I made high-pitched noises like a crazed animal, trying to scratch out the face in the mirror.

---

2. **Nairobi** (nī·rō′bē): capital of Kenya, a nation in Africa.

INTERPRET
What is narrator's **motivation** for trying to become a prodigy?

She doesn't want her to clean houses for a living.

INTERPRET
What does this passage tell you about the **character** of the mother? List details that support your interpretation.

That she doesn't care about nurturing her she is just trying to make her daughter get famous so that she can get rich.

What change has taken place in the narrator?

She is starting to give up hope on being famous and doesn't care anymore.

listlessly (list′lis·lē) *adv.*: without energy or interest.

Imagine the picture the **simile** in lines 104–105 creates.

mesmerizing (mez′mər·īz′iŋ) *v.* used as *adj.*: spellbinding; hypnotic; fascinating.

What do you predict will happen after the mother has seen the child's performance?

And then I saw what seemed to be the prodigy side of me—because I had never seen that face before. I looked at my reflection, blinking so I could see more clearly. The girl staring back at me was angry, powerful. This girl and I were the same. I had new thoughts, willful thoughts, or rather thoughts filled with lots of won'ts. I won't let her change me, I promised myself. I won't be what I'm not.

So now, on nights when my mother presented her tests, I performed
90 listlessly, my head propped on one arm. I pretended to be bored. And I was. I got so bored I started counting the bellows of the foghorns out on the bay while my mother drilled me in other areas. The sound was comforting and reminded me of the cow jumping over the moon. And the next day, I played a game with myself, seeing if my mother would give up on me before eight bellows. After a while I usually counted only one, maybe two bellows at most. At last she was beginning to give up hope.

Two or three months had gone by without any mention of my being a prodigy again. And then one day my mother was watching *The Ed Sullivan Show* on TV. The TV was old and the sound kept shorting out.
100 Every time my mother got halfway up from the sofa to adjust the set, the sound would go back on and Ed would be talking. As soon as she sat down, Ed would go silent again. She got up, the TV broke into loud piano music. She sat down. Silence. Up and down, back and forth, quiet and loud. It was like a stiff embraceless dance between her and the TV set. Finally she stood by the set with her hand on the sound dial.

She seemed entranced by the music, a little frenzied piano piece with this mesmerizing quality, sort of quick passages and then teasing, lilting ones before it returned to the quick, playful parts.

"Ni kan," my mother said, calling me over with hurried hand
110 gestures. "Look here."

I could see why my mother was fascinated by the music. It was being pounded out by a little Chinese girl, about nine years old, with a Peter Pan haircut. The girl had the sauciness of a Shirley Temple. She was proudly modest like a proper Chinese child. And she also did this fancy sweep of a curtsy, so that the fluffy skirt of her white dress cascaded slowly to the floor like the petals of a large carnation.

In spite of these warning signs, I wasn't worried. Our family had no piano and we couldn't afford to buy one, let alone reams[3] of sheet music and piano lessons. So I could be generous in my comments when my
120 mother bad-mouthed the little girl on TV.

"Play note right, but doesn't sound good! No singing sound," complained my mother.

---

3. reams: here, great amount. A ream of paper is about five hundred sheets.

"What are you picking on her for?" I said carelessly. "She's pretty good. Maybe she's not the best, but she's trying hard." I knew almost immediately I would be sorry I said that.

"Just like you," she said. "Not the best. Because you not trying." She gave a little huff as she let go of the sound dial and sat down on the sofa.

130 The little Chinese girl sat down also to play an encore of "Anitra's Dance" by Grieg.[4] I remember the song, because later on I had to learn how to play it.

Three days after watching *The Ed Sullivan Show*, my mother told me what my schedule would be for piano lessons and piano practice. She had talked to Mr. Chong, who lived on the first floor of our apartment building. Mr. Chong was a retired piano teacher, and my mother had traded housecleaning services for weekly lessons and a piano for me to practice on every day, two hours a day, from four until six.

When my mother told me this, I felt as though I had been sent to hell. I whined and then kicked my foot a little when I couldn't stand it
140 anymore.

"Why don't you like me the way I am? I'm *not* a genius! I can't play the piano. And even if I could, I wouldn't go on TV if you paid me a million dollars!" I cried.

My mother slapped me. "Who ask you be genius?" she shouted. "Only ask you be your best. For you sake. You think I want you be genius? Hnnh! What for! Who ask you!"

"So ungrateful," I heard her mutter in Chinese. "If she had as much talent as she has temper, she would be famous now."

Mr. Chong, whom I secretly nicknamed Old Chong, was very strange,
150 always tapping his fingers to the silent music of an invisible orchestra. He looked ancient in my eyes. He had lost most of the hair on top of his head and he wore thick glasses and had eyes that always looked tired and sleepy. But he must have been younger than I thought, since he lived with his mother and was not yet married.

I met Old Lady Chong once and that was enough. She had this peculiar smell like a baby that had done something in its pants. And her fingers felt like a dead person's, like an old peach I once found in the back of the refrigerator; the skin just slid off the meat when I picked it up.

I soon found out why Old Chong had retired from teaching piano. He
160 was deaf. "Like Beethoven!" he shouted to me. "We're both listening only in our head!" And he would start to conduct his frantic silent sonatas.

---

4. **Grieg** (grēg): Edvard Grieg (1843–1907), Norwegian composer; "Anitra's Dance" is from his *Peer Gynt Suite*.

INFER

How does the narrator know she has just said the wrong thing?

_____

_____

_____

_____

IDENTIFY

How does the mother arrange for piano lessons? Underline the words giving the answer.

_____

_____

INTERPRET

This is the first time the narrator openly expresses her frustration to her mother. What causes her frustration?

_____

_____

_____

_____

_____

_____

_____

_____

_____

_____

_____

_____

_____

_____

_____

_____

_____

_____

_____

_____

_____

_____

INTERPRET

Why was the narrator lazy in her practice habits as a child?

_____

_____

_____

_____

_____

_____

_____

_____

WORDS TO OWN
discordant (dis·kord′′nt) *adj.:*
clashing; not in harmony.

_____

_____

_____

_____

_____

_____

_____

Our lessons went like this. He would open the book and point to different things, explaining their purpose: "Key! Treble! Bass! No sharps or flats! So this is C major! Listen now and play after me!"

And then he would play the C scale a few times, a simple chord, and then, as if inspired by an old, unreachable itch, he gradually added more notes and running trills and a pounding bass until the music was really something quite grand.

170   I would play after him, the simple scale, the simple chord, and then I just played some nonsense that sounded like a cat running up and down on top of garbage cans. Old Chong smiled and applauded and then said, "Very good! But now you must learn to keep time!"

So that's how I discovered that Old Chong's eyes were too slow to keep up with the wrong notes I was playing. He went through the motions in half-time. To help me keep rhythm, he stood behind me, pushing down on my right shoulder for every beat. He balanced pennies on top of my wrists so I would keep them still as I slowly played scales and arpeggios.[5] He had me curve my hand around an apple and keep

180   that shape when playing chords. He marched stiffly to show me how to make each finger dance up and down, staccato,[6] like an obedient little soldier.

He taught me all these things, and that was how I also learned I could be lazy and get away with mistakes, lots of mistakes. If I hit the wrong notes because I hadn't practiced enough, I never corrected myself. I just kept playing in rhythm. And Old Chong kept conducting his own private reverie.

So maybe I never really gave myself a fair chance. I did pick up the basics pretty quickly, and I might have become a good pianist at that

190   young age. But I was so determined not to try, not to be anybody different, that I learned to play only the most earsplitting preludes, the most discordant hymns.

Over the next year, I practiced like this, dutifully in my own way. And then one day I heard my mother and her friend Lindo Jong both talking in a loud bragging tone of voice so others could hear. It was after church, and I was leaning against the brick wall, wearing a dress with stiff white petticoats. Auntie Lindo's daughter, Waverly, who was about my age, was standing farther down the wall, about five feet away. We had grown up together and shared all the closeness of two sisters

200   squabbling over crayons and dolls. In other words, for the most part, we hated each other. I thought she was snotty. Waverly Jong had gained a certain amount of fame as "Chinatown's Littlest Chinese Chess Champion."

---

5. **arpeggios** (är·pej′ōz): chords whose notes are played quickly one after another, rather than at the same time.
6. **staccato** (stə·kät′ō): with clear-cut breaks between notes.

"She bring home too many trophy," <u>lamented</u> Auntie Lindo that Sunday. "All day she play chess. All day I have no time do nothing but dust off her winnings." She threw a scolding look at Waverly, who pretended not to see her.

"You lucky you don't have this problem," said Auntie Lindo with a sigh to my mother.

210   And my mother squared her shoulders and bragged: "Our problem worser than yours. If we ask Jing-mei wash dish, she hear nothing but music. It's like you can't stop this natural talent."

And right then, I was determined to put a stop to her foolish pride.

A few weeks later, Old Chong and my mother conspired to have me play in a talent show which would be held in the church hall. By then, my parents had saved up enough to buy me a secondhand piano, a black Wurlitzer spinet with a scarred bench. It was the showpiece of our living room.

For the talent show, I was to play a piece called "Pleading Child"
220   from Schumann's[7] *Scenes from Childhood*. It was a simple, moody piece that sounded more difficult than it was. I was supposed to memorize the whole thing, playing the repeat parts twice to make the piece sound longer. But I <u>dawdled</u> over it, playing a few bars and then cheating, looking up to see what notes followed. I never really listened to what I was playing. I daydreamed about being somewhere else, about being someone else.

The part I liked to practice best was the fancy curtsy: right foot out, touch the rose on the carpet with a pointed foot, sweep to the side, left leg bends, look up and smile.

230   My parents invited all the couples from the Joy Luck Club[8] to witness my debut. Auntie Lindo and Uncle Tin were there. Waverly and her two older brothers had also come. The first two rows were filled with children both younger and older than I was. The littlest ones got to go first. They recited simple nursery rhymes, squawked out tunes on miniature violins, twirled Hula-Hoops, pranced in pink ballet tutus, and when they bowed or curtsied, the audience would sigh in unison, "Awww," and then clap enthusiastically.

When my turn came, I was very confident. I remember my childish excitement. It was as if I knew, without a doubt, that the prodigy side
240   of me really did exist. I had no fear whatsoever, no nervousness. I remember thinking to myself, This is it! This is it! I looked out over the audience, at my mother's blank face, my father's yawn, Auntie Lindo's stiff-lipped smile, Waverly's sulky expression. I had on a white dress

---

7. **Schumann**: Robert Schumann (1810–1856), German composer.
8. **Joy Luck Club**: social club to which Jing-mei's mother and three other Chinese mothers belong

WORDS TO OWN
lamented (lə·ment′id) *v.*: said with regret or sorrow. *Lamented* also means "mourned or grieved for" or "regretted deeply."

√ **INFER**
What does this detail reveal about Jing-mei's parents?

WORDS TO OWN
dawdled (dôd′'ld) *v.*: wasted time; lingered.

√ **INFER**
What do these details tell you about Jing-mei's parents and their expectations about her performance?

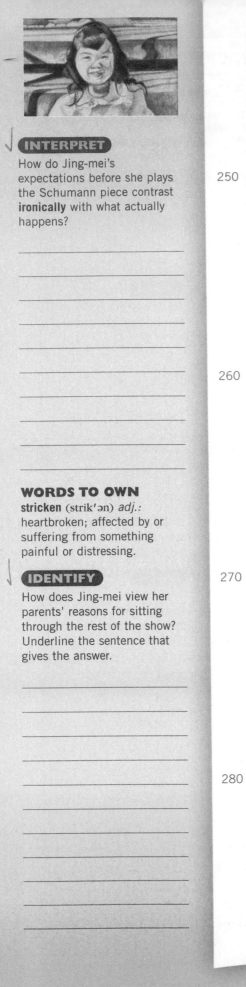

INTERPRET

How do Jing-mei's expectations before she plays the Schumann piece contrast **ironically** with what actually happens?

_____

_____

_____

_____

_____

_____

_____

_____

WORDS TO OWN

stricken (strik'ən) *adj.*: heartbroken; affected by or suffering from something painful or distressing.

IDENTIFY

How does Jing-mei view her parents' reasons for sitting through the rest of the show? Underline the sentence that gives the answer.

_____

_____

_____

_____

_____

_____

_____

layered with sheets of lace, and a pink bow in my Peter Pan haircut. As I sat down I envisioned people jumping to their feet and Ed Sullivan rushing up to introduce me to everyone on TV.

And I started to play. It was so beautiful. I was so caught up in how lovely I looked that at first I didn't worry how I would sound. So it was a surprise to me when I hit the first wrong note and I realized something
250 didn't sound quite right. And then I hit another, and another followed that. A chill started at the top of my head and began to trickle down. Yet I couldn't stop playing, as though my hands were bewitched. I kept thinking my fingers would adjust themselves back, like a train switching to the right track. I played this strange jumble through two repeats, the sour notes staying with me all the way to the end.

When I stood up, I discovered my legs were shaking. Maybe I had just been nervous and the audience, like Old Chong, had seen me go through the right motions and had not heard anything wrong at all. I swept my right foot out, went down on my knee, looked up and smiled.
260 The room was quiet, except for Old Chong, who was beaming and shouting, "Bravo! Bravo! Well done!" But then I saw my mother's face, her stricken face. The audience clapped weakly, and as I walked back to my chair, with my whole face quivering as I tried not to cry, I heard a little boy whisper loudly to his mother, "That was awful," and the mother whispered back, "Well, she certainly tried."

And now I realized how many people were in the audience, the whole world it seemed. I was aware of eyes burning into my back. I felt the shame of my mother and father as they sat stiffly throughout the rest of the show.
270 We could have escaped during intermission. Pride and some strange sense of honor must have anchored my parents to their chairs. And so we watched it all: the eighteen-year-old boy with a fake mustache who did a magic show and juggled flaming hoops while riding a unicycle. The breasted girl with white makeup who sang from *Madama Butterfly*[9] and got honorable mention. And the eleven-year-old boy who won first prize playing a tricky violin song that sounded like a busy bee.

After the show, the Hsus, the Jongs, and the St. Clairs from the Joy Luck Club came up to my mother and father.

"Lots of talented kids," Auntie Lindo said vaguely, smiling broadly.
280 "That was somethin' else," said my father, and I wondered if he was referring to me in a humorous way, or whether he even remembered what I had done.

Waverly looked at me and shrugged her shoulders. "You aren't a genius like me," she said matter-of-factly. And if I hadn't felt so bad, I would have pulled her braids and punched her stomach.

---

9. *Madama Butterfly*: opera by the Italian composer Giacomo Puccini.

But my mother's expression was what devastated me: a quiet, blank look that said she had lost everything. I felt the same way, and it seemed as if everybody were now coming up, like gawkers at the scene of an accident, to see what parts were actually missing. When we got on the bus to go home, my father was humming the busy-bee tune and my mother was silent. I kept thinking she wanted to wait until we got home before shouting at me. But when my father unlocked the door to our apartment, my mother walked in and then went to the back, into the bedroom. No accusations. No blame. And in a way, I felt disappointed. I had been waiting for her to start shouting, so I could shout back and cry and blame her for all my misery.

I assumed my talent-show fiasco meant I never had to play the piano again. But two days later, after school, my mother came out of the kitchen and saw me watching TV.

"Four clock," she reminded me as if it were any other day. I was stunned, as though she were asking me to go through the talent-show torture again. I wedged myself more tightly in front of the TV.

"Turn off TV," she called from the kitchen five minutes later.

I didn't budge. And then I decided. I didn't have to do what my mother said anymore. I wasn't her slave. This wasn't China. I had listened to her before and look what happened. She was the stupid one.

She came out from the kitchen and stood in the arched entryway of the living room. "Four clock," she said once again, louder.

"I'm not going to play anymore," I said nonchalantly. "Why should I? I'm not a genius."

She walked over and stood in front of the TV. I saw her chest was heaving up and down in an angry way.

"No!" I said, and I now felt stronger, as if my true self had finally emerged. So this was what had been inside me all along.

"No! I won't!" I screamed.

She yanked me by the arm, pulled me off the floor, snapped off the TV. She was frighteningly strong, half pulling, half carrying me toward the piano as I kicked the throw rugs under my feet. She lifted me up and onto the hard bench. I was sobbing by now, looking at her bitterly. Her chest was heaving even more and her mouth was open, smiling crazily, as if she were pleased I was crying.

"You want me to be someone that I'm not!" I sobbed. "I'll never be the kind of daughter you want me to be!"

"Only two kinds of daughters," she shouted in Chinese. "Those who are obedient and those who follow their own mind! Only one kind of daughter can live in this house. Obedient daughter!"

"Then I wish I wasn't your daughter. I wish you weren't my mother," I shouted. As I said these things, I got scared. It felt like worms

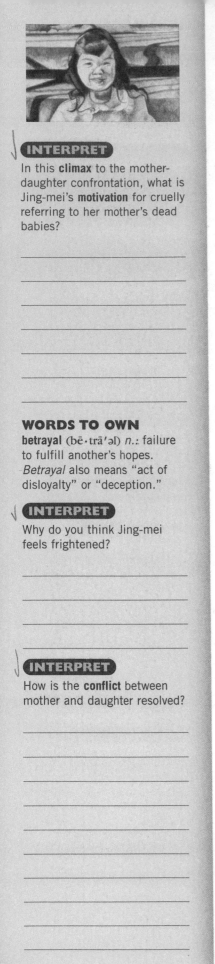

INTERPRET

In this **climax** to the mother-daughter confrontation, what is Jing-mei's **motivation** for cruelly referring to her mother's dead babies?

_____

_____

_____

_____

_____

_____

WORDS TO OWN

betrayal (bĕ·trā′əl) _n._: failure to fulfill another's hopes. _Betrayal_ also means "act of disloyalty" or "deception."

INTERPRET

Why do you think Jing-mei feels frightened?

_____

_____

_____

INTERPRET

How is the **conflict** between mother and daughter resolved?

_____

_____

_____

_____

_____

_____

_____

_____

330 and toads and slimy things crawling out of my chest, but it also felt good, as if this awful side of me had surfaced, at last.

"Too late change this," said my mother shrilly.

And I could sense her anger rising to its breaking point. I wanted to see it spill over. And that's when I remembered the babies she had lost in China, the ones we never talked about. "Then I wish I'd never been born!" I shouted. "I wish I were dead! Like them."

It was as if I had said the magic words. Alakazam!—and her face went blank, her mouth closed, her arms went slack, and she backed out of the room, stunned, as if she were blowing away like a small brown leaf, thin, brittle, lifeless.

340 It was not the only disappointment my mother felt in me. In the years that followed, I failed her so many times, each time asserting my own will, my right to fall short of expectations. I didn't get straight A's. I didn't become class president. I didn't get into Stanford.[10] I dropped out of college.

For unlike my mother, I did not believe I could be anything I wanted to be. I could only be me.

And for all those years, we never talked about the disaster at the recital or my terrible accusations afterward at the piano bench. All that remained unchecked, like a betrayal that was now unspeakable. So I

350 never found a way to ask her why she had hoped for something so large that failure was inevitable.

And even worse, I never asked her what frightened me the most: Why had she given up hope?

For after our struggle at the piano, she never mentioned my playing again. The lessons stopped. The lid to the piano was closed, shutting out the dust, my misery, and her dreams.

So she surprised me. A few years ago, she offered to give me the piano, for my thirtieth birthday. I had not played in all those years. I saw the offer as a sign of forgiveness, a tremendous burden removed.

360 "Are you sure?" I asked shyly. "I mean, won't you and Dad miss it?"

"No, this your piano," she said firmly. "Always your piano. You only one can play."

"Well, I probably can't play anymore," I said. "It's been years."

"You pick up fast," said my mother, as if she knew this was certain. "You have natural talent. You could been genius if you want to."

"No, I couldn't."

"You just not trying," said my mother. And she was neither angry nor sad. She said it as if to announce a fact that could never be disproved. "Take it," she said.

---

10. **Stanford**: high-ranking university in Stanford, California.

370   But I didn't at first. It was enough that she had offered it to me. And after that, every time I saw it in my parents' living room, standing in front of the bay windows, it made me feel proud, as if it were a shiny trophy I had won back.

Last week I sent a tuner over to my parents' apartment and had the piano reconditioned, for purely sentimental reasons. My mother had died a few months before, and I had been getting things in order for my father, a little bit at a time. I put the jewelry in special silk pouches. The sweaters she had knitted in yellow, pink, bright orange—all the colors I hated—I put those in mothproof boxes. I found some old Chinese silk
380 dresses, the kind with little slits up the sides. I rubbed the old silk against my skin, then wrapped them in tissue and decided to take them home with me.

After I had the piano tuned, I opened the lid and touched the keys. It sounded even richer than I remembered. Really, it was a very good piano. Inside the bench were the same exercise notes with handwritten scales, the same secondhand music books with their covers held together with yellow tape.

I opened up the Schumann book to the dark little piece I had played at the recital. It was on the left-hand side of the page, "Pleading Child."
390 It looked more difficult than I remembered. I played a few bars, surprised at how easily the notes came back to me.

And for the first time, or so it seemed, I noticed the piece on the right-hand side. It was called "Perfectly Contented." I tried to play this one as well. It had a lighter melody but the same flowing rhythm and turned out to be quite easy. "Pleading Child" was shorter but slower; "Perfectly Contented" was longer but faster. And after I played them both a few times, I realized they were two halves of the same song.

✓ **INFER**

What does Jing-mei imply in the final sentence of the story?

Motivation

Motivation is a person's reasons for doing something or for behaving in a certain way. Understanding motivation is important for anyone—actor, writer, or reader—who wants to get inside a character's head, or to understand what makes him or her "tick."

1. What do you think motivates the mother to push Jing-mei into being a prodigy? Consider:
   • the mother's life in China
   • her life in America

   _____

   _____

   _____

   _____

2. What do you think motivates Jing-mei to shout and scream at her mother after the fiasco at the talent show?

   _____

   _____

   _____

   _____

3. Do you think someone else's high expectations can make a person *want* to fail, or do you think failure results more often from *low* expectations? Explain your opinion, drawing examples when you can from your own experiences and those of people you know.

   _____

   _____

   _____

   _____

   _____

   _____

   _____

   _____

   _____

   _____

Vocabulary: How to Own a Word

Context Clues

Read the sentences below. Using context clues and definitions from your Words to Own as a guide, circle the word in parentheses that correctly completes the sentence. Underline any context clues that help you arrive at your answer.

> EXAMPLE: My parents entered the concert hall (*listlessly*, *nonchalantly*), masking their concern about whether or not I'd do well.

Word Bank
prodigy
listlessly
mesmerizing
discordant
lamented
dawdled
stricken
fiasco
nonchalantly
betrayal

1. The piano student (*dawdled*, *lamented*) over her assignment, wasting time by daydreaming.

2. Her performance was a (*betrayal*, *fiasco*), but she had to admit that her failure resulted from a lack of practice.

3. The string quartet had a (*discordant*, *mesmerizing*) effect on me, fascinating me with its harmonies and somber mood.

4. She was a noisy child, banging on the keyboard and filling the room with (*listless*, *discordant*) sounds.

5. The parents had great hopes that their son would be a concert pianist, and they felt a certain (*betrayal*, *prodigy*) when he chose a career as a building inspector.

6. "How disappointing!" (*lamented*, *mesmerized*) the teacher. He regretted spending so much time on such a bored and grumpy student.

7. The guitarist's face took on a (*stricken*, *mesmerizing*) expression, as if every chord caused him great heartbreak.

8. Because the musicians played (*listlessly*, *discordantly*), the concert lacked energy and the audience went to sleep.

9. After listening to the young violinist, the maestro pronounced her to be a true (*fiasco*, *prodigy*) with an unusual talent and a rare genius.

10. She was indifferent to praise, for she was quite confident about her talent and accepted it (*nonchalantly*, *listlessly*).

The Pedestrian

Make the Connection

Questioning the Future

Many writers of science fiction, including Ray Bradbury, set their stories in the future. "The Pedestrian" takes place a half century from now in the year 2053.

What will life be like in the year 2053? To spark your thinking, read the phrases in the topic box below. Then, use the lines provided to write four specific questions about life a half century from now.

TOPICS		
family life	television	travel
technology	clothing	education
house design	careers	the environment

1. _____

_____

2. _____

_____

3. _____

_____

4. _____

_____

Ray Bradbury

The Pedestrian

INTERPRET

In the first two paragraphs of the story, what **atmosphere** or **mood** does the author establish? Underline two details that help to create the mood.

_____

_____

_____

_____

WORDS TO OWN

manifest (man′ə·fest′) *v.:* appear; become evident. *Manifest* also means "show" or "reveal."
intermittent (in′tər·mit′′nt) *adj.:* appearing or occurring from time to time.

_____

_____

_____

_____

_____

IDENTIFY

In lines 27–34, circle words or phrases appealing to the senses of touch, sight, hearing, and smell.

_____

_____

_____

_____

_____

_____

_____

_____

To enter out into that silence that was the city at eight o'clock of a misty evening in November, to put your feet upon that buckling concrete walk, to step over grassy seams and make your way, hands in pockets, through the silences, that was what Mr. Leonard Mead most dearly loved to do. He would stand upon the corner of an intersection and peer down long moonlit avenues of sidewalk in four directions, deciding which way to go, but it really made no difference; he was alone in this world of A.D. 2053, or as good as alone, and with a final decision made, a path selected, he would stride off, sending patterns of frosty air before him
10 like the smoke of a cigar.

Sometimes he would walk for hours and miles and return only at midnight to his house. And on his way he would see the cottages and homes with their dark windows, and it was not unequal to walking through a graveyard where only the faintest glimmers of firefly light appeared in flickers behind the windows. Sudden gray phantoms seemed to manifest upon inner room walls where a curtain was still undrawn against the night, or there were whisperings and murmurs where a window in a tomblike building was still open.

Mr. Leonard Mead would pause, cock his head, listen, look, and
20 march on, his feet making no noise on the lumpy walk. For long ago he had wisely changed to sneakers when strolling at night, because the dogs in intermittent squads would parallel his journey with barkings if he wore hard heels, and lights might click on and faces appear and an entire street be startled by the passing of a lone figure, himself, in the early November evening.

On this particular evening he began his journey in a westerly direction, toward the hidden sea. There was a good crystal frost in the air; it cut the nose and made the lungs blaze like a Christmas tree inside; you could feel the cold light going on and off, all the branches filled with
30 invisible snow. He listened to the faint push of his soft shoes through autumn leaves with satisfaction and whistled a cold, quiet whistle between his teeth, occasionally picking up a leaf as he passed, examining its skeletal pattern in the infrequent lamplights as he went on, smelling its rusty smell.

"Hello, in there," he whispered to every house on every side as he moved. "What's up tonight on Channel 4, Channel 7, Channel 9? Where are the cowboys rushing, and do I see the United States Cavalry over the next hill to the rescue?"

The street was silent and long and empty, with only his shadow
40 moving like the shadow of a hawk in midcountry. If he closed his eyes and stood very still, frozen, he could imagine himself upon the center of a plain, a wintry, windless Arizona desert with no house in a thousand miles, and only dry riverbeds, the streets, for company.

"What is it now?" he asked the houses, noticing his wristwatch.
"Eight-thirty P.M.? Time for a dozen assorted murders? A quiz? A revue?
A comedian falling off the stage?"

Was that a murmur of laughter from within a moon-white house? He
hesitated but went on when nothing more happened. He stumbled over
a particularly uneven section of sidewalk. The cement was vanishing
50   under flowers and grass. In ten years of walking by night or day, for
thousands of miles, he had never met another person walking, not one
in all that time.

He came to a cloverleaf intersection which stood silent where two
main highways crossed the town. During the day it was a thunderous
surge of cars, the gas stations open, a great insect rustling, and a
ceaseless jockeying for position as the scarab beetles,[1] a faint incense
puttering from their exhausts, skimmed homeward to the far directions.
But now these highways, too, were like streams in a dry season, all stone
and bed and moon radiance.

60   He turned back on a side street, circling around toward his home. He
was within a block of his destination when the lone car turned a corner
quite suddenly and flashed a fierce white cone of light upon him. He
stood entranced, not unlike a night moth, stunned by the illumination
and then drawn toward it.

A metallic voice called to him:

"Stand still. Stay where you are! Don't move!"

He halted.

"Put up your hands!"

"But———" he said.

70   "Your hands up! Or we'll shoot!"

The police, of course, but what a rare, incredible thing; in a city of
three million, there was only *one* police car left, wasn't that correct? Ever
since a year ago, 2052, the election year, the force had been cut down
from three cars to one. Crime was ebbing; there was no need now for the
police, save for this one lone car wandering and wandering the empty
streets.

"Your name?" said the police car in a metallic whisper. He couldn't
see the men in it for the bright light in his eyes.

"Leonard Mead," he said.

80   "Speak up!"

"Leonard Mead!"

"Business or profession?"

"I guess you'd call me a writer."

"No profession," said the police car, as if talking to itself. The light
held him fixed, like a museum specimen, needle thrust through chest.

---

1. **scarab beetles:** stout-bodied, brilliantly colored beetles. Bradbury is using the term as a
   metaphor for automobiles.

INFER

How does the writer create
suspense in lines 60–64?

WORDS TO OWN

ebbing (eb′iŋ) *v.:* lessening or
weakening. The ebb is the flow
of water away from the land as
the tide falls.

INFER

What is Bradbury's **purpose** in
having the police say writing is
"No profession"?

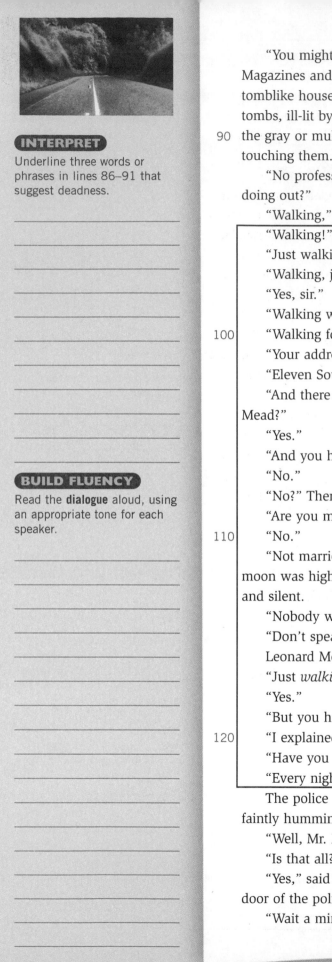

INTERPRET

Underline three words or phrases in lines 86–91 that suggest deadness.

_____

_____

_____

_____

_____

_____

_____

_____

_____

_____

BUILD FLUENCY

Read the **dialogue** aloud, using an appropriate tone for each speaker.

_____

_____

_____

_____

_____

_____

_____

_____

_____

_____

_____

_____

_____

_____

_____

_____

_____

"You might say that," said Mr. Mead. He hadn't written in years. Magazines and books didn't sell anymore. Everything went on in the tomblike houses at night now, he thought, continuing his fancy. The tombs, ill-lit by television light, where the people sat like the dead,

90 the gray or multicolored lights touching their faces, but never really touching them.

"No profession," said the phonograph voice, hissing. "What are you doing out?"

"Walking," said Leonard Mead.

"Walking!"

"Just walking," he said simply, but his face felt cold.

"Walking, just walking, walking?"

"Yes, sir."

"Walking where? For what?"

100 "Walking for air. Walking to *see*."

"Your address!"

"Eleven South Saint James Street."

"And there is air *in* your house, you have an air *conditioner*, Mr. Mead?"

"Yes."

"And you have a viewing screen in your house to see with?"

"No."

"No?" There was a crackling quiet that in itself was an accusation.

"Are you married, Mr. Mead?"

110 "No."

"Not married," said the police voice behind the fiery beam. The moon was high and clear among the stars and the houses were gray and silent.

"Nobody wanted me," said Leonard Mead with a smile.

"Don't speak unless you're spoken to!"

Leonard Mead waited in the cold night.

"Just *walking*, Mr. Mead?"

"Yes."

"But you haven't explained for what purpose."

120 "I explained: for air, and to see, and just to walk."

"Have you done this often?"

"Every night for years."

The police car sat in the center of the street with its radio throat faintly humming.

"Well, Mr. Mead," it said.

"Is that all?" he asked politely.

"Yes," said the voice. "Here." There was a sigh, a pop. The back door of the police car sprang wide. "Get in."

"Wait a minute, I haven't done anything!"

130   "Get in."

"I protest!"

"Mr. Mead."

He walked like a man suddenly drunk. As he passed the front window of the car, he looked in. As he had expected, there was no one in the front seat, no one in the car at all.

"Get in."

He put his hand to the door and peered into the back seat, which was a little cell, a little black jail with bars. It smelled of riveted[2] steel. It smelled of harsh antiseptic; it smelled too clean and hard and metallic.

140 There was nothing soft there.

"Now, if you had a wife to give you an alibi," said the iron voice. "But———"

"Where are you taking me?"

The car hesitated, or rather gave a faint, whirring click, as if information, somewhere, was dropping card by punch-slotted card under electric eyes. "To the Psychiatric Center for Research on Regressive Tendencies."

He got in. The door shut with a soft thud. The police car rolled through the night avenues, flashing its dim lights ahead.

150   They passed one house on one street a moment later, one house in an entire city of houses that were dark, but this one particular house had all of its electric lights brightly lit, every window a loud yellow illumination, square and warm in the cool darkness.

"That's *my* house," said Leonard Mead.

No one answered him.

The car moved down the empty riverbed streets and off away, leaving the empty streets with the empty sidewalks and no sound and no motion all the rest of the chill November night.

INFER

What is the author's **purpose** in adding this description of Mead's house?

EVALUATE

What feelings does this final paragraph leave you with? Circle three key words or phrases that help to create these feelings.

---

2. **riveted** (riv'it·id): held together by rivets (metal bolts or pins).

Setting

The **setting** of a story establishes the time and place of the action. Setting can be used to establish a **mood** or **atmosphere**, and also to suggest the writer's particular worldview or outlook on human life and behavior.

Descriptions of setting may contain words with powerful **connotations**, or emotional overtones. Such words affect the reader's response to the setting and often help to create a particular atmosphere. Here are some passages from "The Pedestrian" that use words with strong connotations. On the lines below each passage, write down what you think is the strongest word or phrase. Then, describe briefly what the word or phrase suggests to you and how it makes you feel.

1. And on his way he would see the cottages and homes with their dark windows, and it was not unequal to walking through a graveyard. . . . (page 56)

   _____

   _____

   _____

2. Sudden gray phantoms seemed to manifest upon inner room walls . . . , or there were whisperings and murmurs where a window in a tomblike building was still open. (page 56)

   _____

   _____

   _____

3. The street was silent and long and empty, with only his shadow moving like the shadow of a hawk in midcountry. (page 56)

   _____

   _____

   _____

4. It [the inside of the car] smelled of harsh antiseptic; it smelled too clean and hard and metallic. There was nothing soft there. (page 59)

   _____

   _____

   _____

Vocabulary: How to Own a Word

Question and Answer

Answer the following questions about "The Pedestrian," using context clues to show that you understand the meaning of the italicized Words to Own.

1. Does the story *manifest* its eerie subject matter right away?

     _____

     _____

     _____

2. Which activity does the police car consider *regressive*: watching television or walking at night?

     _____

     _____

     _____

3. Which could be described as *intermittent* in the story: the sound of people laughing or the silence?

     _____

     _____

     _____

4. Which is *ebbing* in the story: television viewing or crime?

     _____

     _____

     _____

Where Have You Gone, Charming Billy?

Make the Connection

Meeting a Challenge

In this story, Tim O'Brien, who served in Vietnam, describes the experiences of a young soldier who has come straight from training camp to join his platoon. Throughout his long day on maneuvers with a group of soldiers whom he hardly knows, Private First Class Paul Berlin experiences the realities of war for the first time.

Have you ever been in a frightening situation: an accident, a flood, maybe even war? What did you do to make yourself feel better? On the chart below, record a few notes about your experience. If you don't want to write about yourself, write about someone you know.

Challenging Situation	Ways to Cope/Feel Better

Where Have You Gone, Charming Billy?

Tim O'Brien

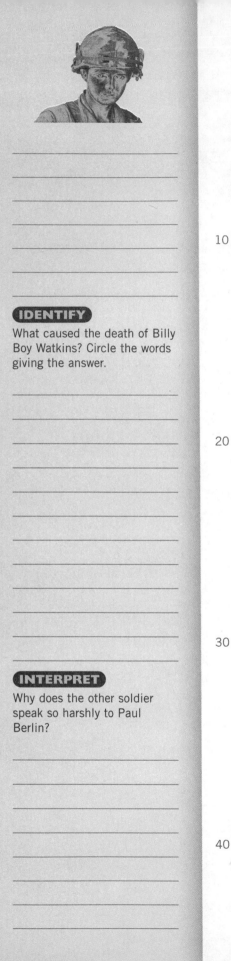

IDENTIFY

What caused the death of Billy Boy Watkins? Circle the words giving the answer.

INTERPRET

Why does the other soldier speak so harshly to Paul Berlin?

The platoon of twenty-six soldiers moved slowly in the dark, single file, not talking. One by one, like sheep in a dream, they passed through the hedgerow, crossed quietly over a meadow, and came down to the rice paddy. There they stopped. Their leader knelt down, motioning with his hand, and one by one the other soldiers squatted in the shadows, vanishing in the primitive stealth of warfare. For a long time they did not move. Except for the sounds of their breathing, the twenty-six men were very quiet: some of them excited by the adventure, some of them afraid, some of them exhausted from the long night march, some of them
10 looking forward to reaching the sea, where they would be safe. At the rear of the column, Private First Class Paul Berlin lay quietly with his forehead resting on the black plastic stock of his rifle, his eyes closed. He was pretending he was not in the war, pretending he had not watched Billy Boy Watkins die of a heart attack that afternoon. He was pretending he was a boy again, camping with his father in the midnight summer along the Des Moines River. In the dark, with his eyes pinched shut, he pretended. He pretended that when he opened his eyes, his father would be there by the campfire and they would talk softly about whatever came to mind and then roll into their sleeping bags, and that later they'd wake
20 up and it would be morning and there would not be a war, and that Billy Boy Watkins had not died of a heart attack that afternoon. He pretended he was not a soldier.

In the morning, when they reached the sea, it would be better. The hot afternoon would be over, he would bathe in the sea, and he would forget how frightened he had been on his first day at the war. The second day would not be so bad. He would learn.

There was a sound beside him, a movement, and then a breathed "Hey!"

He opened his eyes, shivering as if emerging from a deep nightmare.
30 "Hey!" a shadow whispered. "We're *moving*. Get up."

"Okay."

"You sleepin', or something?"

"No." He could not make out the soldier's face. With clumsy, concrete hands he clawed for his rifle, found it, found his helmet.

The soldier shadow grunted. "You got a lot to learn, buddy. I'd shoot you if I thought you was sleepin'. Let's go."

Private First Class Paul Berlin blinked.

Ahead of him, silhouetted against the sky, he saw the string of soldiers wading into the flat paddy, the black outline of their shoulders
40 and packs and weapons. He was comfortable. He did not want to move. But he was afraid, for it was his first night at the war, so he hurried to catch up, stumbling once, scraping his knee, groping as though blind; his boots sank into the thick paddy water, and he smelled it all around him. He would tell his mother how it smelled: mud and algae and cattle

manure and chlorophyll;[1] decay, breeding mosquitoes and leeches as big as mice; the <u>fecund</u> warmth of the paddy waters rising up to his cut knee. But he would not tell how frightened he had been.

Once they reached the sea, things would be better. They would have their rear guarded by three thousand miles of ocean, and they would
50 swim and dive into the breakers and hunt crayfish and smell the salt, and they would be safe.

He followed the shadow of the man in front of him. It was a clear night. Already the Southern Cross[2] was out. And other stars he could not yet name—soon, he thought, he would learn their names. And puffy night clouds. There was not yet a moon. Wading through the paddy, his boots made sleepy, sloshing sounds, like a lullaby, and he tried not to think. Though he was afraid, he now knew that fear came in many degrees and types and peculiar categories, and he knew that his fear now was not so bad as it had been in the hot afternoon, when poor Billy
60 Boy Watkins got killed by a heart attack. His fear now was diffuse and unformed: ghosts in the tree line, nighttime fears of a child, a boogeyman in the closet that his father would open to show empty, saying, "See? Nothing there, champ. Now you can sleep." In the afternoon it had been worse: The fear had been bundled and tight and he'd been on his hands and knees, crawling like an insect, an ant escaping a giant's footsteps, and thinking nothing, brain flopping like wet cement in a mixer, not thinking at all, watching while Billy Boy Watkins died.

Now, as he stepped out of the paddy onto a narrow dirt path, now the fear was mostly the fear of being so terribly afraid again.

70 He tried not to think.

There were tricks he'd learned to keep from thinking. Counting: He counted his steps, concentrating on the numbers, pretending that the steps were dollar bills and that each step through the night made him richer and richer, so that soon he would become a wealthy man, and he kept counting and considered the ways he might spend the money after the war and what he would do. He would look his father in the eye and shrug and say, "It was pretty bad at first, but I learned a lot and I got used to it." Then he would tell his father the story of Billy Boy Watkins. But he would never let on how frightened he had been. "Not so bad,"
80 he would say instead, making his father feel proud.

Songs, another trick to stop from thinking: *Where have you gone, Billy Boy, Billy Boy, oh, where have you gone, charming Billy? I have gone to seek a wife, she's the joy of my life, but she's a young thing and cannot leave her mother*, and other songs that he sang in his thoughts as he walked toward the sea. And when he reached the sea, he would dig a

VISUALIZE

Underline words and phrases in lines 60–67 that help you visualize Paul's fear.

PREDICT

Based on what you've learned about the main **character** so far, what do you predict the **theme** of this story will be?

1. **chlorophyll** (klôr′ə·fil′): green substance found in plant cells.
2. **Southern Cross:** constellation, or group of stars, in the Southern Hemisphere.

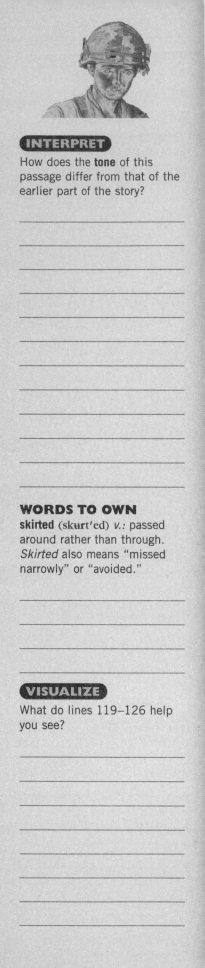

INTERPRET

How does the **tone** of this passage differ from that of the earlier part of the story?

_____

_____

_____

_____

_____

_____

_____

_____

_____

_____

WORDS TO OWN
skirted (skʉrt′ed) v.: passed around rather than through. *Skirted* also means "missed narrowly" or "avoided."

_____

_____

_____

VISUALIZE

What do lines 119–126 help you see?

_____

_____

_____

_____

_____

_____

_____

deep hole in the sand and he would sleep like the high clouds and he would not be afraid anymore.

The moon came out. Pale and shrunken to the size of a dime.

The helmet was heavy on his head. In the morning he would adjust
90 the leather binding. He would clean his rifle, too. Even though he had been frightened to shoot it during the hot afternoon, he would carefully clean the breech and the muzzle and the ammunition so that next time he would be ready and not so afraid. In the morning, when they reached the sea, he would begin to make friends with some of the other soldiers. He would learn their names and laugh at their jokes. Then when the war was over, he would have war buddies, and he would write to them once in a while and exchange memories.

Walking, sleeping in his walking, he felt better. He watched the moon come higher.

100 Once they skirted a sleeping village. The smells again—straw, cattle, mildew. The men were quiet. On the far side of the village, buried in the dark smells, a dog barked. The column stopped until the barking died away; then they marched fast away from the village, through a graveyard filled with conical-shaped burial mounds and tiny altars made of clay and stone. The graveyard had a perfumy smell. A nice place to spend the night, he thought. The mounds would make fine battlements, and the smell was nice and the place was quiet. But they went on, passing through a hedgerow and across another paddy and east toward the sea.

He walked carefully. He remembered what he'd been taught: Stay
110 off the center of the path, for that was where the land mines and booby traps were planted, where stupid and lazy soldiers like to walk. Stay alert, he'd been taught. Better alert than inert. Ag-ile, mo-bile, hos-tile. He wished he'd paid better attention to the training. He could not remember what they'd said about how to stop being afraid; they hadn't given any lessons in courage—not that he could remember—and they hadn't mentioned how Billy Boy Watkins would die of a heart attack, his face turning pale and the veins popping out.

Private First Class Paul Berlin walked carefully.

Stretching ahead of him like dark beads on an invisible chain, the
120 string of shadow soldiers whose names he did not yet know moved with the silence and slow grace of smoke. Now and again moonlight was reflected off a machine gun or a wristwatch. But mostly the soldiers were quiet and hidden and faraway-seeming in a peaceful night, strangers on a long street, and he felt quite separate from them, as if trailing behind like the caboose on a night train, pulled along by inertia,[3] sleepwalking, an afterthought to the war.

---

3. inertia (in·ʉr′shə): tendency to remain either at rest or in motion.

So he walked carefully, counting his steps. When he had counted to 3,485, the column stopped.

One by one the soldiers knelt or squatted down.

130 The grass along the path was wet. Private First Class Paul Berlin lay back and turned his head so that he could lick at the dew with his eyes closed, another trick to forget the war. He might have slept. "I *wasn't* afraid," he was screaming or dreaming, facing his father's stern eyes. "I wasn't afraid," he was saying. When he opened his eyes, a soldier was sitting beside him, quietly chewing a stick of Doublemint gum.

"You sleepin' again?" the soldier whispered.

"No," said Private First Class Paul Berlin. "Hell, no."

The soldier grunted, chewing his gum. Then he twisted the cap off his canteen, took a swallow, and handed it through the dark.

140 "Take some," he whispered.

"Thanks."

"You're the new guy?"

"Yes." He did not want to admit it, being new to the war.

The soldier grunted and handed him a stick of gum. "Chew it quiet—OK? Don't blow no bubbles or nothing."

"Thanks. I won't." He could not make out the man's face in the shadows.

They sat still and Private First Class Paul Berlin chewed the gum until all the sugars were gone; then the soldier said, "Bad day today,
150 buddy."

Private First Class Paul Berlin nodded wisely, but he did not speak.

"Don't think it's always so bad," the soldier whispered. "I don't wanna scare you. You'll get used to it soon enough. . . . They been fighting wars a long time, and you get used to it."

"Yeah."

"You will."

They were quiet awhile. And the night was quiet, no crickets or birds, and it was hard to imagine it was truly a war. He searched for the soldier's face but could not find it. It did not matter much. Even if
160 he saw the fellow's face, he would not know the name; and even if he knew the name, it would not matter much.

"Haven't got the time?" the soldier whispered.

"No."

"Rats. . . . Don't matter, really. Goes faster if you don't know the time, anyhow."

"Sure."

"What's your name, buddy?"

"Paul."

INTERPRET

According to lines 132–134, what is Paul anxious about?

_____

_____

_____

_____

_____

_____

_____

_____

_____

_____

_____

_____

_____

_____

_____

_____

_____

INFER

Why do you think the soldier's name and what he looks like are not important to Paul?

_____

_____

_____

_____

_____

_____

INTERPRET

Slang is very informal speech that gives new meanings to words. What does the word *croaking* mean in line 178?

_____

_____

_____

_____

_____

_____

_____

_____

_____

_____

_____

_____

_____

RETELL

This long sentence reveals what happened to Billy. Briefly summarize the events.

_____

_____

_____

_____

_____

_____

_____

_____

_____

_____

_____

"Nice to meet ya," he said, and in the dark beside the path, they
170 shook hands. "Mine's Toby. Everybody calls me Buffalo, though." The
soldier's hand was strangely warm and soft. But it was a very big hand.
"Sometimes they just call me Buff," he said.

And again they were quiet. They lay in the grass and waited. The
moon was very high now and very bright, and they were waiting for
cloud cover. The soldier suddenly snorted.

"What is it?"

"Nothin'," he said, but then he snorted again. "A bloody *heart
attack*!" the soldier said. "Can't get over it—old Billy Boy croaking from
a lousy heart attack. . . . A heart attack—can you believe it?"

180 The idea of it made Private First Class Paul Berlin smile. He couldn't
help it.

"Ever hear of such a thing?"

"Not till now," said Private First Class Paul Berlin, still smiling.

"Me neither," said the soldier in the dark. "Gawd, dying of a heart
attack. Didn't know him, did you."

"No."

"Tough as nails."

"Yeah."

"And what happens? A heart attack. Can you imagine it?"

190 "Yes," said Private First Class Paul Berlin. He wanted to laugh. "I can
imagine it." And he imagined it clearly. He giggled—he couldn't help it.
He imagined Billy's father opening the telegram: SORRY TO INFORM YOU THAT
YOUR SON BILLY BOY WAS YESTERDAY SCARED TO DEATH IN ACTION IN THE REPUBLIC
OF VIETNAM, VALIANTLY SUCCUMBING TO A HEART ATTACK SUFFERED WHILE UNDER
ENORMOUS STRESS, AND IT IS WITH GREATEST SYMPATHY THAT . . . He giggled
again. He rolled onto his belly and pressed his face into his arms. His
body was shaking with giggles.

The big soldier hissed at him to shut up, but he could not stop
giggling and remembering the hot afternoon, and poor Billy Boy, and
200 how they'd been drinking Coca-Cola from bright-red aluminum cans, and
how they'd started on the day's march, and how a little while later poor
Billy Boy stepped on the mine, and how it made a tiny little sound—
poof—and how Billy Boy stood there with his mouth wide open, looking
down at where his foot had been blown off, and how finally Billy Boy
sat down very casually, not saying a word, with his foot lying behind
him, most of it still in the boot.

He giggled louder—he could not stop. He bit his arm, trying to stifle
it, but remembering: "War's over, Billy," the men had said in consolation,
but Billy Boy got scared and started crying and said he was about to
210 die. "Nonsense," the medic said, Doc Peret, but Billy Boy kept bawling,
tightening up, his face going pale and transparent and his veins popping
out. Scared stiff. Even when Doc Peret stuck him with morphine, Billy
Boy kept crying.

"Shut up!" the big soldier hissed, but Private First Class Paul Berlin could not stop. Giggling and remembering, he covered his mouth. His eyes stung, remembering how it was when Billy Boy died of fright.

"Shut up!"

But he could not stop giggling, the same way Billy Boy could not stop bawling that afternoon.

220   Afterward Doc Peret had explained: "You see, Billy Boy really died of a heart attack. He was scared he was gonna die—so scared he had himself a heart attack—and that's what really killed him. I seen it before."

So they wrapped Billy in a plastic poncho, his eyes still wide open and scared stiff, and they carried him over the meadow to a rice paddy, and then when the Medevac helicopter arrived, they carried him through the paddy and put him aboard, and the mortar rounds were falling everywhere, and the helicopter pulled up, and Billy Boy came tumbling out, falling slowly and then faster, and the paddy water sprayed up as

230 if Billy Boy had just executed a long and dangerous dive, as if trying to escape Graves Registration, where he would be tagged and sent home under a flag, dead of a heart attack.

"Shut up!" the soldier hissed, but Paul Berlin could not stop giggling, remembering: scared to death.

Later they waded in after him, probing for Billy Boy with their rifle butts, elegantly and delicately probing for Billy Boy in the stinking paddy, singing—some of them—*Where have you gone, Billy Boy, Billy Boy, oh, where have you gone, charming Billy?* Then they found him. Green and covered with algae, his eyes still wide open and scared stiff,

240 dead of a heart attack suffered while———

"Shut up!" the soldier said loudly, shaking him.

But Private First Class Paul Berlin could not stop. The giggles were caught in his throat, drowning him in his own laughter: scared to death like Billy Boy.

Giggling, lying on his back, he saw the moon move, or the clouds moving across the moon. Wounded in action, dead of fright. A fine war story. He would tell it to his father, how Billy Boy had been scared to death, never letting on . . . He could not stop.

The soldier smothered him. He tried to fight back, but he was weak

250 from the giggles.

The moon was under the clouds and the column was moving. The soldier helped him up. "You OK now, buddy?"

"Sure."

"What was so bloody funny?"

"Nothing."

"You can get killed, laughing that way."

INTERPRET

Why is Paul unable to control his giggling?

_____

_____

_____

_____

_____

_____

_____

_____

_____

_____

_____

INTERPRET

Why do the soldiers sing?

_____

_____

_____

_____

_____

_____

_____

_____

_____

_____

_____

_____

INTERPRET

What is the principal **conflict** in this story? What do you think Paul has learned about war?

"I know. I know that."

"You got to stay calm, buddy." The soldier handed him his rifle. "Half the battle, just staying calm. You'll get better at it," he said. "Come
260 on, now."

He turned away and Private First Class Paul Berlin hurried after him. He was still shivering.

He would do better once he reached the sea, he thought, still smiling a little. A funny war story that he would tell to his father, how Billy Boy Watkins was scared to death. A good joke. But even when he smelled salt and heard the sea, he could not stop being afraid.

Theme and Character

The **theme** of a story is its central idea or underlying message about human life or behavior. You should be careful to distinguish a story's theme from its subject, or what it is about. The subject of Tim O'Brien's story is clearly a soldier's first night in the field, but the story's theme is much more complex.

One way of identifying the theme of a story is to look at how the main character changes in the course of the tale, or what he or she has learned by the story's end. Often, what this character has discovered about life is the truth the writer wants to reveal to us, too.

To explore the links between theme and character, fill out the chart below. In the left column, write words and phrases that identify what Paul has discovered about himself during his initiation into combat. In the right column, write one or two complete sentences that express the story's theme, or central idea, relating to war.

Character: What Paul Learns	Story's Theme

Vocabulary: How to Own a Word

Word Connections

The word *fecund* comes from Latin *fecundus*, which also means "fruitful" or "fertile." *Fruitful* comes from *fructus*, meaning "to enjoy," especially to enjoy something harvested. *Fertile* comes from *fertilis*, which means "to give birth to." *Fecund*, *fruitful*, and *fertile* are synonyms, all originating in Latin.

The differences in these words are found in their connotations. *Fruitful* has a positive, pleasant connotation, whereas *fertile* has a more neutral one and is a bit scientific. Finally, *fecund* has a somewhat negative connotation, suggesting overripeness.

Check the item(s) below that could be considered fecund.

_____ an apple tree laden with fruit

_____ layers of composting plums beneath a tree

_____ a hen sitting on eggs

_____ a moldy, musty-smelling basement

_____ rich soil

During the Middle Ages, words from Old Norse came to be adopted into Old English. *Skirt* and *shirt* are two such words. They are related to *short*, which probably meant a short item of clothing. Over time, *skirt* came to mean also the lower section of a coat and then the lower part or edge of something. By the early 1400s, it also referred to the border of an area. Eventually, *skirt* came to be used, as in this story, to mean "to go around the edge of."

Write a sentence about each of the people listed below. Tell what each person might want to skirt and for what reason.

1. a hunter _____

_____

2. a police officer _____

_____

3. a shy boy at a dance _____

_____

4. a bodyguard _____

_____

5. a politician _____

_____

Selection: _____

Analyzing a Story's Theme

Questions to Help Clarify Theme	Responses (with Examples from the Story)
1. Does the title signify something about the story? Does it point to the truth the story reveals about life?	
2. Does the main character change in the course of the story? Does the main character realize something he or she did not know before?	
3. Are any important statements about life or people made in the story, either by the narrator or characters in the story?	
4. Is the theme ever directly stated? If so, where is it stated?	
5. In one sentence, state the story's theme. Do you agree with the theme? Is the writer presenting a truth about life or forcing us to accept a false view?	

The Bet

Make the Connection

Being Alone

In this story, a character bets that he can live all alone for fifteen years. His motivation is to win an enormous fortune. His voluntary solitude raises some big questions—for him and for readers.

Think about a time you chose to be alone for a while. Maybe you needed to study for a test, or maybe you wanted to think about an important question or decision. In the space below, jot down the details of your experience. What did you learn from being alone?

_____

_____

_____

_____

_____

_____

_____

_____

_____

_____

_____

_____

_____

_____

_____

Anton Chekhov

THE BET

Translated by **Constance Garnett**

IDENTIFY

Underline the context clue that suggests the meaning of the phrase *capital punishment*.

_____

_____

_____

_____

_____

_____

_____

_____

_____

_____

_____

_____

PREDICT

Based on this early passage, what do you think the story's **theme** will be?

_____

_____

_____

_____

_____

_____

_____

_____

_____

_____

_____

1

It was a dark autumn night. The old banker was walking up and down his study and remembering how, fifteen years before, he had given a party one autumn evening. There had been many clever men there, and there had been interesting conversations. Among other things, they had talked of capital punishment. The majority of the guests, among whom were many journalists and intellectual men, disapproved of the death penalty. They considered that form of punishment out of date, immoral, and unsuitable for Christian states.[1] In the opinion of some of them, the death penalty ought to be replaced everywhere by
10 imprisonment for life.

"I don't agree with you," said their host, the banker. "I have not tried either the death penalty or imprisonment for life, but if one may judge a priori,[2] the death penalty is more moral and more humane than imprisonment for life. Capital punishment kills a man at once, but lifelong imprisonment kills him slowly. Which executioner is the more humane, he who kills you in a few minutes or he who drags the life out of you in the course of many years?"

"Both are equally immoral," observed one of the guests, "for they both have the same object—to take away life. The state is not God. It has
20 not the right to take away what it cannot restore when it wants to."

Among the guests was a young lawyer, a young man of five-and-twenty. When he was asked his opinion, he said: "The death sentence and the life sentence are equally immoral, but if I had to choose between the death penalty and imprisonment for life, I would certainly choose the second. To live anyhow is better than not at all."

A lively discussion arose. The banker, who was younger and more nervous in those days, was suddenly carried away by excitement; he struck the table with his fist and shouted at the young man: "It's not true! I'll bet you two million you wouldn't stay in solitary confinement
30 for five years."

"If you mean that in earnest," said the young man, "I'll take the bet, but I would stay not five, but fifteen years."

"Fifteen? Done!" cried the banker. "Gentlemen, I stake two million!"

"Agreed! You stake your millions and I stake my freedom!" said the young man.

And this wild, senseless bet was carried out! The banker, spoiled and frivolous, with millions beyond his reckoning, was delighted at the bet. At supper he made fun of the young man and said: "Think better of it, young man, while there is still time. To me two million is a trifle, but you are
40 losing three or four of the best years of your life. I say three or four,

---

1. **Christian states:** countries in which Christianity is the main religion.
2. **a priori** (ā′prī·ôr′ī): here, on the basis of theory rather than experience.

because you won't stay longer. Don't forget either, you unhappy man, that voluntary confinement is a great deal harder to bear than <u>compulsory</u>. The thought that you have the right to step out in liberty at any moment will poison your whole existence in prison. I am sorry for you."

And now the banker, walking to and fro, remembered all this and asked himself: "What was the object of that bet? What is the good of that man's losing fifteen years of his life and my throwing away two million? Can it prove that the death penalty is better or worse than imprisonment for life? No, no. It was all nonsensical and meaningless.
50 On my part it was the <u>caprice</u> of a pampered man, and on his part simple greed for money. . . ."

Then he remembered what followed that evening. It was decided that the young man should spend the years of his captivity under the strictest supervision in one of the lodges in the banker's garden. It was agreed that for fifteen years he should not be free to cross the threshold of the lodge, to see human beings, to hear the human voice, or to receive letters and newspapers. He was allowed to have a musical instrument and books and was allowed to write letters, to drink wine, and to smoke. By the terms of the agreement, the only relations he could have with the
60 outer world were by a little window made purposely for that object. He might have anything he wanted—books, music, wine, and so on—in any quantity he desired, by writing an order, but could receive them only through the window. The agreement provided for every detail and every trifle that would make his imprisonment strictly solitary, and bound the young man to stay there *exactly* fifteen years, beginning from twelve o'clock of November 14, 1870, and ending at twelve o'clock of November 14, 1885. The slightest attempt on his part to break the conditions, if only two minutes before the end, released the banker from the obligation to pay him two million.

70 For the first year of his confinement, as far as one could judge from his brief notes, the prisoner suffered severely from loneliness and depression. The sounds of the piano could be heard continually day and night from his lodge. He refused wine and tobacco. Wine, he wrote, excites the desires, and desires are the worst foes of the prisoner; and besides, nothing could be more dreary than drinking good wine and seeing no one. And tobacco spoiled the air of his room. In the first year the books he sent for were principally of a light character—novels with a complicated love plot, sensational and fantastic stories, and so on.

In the second year the piano was silent in the lodge, and the prisoner
80 asked only for the classics. In the fifth year music was <u>audible</u> again, and the prisoner asked for wine. Those who watched him through the window said that all that year he spent doing nothing but eating and drinking and lying on his bed, frequently yawning and talking angrily to himself. He did not read books. Sometimes at night he would sit down to

WORDS TO OWN
compulsory (kəm·pul′sə·rē)
adj.: required; enforced.

EVALUATE

Do you think such a bet would ever be carried out in real life? Why or why not?

_____

_____

_____

_____

WORDS TO OWN
caprice (kə·prēs′) *n.*: sudden notion or desire.

INTERPRET

Although the **plot** appears simple on the surface, it is complicated by the **conflicts** between and within characters. List the conflicts you have identified so far. Are they **internal** or **external**?

_____

_____

_____

_____

_____

_____

_____

_____

_____

_____

WORDS TO OWN
audible (ô′də·bəl) *adj.*: capable of being heard.

INFER

What **theme** is suggested by
the catalog of the prisoner's
activities in lines 87–91?

_____

_____

_____

_____

_____

_____

_____

_____

_____

_____

_____

IDENTIFY

Most of Part 1 is a **flashback**.
In Part 2, the story moves
back into the present. When
did the events leading to the
bet occur?

_____

_____

_____

_____

_____

write; he would spend hours writing and in the morning tear up all that
he had written. More than once he could be heard crying.

In the second half of the sixth year the prisoner began zealously
studying languages, philosophy, and history. He threw himself eagerly
into these studies—so much so that the banker had enough to do to get
90 him the books he ordered. In the course of four years, some six hundred
volumes were procured at his request. It was during this period that the
banker received the following letter from his prisoner:

"My dear Jailer, I write you these lines in six languages. Show them
to people who know the languages. Let them read them. If they find not
one mistake, I implore you to fire a shot in the garden. That shot will
show me that my efforts have not been thrown away. The geniuses of all
ages and of all lands speak different languages, but the same flame burns
in them all. Oh, if you only knew what unearthly happiness my soul
feels now from being able to understand them!" The prisoner's desire
100 was fulfilled. The banker ordered two shots to be fired in the garden.

Then, after the tenth year, the prisoner sat immovably at the table
and read nothing but the Gospels. It seemed strange to the banker that
a man who in four years had mastered six hundred learned volumes
should waste nearly a year over one thin book easy of comprehension.
Theology[3] and histories of religion followed the Gospels.

In the last two years of his confinement, the prisoner read an
immense quantity of books quite indiscriminately. At one time he
was busy with the natural sciences; then he would ask for Byron[4] or
Shakespeare. There were notes in which he demanded at the same
110 time books on chemistry, and a manual of medicine, and a novel, and
some treatise on philosophy or theology. His reading suggested a man
swimming in the sea among the wreckage of his ship and trying to save
his life by greedily clutching first at one spar[5] and then at another.

2

The old banker remembered all this and thought: "Tomorrow at twelve
o'clock he will regain his freedom. By our arrangement I ought to pay
him two million. If I do pay him, it is all over with me: I shall be utterly
ruined."

Fifteen years before, his millions had been beyond his reckoning;
now he was afraid to ask himself which were greater, his debts or his
120 assets. Desperate gambling on the Stock Exchange, wild speculation, and
the excitability which he could not get over even in advancing years had

---

3. **theology** (thē·äl'ə·jē): the study of religious teachings concerning God and God's relation
to the world.
4. **Byron:** George Gordon Byron (1788–1824), known as Lord Byron, English Romantic poet.
5. **spar:** pole that supports or extends a ship's sail.

by degrees led to the decline of his fortune, and the proud, fearless, self-confident millionaire had become a banker of middling rank, trembling at every rise and fall in his investments. "Cursed bet!" muttered the old man, clutching his head in despair. "Why didn't the man die? He is only forty now. He will take my last penny from me, he will marry, will enjoy life, will gamble on the Exchange, while I shall look at him with envy like a beggar and hear from him every day the same sentence: 'I am indebted to you for the happiness of my life; let me help you!' No, it is
130 too much! The one means of being saved from bankruptcy and disgrace is the death of that man!"

It struck three o'clock. The banker listened; everyone was asleep in the house, and nothing could be heard outside but the rustling of the chilled trees. Trying to make no noise, he took from a fireproof safe the key of the door which had not been opened for fifteen years, put on his overcoat, and went out of the house.

It was dark and cold in the garden. Rain was falling. A damp, cutting wind was racing about the garden, howling and giving the trees no rest. The banker strained his eyes but could see neither the earth nor the
140 white statues, nor the lodge, nor the trees. Going to the spot where the lodge stood, he twice called the watchman. No answer followed. Evidently the watchman had sought shelter from the weather and was now asleep somewhere either in the kitchen or in the greenhouse.

"If I had the pluck to carry out my intention," thought the old man, "suspicion would fall first upon the watchman."

He felt in the darkness for the steps and the door and went into the entry of the lodge. Then he groped his way into a little passage and lighted a match. There was not a soul there. There was a bedstead with no bedding on it, and in the corner there was a dark cast-iron stove. The
150 seals on the door leading to the prisoner's rooms were intact.

When the match went out, the old man, trembling with emotion, peeped through the little window. A candle was burning dimly in the prisoner's room. He was sitting at the table. Nothing could be seen but his back, the hair on his head, and his hands. Open books were lying on the table, on the two easy chairs, and on the carpet near the table.

Five minutes passed and the prisoner did not once stir. Fifteen years' imprisonment had taught him to sit still. The banker tapped at the window with his finger, and the prisoner made no movement whatever in response. Then the banker cautiously broke the seals off the door and
160 put the key in the keyhole. The rusty lock gave a grating sound and the door creaked. The banker expected to hear at once footsteps and a cry of astonishment, but three minutes passed and it was as quiet as ever in the room. He made up his mind to go in.

At the table a man unlike ordinary people was sitting motionless. He was a skeleton with the skin drawn tight over his bones, with long curls

PREDICT

Does this passage change your prediction of what the story's **theme** will be? Explain.

_____

_____

_____

_____

_____

_____

BUILD FLUENCY

Read this paragraph aloud as expressively as you can. Through your reading, try to suggest the **atmosphere** or **mood** of this part of the story.

_____

_____

_____

_____

_____

_____

_____

_____

_____

_____

_____

_____

_____

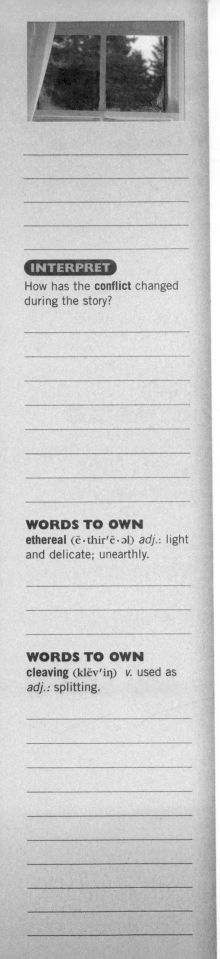

INTERPRET

How has the **conflict** changed during the story?

WORDS TO OWN
ethereal (ē·thir′ē·əl) *adj.*: light and delicate; unearthly.

WORDS TO OWN
cleaving (klēv′iŋ) *v.* used as *adj.*: splitting.

like a woman's, and a shaggy beard. His face was yellow with an earthy tint in it, his cheeks were hollow, his back long and narrow, and the hand on which his shaggy head was propped was so thin and delicate that it was dreadful to look at it. His hair was already streaked with
170 silver, and seeing his emaciated, aged-looking face, no one would have believed that he was only forty. He was asleep. . . . In front of his bowed head there lay on the table a sheet of paper, on which there was something written in fine handwriting.

"Poor creature!" thought the banker, "he is asleep and most likely dreaming of the millions. And I have only to take this half-dead man, throw him on the bed, stifle him a little with the pillow, and the most conscientious expert would find no sign of a violent death. But let us first read what he has written here. . . ."

The banker took the page from the table and read as follows:
180 "Tomorrow at twelve o'clock I regain my freedom and the right to associate with other men, but before I leave this room and see the sunshine, I think it necessary to say a few words to you. With a clear conscience I tell you, as before God, who beholds me, that I despise freedom and life and health and all that in your books is called the good things of the world.

"For fifteen years I have been intently studying earthly life. It is true I have not seen the earth or men, but in your books I have drunk fragrant wine, I have sung songs, I have hunted stags and wild boars in the forests, I have loved women. . . . Beauties as <u>ethereal</u> as clouds, created
190 by the magic of your poets and geniuses, have visited me at night and have whispered in my ears wonderful tales that have set my brain in a whirl. In your books I have climbed to the peaks of Elburz and Mont Blanc,[6] and from there I have seen the sun rise and have watched it at evening flood the sky, the ocean, and the mountaintops with gold and crimson. I have watched from there the lightning flashing over my head and <u>cleaving</u> the storm clouds. I have seen green forests, fields, rivers, lakes, towns. I have heard the singing of the sirens,[7] and the strains of the shepherds' pipes; I have touched the wings of comely devils who flew down to converse with me of God. . . . In your books I have flung
200 myself into the bottomless pit, performed miracles, slain, burned towns, preached new religions, conquered whole kingdoms. . . .

"Your books have given me wisdom. All that the unresting thought of man has created in the ages is compressed into a small compass in my brain. I know that I am wiser than all of you.

---

6. **Elburz** (el·boorz′) **and Mont Blanc** (mōn blän′): Elburz is a mountain range in northern Iran; Mont Blanc, in France, is the highest mountain in the Alps.
7. **sirens:** in Greek mythology, partly human female creatures who lived on an island and lured sailors to their death with their beautiful singing.

"And I despise your books, I despise wisdom and the blessings of this world. It is all worthless, fleeting, illusory, and deceptive, like a mirage. You may be proud, wise, and fine, but death will wipe you off the face of the earth as though you were no more than mice burrowing under the floor, and your posterity, your history, your immortal geniuses will burn or freeze together with the earthly globe.

"You have lost your reason and taken the wrong path. You have taken lies for truth and hideousness for beauty. You would marvel if, owing to strange events of some sort, frogs and lizards suddenly grew on apple and orange trees instead of fruit or if roses began to smell like a sweating horse; so I marvel at you who exchange heaven for earth. I don't want to understand you.

"To prove to you in action how I despise all that you live by, I renounce the two million of which I once dreamed as of paradise and which now I despise. To deprive myself of the right to the money, I shall go out from here five minutes before the time fixed and so break the compact. . . ."

When the banker had read this, he laid the page on the table, kissed the strange man on the head, and went out of the lodge, weeping. At no other time, even when he had lost heavily on the Stock Exchange, had he felt so great a contempt for himself. When he got home, he lay on his bed, but his tears and emotion kept him for hours from sleeping.

Next morning the watchmen ran in with pale faces and told him they had seen the man who lived in the lodge climb out of the window into the garden, go to the gate, and disappear. The banker went at once with the servants to the lodge and made sure of the flight of his prisoner. To avoid arousing unnecessary talk, he took from the table the writing in which the millions were renounced and, when he got home, locked it up in the fireproof safe.

WORDS TO OWN
illusory (i·lōō′sə·rē) *adj.:* not real; based on false ideas.
posterity (päs·ter′ə·tē) *n.:* descendants or all future generations.

_____

_____

WORDS TO OWN
renounce (ri·nouns′) *v.:* give up, especially by formal statement; reject.

INFER
What does the letter imply about the **theme** of the story?

_____
_____
_____
_____

INFER
Why does the banker lock up the prisoner's letter in a fireproof safe?

_____
_____
_____
_____
_____
_____
_____
_____
_____
_____
_____

Ambiguous Theme

The **theme**, or overall meaning, of a story is **ambiguous** when the elements that make up the story are open to two or more interpretations. In "The Bet," for example, it seems at first that the story's central message may concern the morality of capital punishment or the folly and futility of the wager between the banker and the lawyer. As the story unfolds, however, events suggest that the theme may lie elsewhere. Chekhov's central idea may involve the nature of true knowledge and wisdom, or perhaps it may concern the universal human quest for the meaning of life.

What do *you* think is the story's most important passage? How would *you* interpret the story's theme? Discuss your statement of theme with other readers. Are several thematic focuses possible? Summarize your opinions and discussions on the lines provided below.

Vocabulary: How to Own a Word

Word Maps

Fill in the ovals with a synonym, an antonym, and the connotation—positive, negative, or neutral—of each word in the Word Bank. Also provide the dictionary definition, and write a sentence using the word correctly. Be sure that the sentence you write reflects the connotation of the word. If you think an oval does not apply, write "none." An example has been partially completed for you.

Word Bank
compulsory
caprice
audible
zealously
indiscriminately
ethereal
cleaving
illusory
posterity
renounce

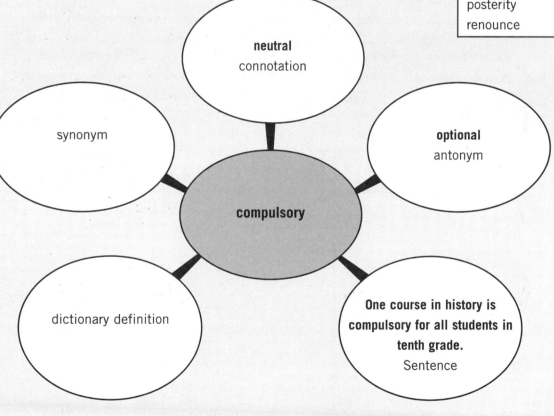

neutral
connotation

synonym

optional
antonym

compulsory

dictionary definition

One course in history is compulsory for all students in tenth grade.
Sentence

Through the Tunnel

Make the Connection

The Road to Achievement

Sometimes you need to prove yourself. Maybe you want so badly to play on a school team that you force yourself to practice several hours a day. Maybe you practice for days to learn a new dance. If what you want is really important to you, you may suffer tedium and maybe even physical pain in order to make the breakthrough and reach your goal.

Use the chart below to analyze your experience during a time when you committed yourself to achieving a goal. In the first column, identify your objective and your reasons for wanting to achieve it. In the second column, use words or phrases to describe the steps you took to attain your goal. In the third column, describe your feelings at the end, when you either overcame the challenge or decided to give up your goal.

Goal/Reasons	Steps Toward Achievement	Feelings at the End

Doris Lessing

Through the Tunnel

Underline descriptions in lines 1–16 that indicate the story is told by an **omniscient narrator** who knows the inner thoughts and feelings of all the characters.

_____

_____

WORDS TO OWN
contrition (kən·trish′ən) *n.:* regret or sense of guilt at having done wrong.

_____

_____

INFER

An omniscient narrator can express **internal conflicts** in more than one character. What conflict does Jerry experience? What is his mother's internal conflict?

_____

_____

_____

_____

_____

_____

_____

_____

_____

_____

_____

_____

_____

_____

Going to the shore on the first morning of the vacation, the young English boy stopped at a turning of the path and looked down at a wild and rocky bay and then over to the crowded beach he knew so well from other years. His mother walked on in front of him, carrying a bright striped bag in one hand. Her other arm, swinging loose, was very white in the sun. The boy watched that white naked arm and turned his eyes, which had a frown behind them, toward the bay and back again to his mother. When she felt he was not with her, she swung around. "Oh, there you are, Jerry!" she said. She looked impatient, then smiled. "Why,
10 darling, would you rather not come with me? Would you rather——" She frowned, conscientiously worrying over what amusements he might secretly be longing for, which she had been too busy or too careless to imagine. He was very familiar with that anxious, apologetic smile. Contrition sent him running after her. And yet, as he ran, he looked back over his shoulder at the wild bay; and all morning, as he played on the safe beach, he was thinking of it.

Next morning, when it was time for the routine of swimming and sunbathing, his mother said, "Are you tired of the usual beach, Jerry? Would you like to go somewhere else?"

20 "Oh, no!" he said quickly, smiling at her out of that unfailing impulse of contrition—a sort of chivalry. Yet, walking down the path with her, he blurted out, "I'd like to go and have a look at those rocks down there."

She gave the idea her attention. It was a wild-looking place, and there was no one there, but she said, "Of course, Jerry. When you've had enough, come to the big beach. Or just go straight back to the villa, if you like." She walked away, that bare arm, now slightly reddened from yesterday's sun, swinging. And he almost ran after her again, feeling it unbearable that she should go by herself, but he did not.

30 She was thinking, Of course he's old enough to be safe without me. Have I been keeping him too close? He mustn't feel he ought to be with me. I must be careful.

He was an only child, eleven years old. She was a widow. She was determined to be neither possessive nor lacking in devotion. She went worrying off to her beach.

As for Jerry, once he saw that his mother had gained her beach, he began the steep descent to the bay. From where he was, high up among red-brown rocks, it was a scoop of moving bluish green fringed with white. As he went lower, he saw that it spread among small
40 promontories and inlets of rough, sharp rock, and the crisping, lapping surface showed stains of purple and darker blue. Finally, as he ran sliding and scraping down the last few yards, he saw an edge of white surf and the shallow, luminous movement of water over white sand and, beyond that, a solid, heavy blue.

He ran straight into the water and began swimming. He was a good swimmer. He went out fast over the gleaming sand, over a middle region where rocks lay like discolored monsters under the surface, and then he was in the real sea—a warm sea where irregular cold currents from the deep water shocked his limbs.

50   When he was so far out that he could look back not only on the little bay but past the promontory that was between it and the big beach, he floated on the buoyant surface and looked for his mother. There she was, a speck of yellow under an umbrella that looked like a slice of orange peel. He swam back to shore, relieved at being sure she was there, but all at once very lonely.

On the edge of a small cape that marked the side of the bay away from the promontory was a loose scatter of rocks. Above them, some boys were stripping off their clothes. They came running, naked, down to the rocks. The English boy swam toward them but kept his distance

60   at a stone's throw. They were of that coast; all of them were burned smooth dark brown and speaking a language he did not understand. To be with them, of them, was a craving that filled his whole body. He swam a little closer; they turned and watched him with narrowed, alert dark eyes. Then one smiled and waved. It was enough. In a minute, he had swum in and was on the rocks beside them, smiling with a desperate, nervous <u>supplication</u>. They shouted cheerful greetings at him; and then, as he preserved his nervous, uncomprehending smile, they understood that he was a foreigner strayed from his own beach, and they proceeded to forget him. But he was happy. He was with them.

70   They began diving again and again from a high point into a well of blue sea between rough, pointed rocks. After they had dived and come up, they swam around, hauled themselves up, and waited their turn to dive again. They were big boys—men, to Jerry. He dived, and they watched him; and when he swam around to take his place, they made way for him. He felt he was accepted and he dived again, carefully, proud of himself.

Soon the biggest of the boys poised himself, shot down into the water, and did not come up. The others stood about, watching. Jerry, after waiting for the sleek brown head to appear, let out a yell of

80   warning; they looked at him idly and turned their eyes back toward the water. After a long time, the boy came up on the other side of a big dark rock, letting the air out of his lungs in a sputtering gasp and a shout of triumph. Immediately the rest of them dived in. One moment, the morning seemed full of chattering boys; the next, the air and the surface of the water were empty. But through the heavy blue, dark shapes could be seen moving and groping.

Jerry dived, shot past the school of underwater swimmers, saw a black wall of rock looming at him, touched it, and bobbed up at once to

INTERPRET

One function of **setting** is to create **atmosphere** or **mood**. What atmosphere is created with the following details: "big dark rock," "heavy blue, dark shapes," and "black wall of rock looming at him" (lines 81–88)?

Why is it so important for Jerry to have the other boys' approval?

_____

_____

_____

_____

INTERPRET

How does the footnote for this passage help you to understand that Jerry is trying to attract the boys' attention?

_____

_____

_____

_____

_____

_____

_____

_____

_____

INTERPRET

Do the older boys leave to get away from Jerry, or is this what Jerry thinks?

_____

_____

_____

_____

_____

_____

_____

_____

the surface, where the wall was a low barrier he could see across. There
90 was no one visible; under him, in the water, the dim shapes of the
swimmers had disappeared. Then one and then another of the boys
came up on the far side of the barrier of rock, and he understood that
they had swum through some gap or hole in it. He plunged down again.
He could see nothing through the stinging salt water but the blank rock.
When he came up, the boys were all on the diving rock, preparing to
attempt the feat again. And now, in a panic of failure, he yelled up, in
English, "Look at me! Look!" and he began splashing and kicking in the
water like a foolish dog.

They looked down gravely, frowning. He knew the frown. At moments
100 of failure, when he clowned to claim his mother's attention, it was with
just this grave, embarrassed inspection that she rewarded him. Through
his hot shame, feeling the pleading grin on his face like a scar that he
could never remove, he looked up at the group of big brown boys on the
rock and shouted, "Bonjour! Merci! Au revoir! Monsieur, monsieur!"[1]
while he hooked his fingers round his ears and waggled them.

Water surged into his mouth; he choked, sank, came up. The rock,
lately weighted with boys, seemed to rear up out of the water as their
weight was removed. They were flying down past him now, into the
water; the air was full of falling bodies. Then the rock was empty in
110 the hot sunlight. He counted one, two, three . . .

At fifty, he was terrified. They must all be drowning beneath him, in
the watery caves of the rock! At a hundred, he stared around him at the
empty hillside, wondering if he should yell for help. He counted faster,
faster, to hurry them up, to bring them to the surface quickly, to drown
them quickly—anything rather than the terror of counting on and on into
the blue emptiness of the morning. And then, at a hundred and sixty, the
water beyond the rock was full of boys blowing like brown whales. They
swam back to the shore without a look at him.

He climbed back to the diving rock and sat down, feeling the hot
120 roughness of it under his thighs. The boys were gathering up their bits of
clothing and running off along the shore to another promontory. They
were leaving to get away from him. He cried openly, fists in his eyes.
There was no one to see him, and he cried himself out.

It seemed to him that a long time had passed, and he swam out to
where he could see his mother. Yes, she was still there, a yellow spot
under an orange umbrella. He swam back to the big rock, climbed up,
and dived into the blue pool among the fanged and angry boulders.
Down he went, until he touched the wall of rock again. But the salt
was so painful in his eyes that he could not see.

---

1. **Bonjour! Merci! Au revoir! Monsieur, monsieur!:** French for "Hello! Thank you!
Goodbye! Mr., Mr.!"—probably the only French words Jerry knows.

130   He came to the surface, swam to shore, and went back to the villa to wait for his mother. Soon she walked slowly up the path, swinging her striped bag, the flushed, naked arm dangling beside her. "I want some swimming goggles," he panted, defiant and beseeching.

    She gave him a patient, <u>inquisitive</u> look as she said casually, "Well, of course, darling."

    But now, now, now! He must have them this minute, and no other time. He nagged and pestered until she went with him to a shop. As soon as she had bought the goggles, he grabbed them from her hand as if she were going to claim them for herself, and was off, running down

140 the steep path to the bay.

    Jerry swam out to the big barrier rock, adjusted the goggles, and dived. The impact of the water broke the rubber-enclosed vacuum, and the goggles came loose. He understood that he must swim down to the base of the rock from the surface of the water. He fixed the goggles tight and firm, filled his lungs, and floated, face down, on the water. Now he could see. It was as if he had eyes of a different kind—fish eyes that showed everything clear and delicate and wavering in the bright water.

    Under him, six or seven feet down, was a floor of perfectly clean, shining white sand, rippled firm and hard by the tides. Two grayish

150 shapes steered there, like long, rounded pieces of wood or slate. They were fish. He saw them nose toward each other, poise motionless, make a dart forward, swerve off, and come around again. It was like a water dance. A few inches above them the water sparkled as if sequins were dropping through it. Fish again—myriads of <u>minute</u> fish, the length of his fingernail—were drifting through the water, and in a moment he could feel the innumerable tiny touches of them against his limbs. It was like swimming in flaked silver. The great rock the big boys had swum through rose sheer out of the white sand—black, tufted lightly with greenish weed. He could see no gap in it. He swam down to its base.

160   Again and again he rose, took a big chestful of air, and went down. Again and again he groped over the surface of the rock, feeling it, almost hugging it in the desperate need to find the entrance. And then, once, while he was clinging to the black wall, his knees came up and he shot his feet out forward and they met no obstacle. He had found the hole.

    He gained the surface, clambered about the stones that littered the barrier rock until he found a big one, and with this in his arms, let himself down over the side of the rock. He dropped, with the weight, straight to the sandy floor. Clinging tight to the anchor of stone, he lay on his side and looked in under the dark shelf at the place where his feet

170 had gone. He could see the hole. It was an irregular, dark gap; but he could not see deep into it. He let go of his anchor, clung with his hands to the edges of the hole, and tried to push himself in.

WORDS TO OWN
inquisitive (in·kwiz′ə·tiv) *adj.*: questioning; curious.

_____

_____

VISUALIZE

Underline details that the writer provides to help you visualize the scene in the water.

_____

_____

WORDS TO OWN
minute (mī·nōōt′) *adj.*: small; tiny.

_____

_____

_____

_____

RETELL

Briefly summarize the action in lines 160–172.

_____

_____

_____

_____

_____

_____

_____

_____

_____

_____

_____

_____

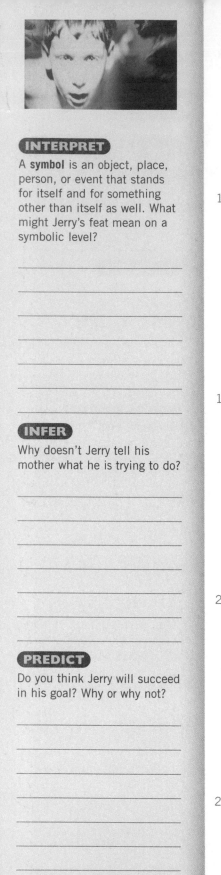

INTERPRET

A **symbol** is an object, place, person, or event that stands for itself and for something other than itself as well. What might Jerry's feat mean on a symbolic level?

_____

_____

_____

_____

_____

_____

INFER

Why doesn't Jerry tell his mother what he is trying to do?

_____

_____

_____

_____

_____

_____

_____

PREDICT

Do you think Jerry will succeed in his goal? Why or why not?

_____

_____

_____

_____

_____

_____

_____

WORDS TO OWN
incredulous (in·krej′oo·ləs)
adj.: disbelieving; skeptical.

He got his head in, found his shoulders jammed, moved them in sidewise, and was inside as far as his waist. He could see nothing ahead. Something soft and clammy touched his mouth; he saw a dark frond moving against the grayish rock, and panic filled him. He thought of octopuses, of clinging weed. He pushed himself out backward and caught a glimpse, as he retreated, of a harmless tentacle of seaweed drifting in the mouth of the tunnel. But it was enough. He reached the
180 sunlight, swam to shore, and lay on the diving rock. He looked down into the blue well of water. He knew he must find his way through that cave, or hole, or tunnel, and out the other side.

First, he thought, he must learn to control his breathing. He let himself down into the water with another big stone in his arms, so that he could lie effortlessly on the bottom of the sea. He counted. One, two, three. He counted steadily. He could hear the movement of blood in his chest. Fifty-one, fifty-two. . . . His chest was hurting. He let go of the rock and went up into the air. He saw that the sun was low. He rushed to the villa and found his mother at her supper. She said only, "Did you
190 enjoy yourself?" and he said, "Yes."

All night the boy dreamed of the water-filled cave in the rock, and as soon as breakfast was over, he went to the bay.

That night, his nose bled badly. For hours he had been underwater, learning to hold his breath, and now he felt weak and dizzy. His mother said, "I shouldn't overdo things, darling, if I were you."

That day and the next, Jerry exercised his lungs as if everything, the whole of his life, all that he would become, depended upon it. Again his nose bled at night, and his mother insisted on his coming with her the next day. It was a torment to him to waste a day of his careful self-
200 training, but he stayed with her on that other beach, which now seemed a place for small children, a place where his mother might lie safe in the sun. It was not his beach.

He did not ask for permission, on the following day, to go to his beach. He went, before his mother could consider the complicated rights and wrongs of the matter. A day's rest, he discovered, had improved his count by ten. The big boys had made the passage while he counted a hundred and sixty. He had been counting fast, in his fright. Probably now, if he tried, he could get through that long tunnel, but he was not going to try yet. A curious, most unchildlike persistence, a controlled
210 impatience, made him wait. In the meantime, he lay underwater on the white sand, littered now by stones he had brought down from the upper air, and studied the entrance to the tunnel. He knew every jut and corner of it, as far as it was possible to see. It was as if he already felt its sharpness about his shoulders.

He sat by the clock in the villa, when his mother was not near, and checked his time. He was <u>incredulous</u> and then proud to find he could

hold his breath without strain for two minutes. The words "two minutes," authorized by the clock, brought close the adventure that was so necessary to him.

220   In another four days, his mother said casually one morning, they must go home. On the day before they left, he would do it. He would do it if it killed him, he said defiantly to himself. But two days before they were to leave—a day of triumph when he increased his count by fifteen—his nose bled so badly that he turned dizzy and had to lie limply over the big rock like a bit of seaweed, watching the thick red blood flow onto the rock and trickle slowly down to the sea. He was frightened. Supposing he turned dizzy in the tunnel? Supposing he died there, trapped? Supposing—his head went around, in the hot sun, and he almost gave up. He thought he would return to the house and lie down,
230   and next summer, perhaps, when he had another year's growth in him—then he would go through the hole.

But even after he had made the decision, or thought he had, he found himself sitting up on the rock and looking down into the water; and he knew that now, this moment, when his nose had only just stopped bleeding, when his head was still sore and throbbing—this was the moment when he would try. If he did not do it now, he never would. He was trembling with fear that he would not go; and he was trembling with horror at the long, long tunnel under the rock, under the sea. Even in the open sunlight, the barrier rock seemed very wide and very heavy;
240   tons of rock pressed down on where he would go. If he died there, he would lie until one day—perhaps not before next year—those big boys would swim into it and find it blocked.

He put on his goggles, fitted them tight, tested the vacuum. His hands were shaking. Then he chose the biggest stone he could carry and slipped over the edge of the rock until half of him was in the cool enclosing water and half in the hot sun. He looked up once at the empty sky, filled his lungs once, twice, and then sank fast to the bottom with the stone. He let it go and began to count. He took the edges of the hole in his hands and drew himself into it, wriggling his shoulders in sidewise
250   as he remembered he must, kicking himself along with his feet.

Soon he was clear inside. He was in a small rock-bound hole filled with yellowish-gray water. The water was pushing him up against the roof. The roof was sharp and pained his back. He pulled himself along with his hands—fast, fast—and used his legs as levers. His head knocked against something; a sharp pain dizzied him. Fifty, fifty-one, fifty-two . . . He was without light, and the water seemed to press upon him with the weight of rock. Seventy-one, seventy-two . . . There was no strain on his lungs. He felt like an inflated balloon, his lungs were so light and easy, but his head was pulsing.

BUILD FLUENCY

Read lines 232–242 aloud, focusing on the author's use of **parallel structures**, **repetition**, and **rhythm**.

IDENTIFY

Underline four **images** appealing to the sense of touch in lines 251–259.

260　　He was being continually pressed against the sharp roof, which felt slimy as well as sharp. Again he thought of octopuses, and wondered if the tunnel might be filled with weed that could tangle him. He gave himself a panicky, convulsive kick forward, ducked his head, and swam. His feet and hands moved freely, as if in open water. The hole must have widened out. He thought he must be swimming fast, and he was frightened of banging his head if the tunnel narrowed.

　　A hundred, a hundred and one . . . The water paled. Victory filled him. His lungs were beginning to hurt. A few more strokes and he would be out. He was counting wildly; he said a hundred and fifteen and then,
270　a long time later, a hundred and fifteen again. The water was a clear jewel-green all around him. Then he saw, above his head, a crack running up through the rock. Sunlight was falling through it, showing the clean, dark rock of the tunnel, a single mussel[2] shell, and darkness ahead.

　　He was at the end of what he could do. He looked up at the crack as if it were filled with air and not water, as if he could put his mouth to it to draw in air. A hundred and fifteen, he heard himself say inside his head—but he had said that long ago. He must go on into the blackness ahead, or he would drown. His head was swelling, his lungs cracking. A
280　hundred and fifteen, a hundred and fifteen, pounded through his head, and he feebly clutched at rocks in the dark, pulling himself forward, leaving the brief space of sunlit water behind. He felt he was dying. He was no longer quite conscious. He struggled on in the darkness between lapses into unconsciousness. An immense, swelling pain filled his head, and then the darkness cracked with an explosion of green light. His hands, groping forward, met nothing; and his feet, kicking back, propelled him out into the open sea.

　　He drifted to the surface, his face turned up to the air. He was gasping like a fish. He felt he would sink now and drown; he could not
290　swim the few feet back to the rock. Then he was clutching it and pulling himself up onto it. He lay face down, gasping. He could see nothing but a red-veined, clotted dark. His eyes must have burst, he thought; they were full of blood. He tore off his goggles and a gout[3] of blood went into the sea. His nose was bleeding, and the blood had filled the goggles.

　　He scooped up handfuls of water from the cool, salty sea, to splash on his face, and did not know whether it was blood or salt water he tasted. After a time, his heart quieted, his eyes cleared, and he sat up. He could see the local boys diving and playing half a mile away. He did not want them. He wanted nothing but to get back home and lie down.
300　　In a short while, Jerry swam to shore and climbed slowly up the path to the villa. He flung himself on his bed and slept, waking at the

---

2. **mussel:** shellfish, similar to a clam or an oyster, that attaches itself to rocks.
3. **gout:** large glob.

sound of feet on the path outside. His mother was coming back. He rushed to the bathroom, thinking she must not see his face with bloodstains, or tearstains, on it. He came out of the bathroom and met her as she walked into the villa, smiling, her eyes lighting up.

"Have a nice morning?" she asked, laying her hand on his warm brown shoulder a moment.

"Oh, yes, thank you," he said.

"You look a bit pale." And then, sharp and anxious, "How did you

310 bang your head?"

"Oh, just banged it," he told her.

She looked at him closely. He was strained; his eyes were glazed-looking. She was worried. And then she said to herself, Oh, don't fuss! Nothing can happen. He can swim like a fish.

They sat down to lunch together.

"Mummy," he said, "I can stay underwater for two minutes—three minutes, at least." It came bursting out of him.

"Can you, darling?" she said. "Well, I shouldn't overdo it. I don't think you ought to swim anymore today."

320 She was ready for a battle of wills, but he gave in at once. It was no longer of the least importance to go to the bay.

INTERPRET

Why do you think Jerry gives in "at once"? Why has going to the bay now become unimportant?

Omniscient Point of View

In a story told from the **omniscient point of view,** the narrator is an all-knowing observer who can reveal the thoughts, feelings, motives, and conflicts of all the characters. Unlike stories written from the first-person point of view, stories with an omniscient point of view give us a more reliable perspective. We know that the narrator knows all, and we trust the narrator's voice.

1. Re-read the passage from the story below. Underline the words and phrases that relate to the mother's perspective. Circle the words and phrases that relate to Jerry's thoughts and feelings.

> She frowned, conscientiously worrying over what amusements he might secretly be longing for, which she had been too busy or too careless to imagine. He was very familiar with that anxious, apologetic smile. Contrition sent him running after her. And yet, as he ran, he looked back over his shoulder at the wild bay; and all morning, as he played on the safe beach, he was thinking of it.

2. How do you think the story would be different if Jerry's mother, rather than the omniscient narrator, were telling it?

_____

_____

_____

_____

_____

Vocabulary: How to Own a Word

Using Word Parts to Build Meaning

For each Word to Own, create your own definition by combining the meanings given in the boxes below for each word's root, prefix, and suffix. If there is more than one meaning given for any word part, underline the meaning that best suits the word you are defining. Then, give an explanation of the word's meaning. Finally, write a sentence using the Word to Own in the proper context. You may use a dictionary if you wish. The first one has been partially completed for you as an example.

Word Bank	
contrition	minute
supplication	incredulous
inquisitive	

Word to Own	Root	Prefix	Suffix
contrition	*tritus*, past participle of *terere*, to rub	*con–*, with, <u>together</u>	*–ion*, the result, <u>act</u>, or condition of

Meaning: <u>con</u> (together) + <u>tritus</u> (to rub) + <u>-ion</u> (act of)—act of rubbing together. <u>Contrition</u> combines a feeling of guilt with a determination to make amends. These feelings "rub together," or have a scrubbing or cleansing effect on the person who regrets the action.

Sentence: _____

_____

_____

_____

supplication	*plicare*, to fold	*sup– (sub-)*, under	*–ion*, the result, <u>act</u>, or condition of

Meaning: _____

_____

_____

_____

Sentence: _____

_____

_____

_____

Vocabulary: How to Own a Word (continued)

inquisitive	*quaerere,* to seek	*in–,* into, toward on	*–ive,* belonging to quality of

Meaning: _____

_____

_____

_____

Sentence: _____

_____

_____

_____

minute	*minuere,* to lessen		*–tus,* degree of, characteristic of

Meaning: _____

_____

_____

_____

Sentence: _____

_____

_____

_____

incredulous	*credere,* to believe	*in–,* no, not, without	*–ous,* having, full of, characterized by

Meaning: _____

_____

_____

_____

Sentence: _____

_____

_____

_____

Selection: _____

Analyzing Point of View in a Story

1. Who is the narrator?	
2. From which of the following three points of view is the story told: omniscient, third-person limited, or first person?	
3. What does the narrator know that no one else coud?	
4. What does the narrator not know?	
5. What are the narrator's biases, if any?	
6. How does the point of view affect the way you feel about the characters? Does it make you sympathize more with one character than with another?	
7. Choose a different point of view from which the story could be told. How would the story change if this point of view were used?	

The Pit and the Pendulum

Make the Connection

Our Deepest Fears

Fear often heightens awareness of our surroundings. Suppose, for example, you are lying awake in the dark. You may see things you never noticed before. It might be the way shadows play on familiar objects and make them seem menacing. You may hear sounds that you would normally disregard, such as the ticking of a clock or creaking from the woodwork.

Use the diagram below to help you understand how fear heightens the senses. In the left-hand column is a list of senses (sight, hearing, touch, smell, taste). In the right-hand column, record objects or sensations that you might detect when you feel frightened. You may use words, symbols, or sketches.

Senses	Objects or Sensations
Sight	
Hearing	
Touch	
Smell	
Taste	

The Pit and the Pendulum

Edgar Allan Poe

INFER

Who is telling the story? What is happening to him in lines 2–5?

_____

_____

_____

_____

_____

_____

_____

WORDS TO OWN

imperceptible (im′pər·sep′ tə·bəl) *adj.:* not clear or obvious to the senses or the mind; too slight or gradual to be noticeable.

INTERPRET

What **symbolic meaning** do the candles have for the narrator? Underline the passage that gives the answer.

_____

_____

_____

_____

_____

_____

_____

_____

_____

_____

_____

_____

I was sick—sick unto death with that long agony; and when they at length unbound me, and I was permitted to sit, I felt that my senses were leaving me. The sentence—the dread sentence of death—was the last of distinct accentuation which reached my ears. After that, the sound of the Inquisitorial voices seemed merged in one dreamy, indeterminate hum. It conveyed to my soul the idea of *revolution*[1]—perhaps from its association in fancy[2] with the burr of a mill wheel. This only for a brief period, for presently I heard no more. Yet for a while, I saw—but with how terrible an exaggeration! I saw the lips of the black-robed judges. They appeared
10 to me white—whiter than the sheet upon which I trace these words—and thin even to grotesqueness; thin with the intensity of their expression of firmness—of immovable resolution—of stern contempt of human torture. I saw that the decrees of what to me was Fate were still issuing from those lips. I saw them writhe with a deadly locution.[3] I saw them fashion the syllables of my name; and I shuddered because no sound succeeded.[4] I saw, too, for a few moments of delirious horror, the soft and nearly imperceptible waving of the sable draperies which enwrapped the walls of the apartment. And then my vision fell upon the seven tall candles upon the table. At first they wore the aspect of charity and seemed white,
20 slender angels who would save me; but then, all at once, there came a most deadly nausea over my spirit, and I felt every fiber in my frame thrill as if I had touched the wire of a galvanic battery, while the angel forms became meaningless specters, with heads of flame, and I saw that from them there would be no help. And then there stole into my fancy, like a rich musical note, the thought of what sweet rest there must be in the grave. The thought came gently and stealthily, and it seemed long before it attained full appreciation; but just as my spirit came at length properly to feel and entertain it, the figures of the judges vanished, as if magically, from before me; the tall candles sank into nothingness! Their flames went
30 out utterly; the blackness of darkness supervened; all sensations appeared swallowed up in a mad rushing descent, as of the soul into Hades. Then silence, and stillness, and night were the universe.

I had swooned;[5] but still will not say that all of consciousness was lost. What of it there remained I will not attempt to define, or even to describe; yet all was not lost. In the deepest slumber—no! In delirium— no! In a swoon—no! In death—no! Even in the grave all *is not* lost. Else there is no immortality for man. Arousing from the most profound of slumbers, we break the gossamer web of *some* dream. Yet in a second afterward (so frail may that web have been), we remember not that we

---

1. **revolution:** here, rotation; turning motion.
2. **fancy:** here, imagination.
3. **locution** (lō·kyōō′shən): utterance; statement.
4. **succeeded:** here, followed.
5. **swooned:** fainted.

have dreamed. In the return to life from the swoon, there are two stages: first, that of the sense of mental or spiritual; second, that of the sense of physical existence. It seems probable that if, upon reaching the second stage, we could recall the impressions of the first, we should find these impressions eloquent in memories of the gulf beyond. And that gulf is— what? How at least shall we distinguish its shadows from those of the tomb? But if the impressions of what I have termed the first stage are not, at will, recalled, yet, after long interval, do they not come unbidden, while we marvel whence they come? He who has never swooned is not he who finds strange palaces and wildly familiar faces in coals that glow; is not he who beholds floating in midair the sad visions that the many may not view; is not he who ponders over the perfume of some novel flower; is not he whose brain grows bewildered with the meaning of some musical cadence which has never before arrested his attention.

Amid frequent and thoughtful endeavors to remember, amid earnest struggles to regather some token of the state of seeming nothingness into which my soul had lapsed, there have been moments when I have dreamed of success; there have been brief, very brief, periods when I have conjured up remembrances which the lucid reason of a later epoch assures me could have had reference only to that condition of seeming unconsciousness. These shadows of memory tell, indistinctly, of tall figures that lifted and bore me in silence down—down—still down—till a hideous dizziness oppressed me at the mere idea of the interminableness of the descent. They tell also of a vague horror at my heart, on account of that heart's unnatural stillness. Then comes a sense of sudden motionlessness throughout all things; as if those who bore me (a ghastly train!) had outrun, in their descent, the limits of the limitless, and paused from the wearisomeness of their toil. After this I call to mind flatness and dampness; and then all is *madness*—the madness of a memory which busies itself among forbidden things.

Very suddenly there came back to my soul motion and sound—the tumultuous motion of the heart and, in my ears, the sound of its beating. Then a pause in which all is blank. Then again sound, and motion, and touch—a tingling sensation pervading my frame. Then the mere consciousness of existence, without thought—a condition which lasted long. Then, very suddenly, *thought*, and shuddering terror, and earnest endeavor to comprehend my true state. Then a strong desire to lapse into insensibility. Then a rushing revival of soul and a successful effort to move. And now a full memory of the trial, of the judges, of the sable draperies, of the sentence, of the sickness, of the swoon. Then entire forgetfulness of all that followed; of all that a later day and much earnestness of endeavor have enabled me vaguely to recall.

So far, I had not opened my eyes. I felt that I lay upon my back, unbound. I reached out my hand, and it fell heavily upon something damp

IDENTIFY

According to the narrator, what are the two stages of returning to life from a swoon? Underline the words giving the answer.

WORDS TO OWN
ponders (pän′dərz) v.: thinks deeply.

_____

_____

_____

WORDS TO OWN
lucid (loo′sid) adj.: clearheaded; not confused. *Lucid* also means "understandable" or "bright and shining."

_____

_____

_____

INTERPRET

What word is repeated in lines 67–69? What is the effect of this **repetition**?

_____

_____

_____

_____

_____

_____

_____

WORDS TO OWN
tumultuous (too·mul′choo·əs) adj.: violent; greatly agitated or disturbed. *Tumultuous* also means "wild, noisy, and confused."

BUILD FLUENCY

Read lines 82–104 aloud as expressively as you can. Use the punctuation as a guide to units of meaning, and focus on **repetition** and **parallel phrasing**.

EVALUATE

Do you agree with the narrator that seeing nothing would be worse than seeing horrible things? Why or why not?

_____

_____

_____

_____

_____

_____

_____

_____

_____

IDENTIFY

What does the narrator consider "the most hideous of fates?" Underline the words giving the answer.

_____

_____

_____

_____

_____

_____

_____

_____

_____

and hard. There I suffered[6] it to remain for many minutes, while I strove to imagine where and *what* I could be. I longed, yet dared not, to employ my vision. I dreaded the first glance at objects around me. It was not that I feared to look upon things horrible, but that I grew aghast lest there should be *nothing* to see. At length, with a wild desperation at heart, I quickly unclosed my eyes. My worst thoughts, then, were confirmed. The

90 blackness of eternal night encompassed me. I struggled for breath. The intensity of the darkness seemed to oppress and stifle me. The atmosphere was intolerably close. I still lay quietly, and made effort to exercise my reason. I brought to mind the Inquisitorial proceedings and attempted from that point to deduce my real condition. The sentence had passed; and it appeared to me that a very long interval of time had since elapsed. Yet not for a moment did I suppose myself actually dead. Such a supposition, notwithstanding what we read in fiction, is altogether inconsistent with real existence—but where and in what state was I? The condemned to death, I knew, perished usually at the autos-da-fé, and one of these had

100 been held on the very night of the day of my trial. Had I been remanded to my dungeon, to await the next sacrifice, which would not take place for many months? This I at once saw could not be. Victims had been in immediate demand. Moreover, my dungeon, as well as all the condemned cells at Toledo, had stone floors, and light was not altogether excluded.

A fearful idea now suddenly drove the blood in torrents upon my heart, and for a brief period I once more relapsed into insensibility. Upon recovering, I at once started to my feet, trembling convulsively in every fiber. I thrust my arms wildly above and around me in all directions. I felt nothing; yet dreaded to move a step, lest I should be impeded by the

110 walls of a *tomb*. Perspiration burst from every pore and stood in cold, big beads upon my forehead. The agony of suspense grew at length intolerable, and I cautiously moved forward, with my arms extended and my eyes straining from their sockets in the hope of catching some faint ray of light. I proceeded for many paces; but still all was blackness and vacancy. I breathed more freely. It seemed evident that mine was not, at least, the most hideous of fates.

And now, as I still continued to step cautiously onward, there came thronging upon my recollection a thousand vague rumors of the horrors of Toledo. Of the dungeons there had been strange things narrated—

120 fables I had always deemed them—but yet strange, and too ghastly to repeat, save in a whisper. Was I left to perish of starvation in the subterranean world of darkness; or what fate, perhaps even more fearful, awaited me? That the result would be death, and a death of more than customary bitterness, I knew too well the character of my judges to doubt. The mode and the hour were all that occupied or distracted me.

---

6. **suffered:** here, allowed; tolerated.

My outstretched hands at length encountered some solid obstruction. It was a wall, seemingly of stone masonry—very smooth, slimy, and cold. I followed it up, stepping with all the careful distrust with which certain antique narratives had inspired me. This process, however,
130 afforded me no means of ascertaining the dimensions of my dungeon, as I might make its circuit and return to the point whence I set out without being aware of the fact, so perfectly uniform seemed the wall. I therefore sought the knife which had been in my pocket when led into the Inquisitorial chamber, but it was gone; my clothes had been exchanged for a wrapper of coarse serge. I had thought of forcing the blade in some minute crevice of the masonry, so as to identify my point of departure. The difficulty, nevertheless, was but trivial; although, in the disorder of my fancy, it seemed at first insuperable. I tore a part of the hem from the robe and placed the fragment at full length and at right angles to the
140 wall. In groping my way around the prison, I could not fail to encounter this rag upon completing the circuit. So, at least, I thought; but I had not counted upon the extent of the dungeon, or upon my own weakness. The ground was moist and slippery. I staggered onward for some time, when I stumbled and fell. My excessive fatigue induced me to remain prostrate; and sleep soon overtook me as I lay.

Upon awaking and stretching forth an arm, I found beside me a loaf and a pitcher with water. I was too much exhausted to reflect upon this circumstance, but ate and drank with avidity.[7] Shortly afterward, I resumed my tour around the prison and, with much toil, came at last
150 upon the fragment of the serge. Up to the period when I fell, I had counted fifty-two paces, and upon resuming my walk, I had counted forty-eight more—when I arrived at the rag. There were in all, then, a hundred paces; and, admitting two paces to the yard, I presumed the dungeon to be fifty yards in circuit. I had met, however, with many angles in the wall, and thus I could form no guess at the shape of the vault, for vault I could not help supposing it to be.

I had little object—certainly no hope—in these researches; but a vague curiosity prompted me to continue them. Quitting the wall, I resolved to cross the area of the enclosure. At first, I proceeded with
160 extreme caution, for the floor, although seemingly of solid material, was treacherous with slime. At length, however, I took courage and did not hesitate to step firmly—endeavoring to cross in as direct a line as possible. I had advanced some ten or twelve paces in this manner when the remnant of the torn hem of my robe became entangled between my legs. I stepped on it and fell violently on my face.

In the confusion attending my fall, I did not immediately apprehend a somewhat startling circumstance, which yet, in a few seconds afterward

WORDS TO OWN
insuperable (in·soo′pər·ə·bəl) *adj.:* incapable of being overcome or passed over.

WORDS TO OWN
prostrate (präs′trāt′) *adj.:* lying flat. *Prostrate* also means "helpless; overcome" or "lying with the face downward to show devotion or submission."

IDENTIFY

How does the narrator attempt to determine the extent of his prison?

7. **avidity** (ə·vid′ə·tē): great eagerness.

IDENTIFY

How does the narrator discover the existence of the pit? Underline the words giving the answer.

_____

_____

_____

_____

PREDICT

Given the title of the story, as well as what you have been told about the Inquisition, what do you think may happen to the narrator now?

_____

_____

_____

_____

_____

_____

_____

_____

_____

_____

_____

_____

_____

_____

_____

_____

_____

and while I still lay prostrate, arrested my attention. It was this—my chin rested upon the floor of the prison, but my lips and the upper portion of
170 my head, although seemingly at a less elevation than the chin, touched nothing. At the same time, my forehead seemed bathed in a clammy vapor, and the peculiar smell of decayed fungus arose to my nostrils. I put forward my arm, and shuddered to find that I had fallen at the very brink of a circular pit, whose extent, of course, I had no means of ascertaining at the moment. Groping about the masonry just below the margin, I succeeded in dislodging a small fragment and let it fall into the abyss. For many seconds I hearkened to its reverberations as it dashed against the sides of the chasm in its descent; at length, there was a sullen plunge into water, succeeded by loud echoes. At the same moment, there came a
180 sound resembling the quick opening and as rapid closing of a door overhead, while a faint gleam of light flashed suddenly through the gloom and as suddenly faded away.

I saw clearly the doom which had been prepared for me, and congratulated myself upon the timely accident by which I had escaped. Another step before my fall, and the world had seen me no more. And the death just avoided was of that very character which I had regarded as fabulous and frivolous in the tales respecting the Inquisition. To the victims of its tyranny, there was the choice of death with its direst physical agonies or death with its most hideous moral horrors. I had been
190 reserved for the latter. By long suffering, my nerves had been unstrung, until I trembled at the sound of my own voice and had become in every respect a fitting subject for the species of torture which awaited me.

Shaking in every limb, I groped my way back to the wall; resolving there to perish rather than risk the terrors of the wells, of which my imagination now pictured many in various positions about the dungeon. In other conditions of mind, I might have had courage to end my misery at once, by a plunge into one of these abysses; but now I was the veriest[8] of cowards. Neither could I forget what I had read of these pits—that the _sudden_ extinction of life formed no part of their most horrible plan.

200 Agitation of spirit kept me awake for many long hours, but at length I again slumbered. Upon arousing, I found by my side, as before, a loaf and a pitcher of water. A burning thirst consumed me, and I emptied the vessel at a draft. It must have been drugged; for scarcely had I drunk before I became irresistibly drowsy. A deep sleep fell upon me—a sleep like that of death. How long it lasted of course I know not; but when, once again, I unclosed my eyes, the objects around me were visible. By a wild, sulfurous luster,[9] the origin of which I could not at first determine, I was enabled to see the extent and aspect of the prison.

---

8. **veriest** (ver′ē·ist): greatest.
9. **sulfurous** (sul′fər·əs) **luster:** glow like that of burning sulfur, which produces a blue flame. The word _sulfurous_ is also used to mean "suggesting the fires of hell."

In its size I had been greatly mistaken. The whole circuit of its walls
210 did not exceed twenty-five yards. For some minutes this fact occasioned
me a world of vain trouble; vain indeed, for what could be of less
importance, under the terrible circumstances which environed me, than
the mere dimensions of my dungeon? But my soul took a wild interest in
trifles, and I busied myself in endeavors to account for the error I had
committed in my measurement. The truth at length flashed upon me. In
my first attempt at exploration I had counted fifty-two paces, up to the
period when I fell; I must then have been within a pace or two of the
fragment of serge; in fact, I had nearly performed the circuit of the vault.
I then slept, and upon awaking, I must have returned upon my steps—
220 thus supposing the circuit nearly double what it actually was. My
confusion of mind prevented me from observing that I began my tour
with the wall to the left and ended it with the wall to the right.

I had been deceived, too, in respect to the shape of the enclosure.
In feeling my way I had found many angles and thus deduced an idea
of great irregularity; so <u>potent</u> is the effect of total darkness upon one
arousing from <u>lethargy</u> or sleep! The angles were simply those of a few
slight depressions, or niches, at odd intervals. The general shape of the
prison was square. What I had taken for masonry seemed now to be
iron, or some other metal, in huge plates, whose sutures or joints
230 occasioned the depression. The entire surface of this metallic enclosure
was rudely daubed[10] in all the hideous and repulsive devices to which
the charnel[11] superstition of the monks has given rise. The figures of
fiends in aspects of menace, with skeleton forms, and other, more really
fearful images, overspread and disfigured the walls. I observed that the
outlines of these monstrosities were sufficiently distinct, but that the
colors seemed faded and blurred, as if from the effects of a damp
atmosphere. I now noticed the floor, too, which was of stone. In the
center yawned the circular pit from whose jaws I had escaped; but it
was the only one in the dungeon.

240 All this I saw indistinctly and by much effort: for my personal
condition had been greatly changed during slumber. I now lay upon my
back, and at full length, on a species of low framework of wood. To this
I was securely bound by a long strap resembling a surcingle.[12] It passed
in many convolutions about my limbs and body, leaving at liberty only
my head, and my left arm to such extent that I could, by dint of much
exertion, supply myself with food from an earthen dish which lay by my
side on the floor. I saw, to my horror, that the pitcher had been removed.

---

10. **daubed:** painted crudely or unskillfully.
11. **charnel:** suggestive of death. A charnel house is a building or place where bones or bodies are deposited.
12. **surcingle** (sʉr'siŋ'gəl): strap passed around a horse's body to bind on a saddle or a pack.

INFER

Why might the narrator be so interested in the minute details of his cell?

_____

_____

_____

_____

WORDS TO OWN

potent (pōt''nt) *adj.:* powerful or effective.
lethargy (leth'ər·jē) *n.:* abnormal drowsiness. *Lethargy* also means "great lack of energy; dull or indifferent state."

VISUALIZE

Use the details in this paragraph to visualize the scene. What new horrors does the narrator see?

_____

_____

_____

_____

_____

IDENTIFY

In what two ways has the physical condition of the narrator changed? Underline the words giving the answer.

_____

_____

_____

_____

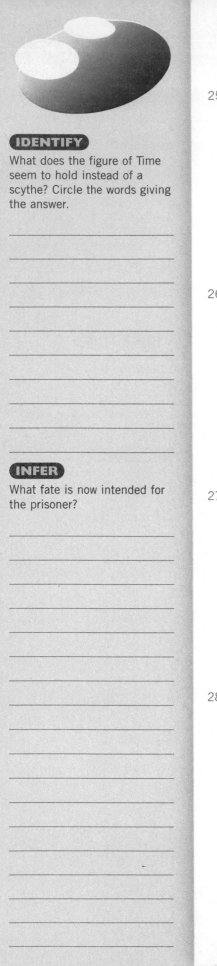

IDENTIFY

What does the figure of Time seem to hold instead of a scythe? Circle the words giving the answer.

_____
_____
_____
_____
_____
_____
_____
_____
_____

INFER

What fate is now intended for the prisoner?

_____
_____
_____
_____
_____
_____
_____
_____
_____
_____
_____
_____
_____
_____
_____
_____

I say to my horror, for I was consumed with intolerable thirst. This thirst it appeared to be the design of my persecutors to stimulate—for the food 250 in the dish was meat pungently seasoned.

Looking upward, I surveyed the ceiling of my prison. It was some thirty or forty feet overhead and constructed much as the side walls. In one of its panels a very singular figure riveted my whole attention. It was the painted figure of Time as he is commonly represented, save[13] that, in lieu of[14] a scythe, he held what, at a casual glance, I supposed to be the pictured image of a huge pendulum, such as we see on antique clocks. There was something, however, in the appearance of this machine which caused me to regard it more attentively. While I gazed directly upward at it (for its position was immediately over my own), I fancied that I saw it 260 in motion. In an instant afterward the fancy was confirmed. Its sweep was brief and of course slow. I watched it for some minutes somewhat in fear, but more in wonder. Wearied at length with observing its dull movement, I turned my eyes upon the other objects in the cell.

A slight noise attracted my notice, and looking to the floor, I saw several enormous rats traversing it. They had issued from the well which lay just within view to my right. Even then, while I gazed, they came up in troops, hurriedly, with ravenous eyes, allured by the scent of the meat. From this it required much effort and attention to scare them away.

It might have been half an hour, perhaps even an hour (for I could 270 take but imperfect note of time), before I again cast my eyes upward. What I then saw confounded and amazed me. The sweep of the pendulum had increased in extent by nearly a yard. As a natural consequence its velocity was also much greater. But what mainly disturbed me was the idea that it had perceptibly _descended_. I now observed—with what horror it is needless to say—that its nether extremity[15] was formed of a crescent of glittering steel, about a foot in length from horn to horn; the horns upward, and the under edge evidently as keen as that of a razor. Like a razor also, it seemed massy and heavy, tapering from the edge into a solid and broad structure 280 above. It was appended to a weighty rod of brass, and the whole _hissed_ as it swung through the air.

I could no longer doubt the doom prepared for me by monkish ingenuity in torture. My cognizance[16] of the pit had become known to the Inquisitorial agents—_the pit_, whose horrors had been destined for so bold a recusant[17] as myself—_the pit_, typical of hell and regarded by rumor as the ultima Thule[18] of all their punishments. The plunge into

---

13. **save:** here, except.
14. **in lieu** (l$\overline{oo}$) **of:** instead of.
15. **nether** (ne_th_'ər) **extremity:** lower end.
16. **cognizance** (käg'nə·zəns): awareness.
17. **recusant** (rek'yoo·zənt): person who refuses to obey an established authority.
18. **ultima Thule** (ul'ti·mə th$\overline{oo}$'lē): most extreme. The term is Latin for "northernmost region of the world."

this pit I had avoided by the merest of accidents, and I knew that surprise, or entrapment into torment, formed an important portion of all the grotesquerie of these dungeon deaths. Having failed to fall, it was no
290 part of the demon plan to hurl me into the abyss, and thus (there being no alternative) a different and a milder destruction awaited me. Milder! I half smiled in my agony as I thought of such application of such a term.

What boots it[19] to tell of the long, long hours of horror more than mortal, during which I counted the rushing vibrations of the steel! Inch by inch—line by line—with a descent only appreciable at intervals that seemed ages—down and still down it came! Days passed—it might have been that many days passed—ere it swept so closely over me as to fan me with its acrid breath. The odor of the sharp steel forced itself into my nostrils. I prayed—I wearied heaven with my prayer for its more speedy
300 descent. I grew frantically mad and struggled to force myself upward against the sweep of the fearful scimitar.[20] And then I fell suddenly calm and lay smiling at the glittering death, as a child at some rare bauble.

There was another interval of utter insensibility; it was brief; for, upon again lapsing into life, there had been no perceptible descent in the pendulum. But it might have been long—for I knew there were demons who took note of my swoon and who could have arrested the vibration at pleasure. Upon my recovery, too, I felt very—oh! inexpressibly—sick and weak, as if through long inanition.[21] Even amid the agonies of that period, the human nature craved food. With painful effort I outstretched
310 my left arm as far as my bonds permitted and took possession of the small remnant which had been spared me by the rats. As I put a portion of it within my lips, there rushed to my mind a half-formed thought of joy—of hope. Yet what business had *I* with hope? It was, as I say, a half-formed thought—man has many such, which are never completed. I felt that it was of joy—of hope; but I felt also that it had perished in its formation. In vain I struggled to perfect—to regain it. Long suffering had nearly annihilated all my ordinary powers of mind. I was an imbecile—an idiot.

The vibration of the pendulum was at right angles to my length.
320 I saw that the crescent was designed to cross the region of the heart. It would fray the serge of my robe—it would return and repeat its operations—again—and again. Notwithstanding its terrifically wide sweep (some thirty feet or more) and the hissing vigor of its descent, sufficient to sunder these very walls of iron, still the fraying of my robe would be all that, for several minutes, it would accomplish. And at this

IDENTIFY

Poe uses **repetition** and **sound effects** to reinforce the emotional effect of his story. Underline examples of **repetition** and **alliteration** in lines 293–302 that emphasize the narrator's suspense and anguish.

---

19. **what boots it:** of what use is it.
20. **scimitar** (sim′ə·tər): sword with a curved blade, used mainly by Arabs and Turks.
21. **inanition** (in′ə·nish′ən): weakness from lack of food.

thought I paused. I dared not go further than this reflection. I dwelt upon it with a pertinacity[22] of attention—as if, in so dwelling, I could arrest[23] *here* the descent of the steel. I forced myself to ponder upon the sound of the crescent as it should pass across the garment—upon the peculiar 330 thrilling sensation which the friction of cloth produces on the nerves. I pondered upon all this frivolity until my teeth were on edge.

Down—steadily down it crept. I took a frenzied pleasure in contrasting its downward with its lateral velocity. To the right—to the left—far and wide—with the shriek of a damned spirit! to my heart, with the stealthy pace of the tiger! I alternately laughed and howled, as the one or the other idea grew predominant.

Down—certainly, relentlessly down! It vibrated within three inches of my bosom! I struggled violently—furiously—to free my left arm. This was free only from the elbow to the hand. I could reach the latter, from 340 the platter beside me, to my mouth, with great effort, but no farther. Could I have broken the fastenings above the elbow, I would have seized and attempted to arrest the pendulum. I might as well have attempted to arrest an avalanche!

Down—still unceasingly—still inevitably down! I gasped and struggled at each vibration. I shrunk convulsively at its every sweep. My eyes followed its outward or upward whorls with the eagerness of the most unmeaning despair; they closed themselves spasmodically at the descent, although death would have been a relief, oh, how unspeakable! Still I quivered in every nerve to think how slight a sinking of the 350 machinery would precipitate that keen, glistening ax upon my bosom. It was *hope* that prompted the nerve to quiver—the frame to shrink. It was *hope*—the hope that triumphs on the rack—that whispers to the death-condemned even in the dungeons of the Inquisition.

I saw that some ten or twelve vibrations would bring the steel in actual contact with my robe, and with this observation there suddenly came over my spirit all the keen, collected calmness of despair. For the first time during many hours—or perhaps days—I *thought*. It now occurred to me that the bandage, or surcingle, which enveloped me, was *unique*. I was tied by no separate cord. The first stroke of the razorlike 360 crescent athwart any portion of the band would so detach it that it might be unwound from my person by means of my left hand. But how fearful, in that case, the proximity of the steel! The result of the slightest struggle, how deadly! Was it likely, moreover, that the minions[24] of the torturer had not foreseen and provided for this possibility? Was it probable that the bandage crossed my bosom in the track of the

WORDS TO OWN
proximity (präk·sim′ə·tē) *n.:* nearness.

---

22. **pertinacity** (pur′tə·nas′ə·tē): stubborn persistence.
23. **arrest:** here, stop.
24. **minions:** servants; followers.

pendulum? Dreading to find my faint and, as it seemed, my last hope frustrated, I so far elevated my head as to obtain a distinct view of my breast. The surcingle enveloped my limbs and body close in all directions—*save in the path of the destroying crescent.*

370 Scarcely had I dropped my head back into its original position when there flashed upon my mind what I cannot better describe than as the unformed half of that idea of deliverance to which I had previously alluded, and of which a moiety[25] only floated indeterminately through my brain when I raised food to my burning lips. The whole thought was now present—feeble, scarcely sane, scarcely definite—but still entire. I proceeded at once, with the nervous energy of despair, to attempt its execution.

For many hours the immediate vicinity of the low framework upon which I lay had been literally swarming with rats. They were wild, bold,
380 ravenous—their red eyes glaring upon me as if they waited but for motionlessness on my part to make me their prey. "To what food," I thought, "have they been accustomed in the well?"

They had devoured, in spite of all my efforts to prevent them, all but a small remnant of the contents of the dish. I had fallen into a habitual seesaw or wave of the hand about the platter; and, at length, the unconscious uniformity of the movement deprived it of effect. In their voracity, the vermin frequently fastened their sharp fangs in my fingers. With the particles of the oily and spicy viand which now remained, I thoroughly rubbed the bandage wherever I could reach it; then, raising
390 my hand from the floor, I lay breathlessly still.

At first, the ravenous animals were startled and terrified at the change—at the cessation of movement. They shrank alarmedly back; many sought the well. But this was only for a moment. I had not counted in vain upon their voracity. Observing that I remained without motion, one or two of the boldest leaped upon the framework and smelled at the surcingle. This seemed the signal for a general rush. Forth from the well they hurried in fresh troops. They clung to the wood—they overran it and leaped in hundreds upon my person. The measured movement of the pendulum disturbed them not at all. Avoiding its
400 strokes, they busied themselves with the anointed bandage. They pressed—they swarmed upon me in ever accumulating heaps. They writhed upon my throat; their cold lips sought my own; I was half stifled by their thronging pressure; disgust for which the world has no name swelled my bosom and chilled, with a heavy clamminess, my heart. Yet one minute, and I felt that the struggle would be over. Plainly I perceived the loosening of the bandage. I knew that in more than one place it must be already severed. With a more than human resolution I lay *still.*

---

25. **moiety** (moi′ə·tē): part.

RETELL

How does the narrator escape
the deadly pendulum?

Nor had I erred in my calculations—nor had I endured in vain. I at length felt that I was *free*. The surcingle hung in ribbons from my body.
410 But the stroke of the pendulum already pressed upon my bosom. It had divided the serge of the robe. It had cut through the linen beneath. Twice again it swung, and a sharp sense of pain shot through every nerve. But the moment of escape had arrived. At a wave of my hand my deliverers hurried tumultuously away. With a steady movement—cautious, sidelong, shrinking, and slow—I slid from the embrace of the bandage and beyond the reach of the scimitar. For the moment, at least, *I was free.*

Free!—and in the grasp of the Inquisition! I had scarcely stepped from my wooden bed of horror upon the stone floor of the prison when the motion of the hellish machine ceased, and I beheld it drawn up, by
420 some invisible force, through the ceiling. This was a lesson which I took desperately to heart. My every motion was undoubtedly watched. Free!—I had but escaped death in one form of agony to be delivered unto worse than death in some other. With that thought I rolled my eyes nervously around on the barriers of iron that hemmed me in. Something unusual—some change which at first I could not appreciate distinctly—it was obvious, had taken place in the apartment. For many minutes of a dreamy and trembling abstraction, I busied myself in vain, unconnected conjecture. During this period, I became aware, for the first time, of the origin of the sulfurous light which illumined the cell. It proceeded from a
430 fissure, about half an inch in width, extending entirely around the prison at the base of the walls, which thus appeared, and were, completely separated from the floor. I endeavored, but of course in vain, to look through the aperture.

As I arose from the attempt, the mystery of the alteration in the chamber broke at once upon my understanding. I had observed that, although the outlines of the figures upon the walls were sufficiently distinct, yet the colors seemed blurred and indefinite. These colors had now assumed and were momentarily assuming, a startling and most intense brilliance that gave to the spectral and fiendish portraitures an
440 aspect that might have thrilled even firmer nerves than my own. Demon eyes, of a wild and ghastly vivacity, glared upon me in a thousand directions where none had been visible before, and gleamed with the lurid luster of a fire that I could not force my imagination to regard as unreal.

Unreal!—even while I breathed, there came to my nostrils the breath of the vapor of heated iron! A suffocating odor pervaded the prison! A deeper glow settled each moment in the eyes that glared at my agonies! A richer tint of crimson diffused itself over the pictured horrors of blood. I panted! I gasped for breath! There could be no doubt of the design of my tormenters—oh! most unrelenting! oh! most demoniac of men! I
450 shrank from the glowing metal to the center of the cell. Amid the thought of the fiery destruction that impended, the idea of the coolness

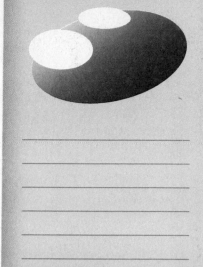

of the well came over my soul like balm. I rushed to its deadly brink.
I threw my straining vision below. The glare from the enkindled roof
illumined its inmost recesses. Yet for a wild moment did my spirit refuse
to comprehend the meaning of what I saw. At length it forced—it
wrestled its way into my soul—it burned itself in upon my shuddering
reason.—Oh! for a voice to speak!—oh! horror!—oh! any horror but
this! With a shriek, I rushed from the margin and buried my face in my
hands—weeping bitterly.

460   The heat rapidly increased, and once again I looked up, shuddering
as with a fit of the ague.[26] There had been a second change in the cell—
and now the change was obviously in the *form*. As before, it was in vain
that I at first endeavored to appreciate or understand what was taking
place. But not long was I left in doubt. The Inquisitorial vengeance had
been hurried by my twofold escape, and there was to be no more
dallying with the King of Terrors. The room had been square. I saw that
two of its iron angles were now acute[27]—two, consequently, obtuse.[28]
The fearful difference quickly increased with a low rumbling or moaning
sound. In an instant the apartment had shifted its form into that of a
470 lozenge.[29] But the alteration stopped not here—I neither hoped nor
desired it to stop. I could have clasped the red walls to my bosom as a
garment of eternal peace. "Death," I said, "any death but that of the pit!"
Fool! Might I not have known that *into the pit* it was the object of the
burning iron to urge me? Could I resist its glow? Or if even that, could I
withstand its pressure? And now, flatter and flatter grew the lozenge,
with a rapidity that left me no time for contemplation. Its center, and of
course its greatest width, came just over the yawning gulf. I shrank
back—but the closing walls pressed me resistlessly onward. At length,
for my seared and writhing body, there was no longer an inch of
480 foothold on the firm floor of the prison. I struggled no more, but the
agony of my soul found vent in one loud, long, and final scream of
despair. I felt that I tottered upon the brink—I averted my eyes——

    There was a discordant hum of human voices! There was a loud
blast as of many trumpets! There was a harsh grating as of a thousand
thunders! The fiery walls rushed back! An outstretched arm caught my
own as I fell, fainting, into the abyss. It was that of General Lasalle. The
French army had entered Toledo. The Inquisition was in the hands of its
enemies.

---

26. **ague** (ā′gyōō′): chills.
27. **acute** (ə·kyōōt′): of less than 90 degrees.
28. **obtuse** (äb·tōōs′): of more than 90 degrees and less than 180 degrees.
29. **lozenge** (läz′ənj): diamond shape.

Symbolic Meaning

A symbol is a person, place, object, or event that stands both for itself and for something other than itself. When we read, we often sense that a story means more than what literally happens on the surface. For example, if a young woman in a story is in serious conflict with her parents over her earrings, we should suspect that these earrings represent something important to her—perhaps independence or attractiveness. The symbolic meaning of a story emerges from an overall interpretation of the story's individual symbols.

On one level, "The Pit and the Pendulum" is a story about a man being tortured by the Inquisition. However, some critics read the story on a symbolic level, as the tale of a man who dies, almost loses his soul to Hell, and is rescued at the end by God. Consider whether the story "works" if it is read symbolically in this fashion. For each symbol from the story listed in the left-hand column, jot down some notes giving your interpretation of the symbolic meaning(s).

Symbol	Symbolic Meaning(s)
1. the pit	_____ _____ _____
2. the pendulum	_____ _____ _____
3. the old man with the scythe	_____ _____ _____
4. the rats	_____ _____ _____
5. the trumpet blasts at the end of the story	_____ _____ _____

Vocabulary: How to Own a Word

Synonyms and Antonyms

Word Bank	
imperceptible	prostrate
ponders	potent
lucid	lethargy
tumultuous	proximity
insuperable	averted

Below are ten word pairs. The first word in each pair is a Word to Own. For each numbered pair write **S** in the blank if the second word in the pair is a synonym for the Word to Own, or **A** if the word is an antonym. You may need a dictionary or a thesaurus for this activity.

_____ 1. imperceptible : obvious

_____ 2. ponders : meditates

_____ 3. lucid : confused

_____ 4. tumultuous : calm

_____ 5. insuperable : insurmountable

_____ 6. prostrate : upright

_____ 7. potent : concentrated

_____ 8. lethargy : listlessness

_____ 9. proximity : distance

_____ 10. averted : prevented

Prefixes

Some of the Words to Own above contain prefixes. These small word parts have meaning and can change the root's definition. Use a dictionary to find the meanings of the prefixes as they are used in the Words to Own above. Write the meaning of the prefix in the space provided. The first one has been done for you as an example.

Prefix	Meaning
per-	through
im-	
in-	
pro-	
a- (ab-)	

Hair

Make the Connection

Keeping Up Appearances

Suppose you are entering a new school and want to make friends quickly and become popular. Is it worth changing your appearance or your identity in order to gain acceptance? Should superficial characteristics such as hair and clothes really matter? You'll explore the idea behind these questions as Malcolm X relates a personal experience in "Hair."

The following opinion scales contain other ideas related to the selection. Before you read, write the word *before* at a place on each scale to indicate how strongly you agree or disagree with each statement. Then, after you have read the selection, write the word *after* on the scale in response to the same statements. You may want to discuss your responses in small groups, both before and after reading, to see if your group can reach agreement.

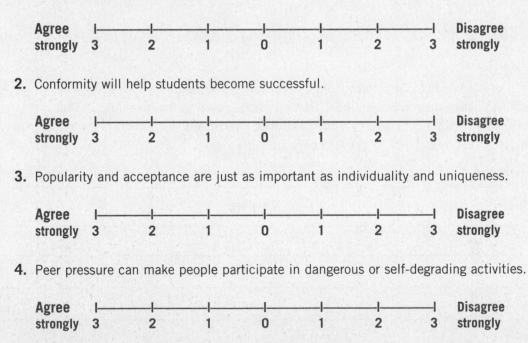

1. Popularity is based on appearances.

    Agree strongly 3 2 1 0 1 2 3 Disagree strongly

2. Conformity will help students become successful.

    Agree strongly 3 2 1 0 1 2 3 Disagree strongly

3. Popularity and acceptance are just as important as individuality and uniqueness.

    Agree strongly 3 2 1 0 1 2 3 Disagree strongly

4. Peer pressure can make people participate in dangerous or self-degrading activities.

    Agree strongly 3 2 1 0 1 2 3 Disagree strongly

HAIR

FROM **The Autobiography of Malcolm X**

Malcolm X with Alex Haley

INTERPRET

Read the first three paragraphs of the selection silently. Which tone of voice—happy, sad, angry— best fits the writing **tone** that you "hear"?

_____

_____

_____

_____

IDENTIFY

Underline one detail in lines 11–12 that shows you the attitude of Malcolm X, as a young man, toward his first conk.

INFER

This passage contains much **colloquial** or informal language, including words and phrases like *glop, real fast,* and *it burns bad.* What **tone** is created by these informal words and phrases?

_____

_____

_____

_____

_____

_____

_____

_____

_____

_____

_____

Shorty soon decided that my hair was finally long enough to be conked. He had promised to school me in how to beat the barbershops' three- and four-dollar price by making up congolene and then conking ourselves.

I took the little list of ingredients he had printed out for me and went to a grocery store, where I got a can of Red Devil lye, two eggs, and two medium-sized white potatoes. Then at a drugstore near the poolroom, I asked for a large jar of Vaseline, a large bar of soap, a large-toothed comb and a fine-toothed comb, one of those rubber hoses with a metal
10 sprayhead, a rubber apron, and a pair of gloves.

"Going to lay on that first conk?" the drugstore man asked me. I proudly told him, grinning, "Right!"

Shorty paid six dollars a week for a room in his cousin's shabby apartment. His cousin wasn't at home. "It's like the pad's mine, he spends so much time with his woman," Shorty said. "Now, you watch me—"

He peeled the potatoes and thin-sliced them into a quart-sized Mason fruit jar, then started stirring them with a wooden spoon as he gradually poured in a little over half the can of lye. "Never use a metal spoon; the
20 lye will turn it black," he told me.

A jellylike, starchy-looking glop resulted from the lye and potatoes, and Shorty broke in the two eggs, stirring real fast—his own conk and dark face bent down close. The congolene turned pale yellowish. "Feel the jar," Shorty said. I cupped my hand against the outside and snatched it away. "Damn right, it's hot, that's the lye," he said. "So you know it's going to burn when I comb it in—it burns *bad.* But the longer you can stand it, the straighter the hair."

He made me sit down, and he tied the string of the new rubber apron tightly around my neck and combed up my bush of hair. Then,
30 from the big Vaseline jar, he took a handful and massaged it hard all through my hair and into the scalp. He also thickly Vaselined my neck, ears, and forehead. "When I get to washing out your head, be sure to tell me anywhere you feel any little stinging," Shorty warned me, washing his hands, then pulling on the rubber gloves and tying on his own rubber apron. "You always got to remember that any congolene left in burns a sore into your head."

The congolene just felt warm when Shorty started combing it in. But then my head caught fire.

I gritted my teeth and tried to pull the sides of the kitchen table
40 together. The comb felt as if it was raking my skin off.

My eyes watered, my nose was running. I couldn't stand it any longer; I bolted to the washbasin. I was cursing Shorty with every name I could think of when he got the spray going and started soap-lathering my head.

He lathered and spray-rinsed, lathered and spray-rinsed, maybe ten or twelve times, each time gradually closing the hot-water faucet, until the rinse was cold, and that helped some.

"You feel any stinging spots?"

"No," I managed to say. My knees were trembling.

50 "Sit back down, then. I think we got it all out OK."

The flame came back as Shorty, with a thick towel, started drying my head, rubbing hard. *"Easy, man, easy!"* I kept shouting.

"The first time's always worst. You get used to it better before long. You took it real good, homeboy. You got a good conk."

When Shorty let me stand up and see in the mirror, my hair hung down in limp, damp strings. My scalp still flamed, but not as badly; I could bear it. He draped the towel around my shoulders, over my rubber apron, and began again Vaselining my hair.

I could feel him combing, straight back, first the big comb, then the
60 fine-toothed one.

Then he was using a razor, very delicately, on the back of my neck. Then, finally, shaping the sideburns.

My first view in the mirror blotted out the hurting. I'd seen some pretty conks, but when it's the first time, on your *own* head, the transformation, after the lifetime of kinks, is staggering.

The mirror reflected Shorty behind me. We both were grinning and sweating. And on top of my head was this thick, smooth sheen of shining red hair—real red—as straight as any white man's.

How ridiculous I was! Stupid enough to stand there simply lost in
70 admiration of my hair now looking "white," reflected in the mirror in Shorty's room. I vowed that I'd never again be without a conk, and I never was for many years.

This was my first really big step toward self-degradation: when I endured all of that pain, literally burning my flesh to have it look like a white man's hair. I had joined that multitude of Negro men and women in America who are brainwashed into believing that the black people are "inferior"—and white people "superior"—that they will even violate and mutilate their God-created bodies to try to look "pretty" by white standards.

HAIR **117**

Tone

The **tone** of a literary work is the writer's attitude toward the audience, the subject matter, or one or more characters in the work. When you read, you can't hear the tone of the speaker's or narrator's voice. Writers have to rely on word choice and specific details in order to communicate their tone. Readers must then piece together these clues to infer, or make an intelligent guess about, the writer's attitudes.

1. How does the tone of "Hair" change sharply in the last two paragraphs?

_____

_____

_____

_____

_____

2. What specific words or phrases help to establish this new tone?

_____

_____

_____

_____

_____

Vocabulary: How to Own a Word

Word Maps

Below is a word map, partially filled out. At the center of the map is a Word to Own. To the north is a space for the definition of the word as it is used in the selection; to the west is a space for a synonym; to the east is a space for an antonym; and to the south is a space for images or feelings you might associate with the word. Create a word map for each Word to Own.

Word Bank
self-degradation
multitude
violate
mutilate

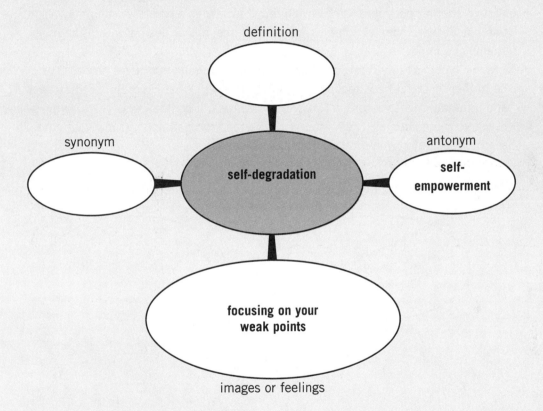

definition

synonym

antonym

self-degradation

self-empowerment

focusing on your
weak points

images or feelings

Typhoid Fever

Make the Connection

Signs of Conflict

The mainspring of most stories and plays is a **conflict,** or struggle between clashing forces. You have learned that a conflict may be **external,** pitting the major character against another person, a force of nature, or society as a whole. A story may also contain one or more **internal** conflicts, or clashing feelings or desires within the main character's mind.

In "Typhoid Fever," two children, a boy named Frank and a girl named Patricia, lie in their hospital beds recuperating from illnesses. What conflicts, both external and internal, might you predict that the narrative will contain? Use the diagram below to list your predictions. Then, after you have read the narrative, review your notes to see how accurately you predicted the story's conflicts.

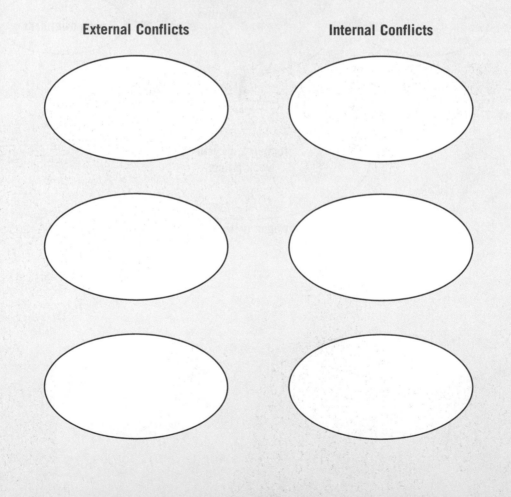

External Conflicts   **Internal Conflicts**

Frank McCourt

TYPHOID FEVER

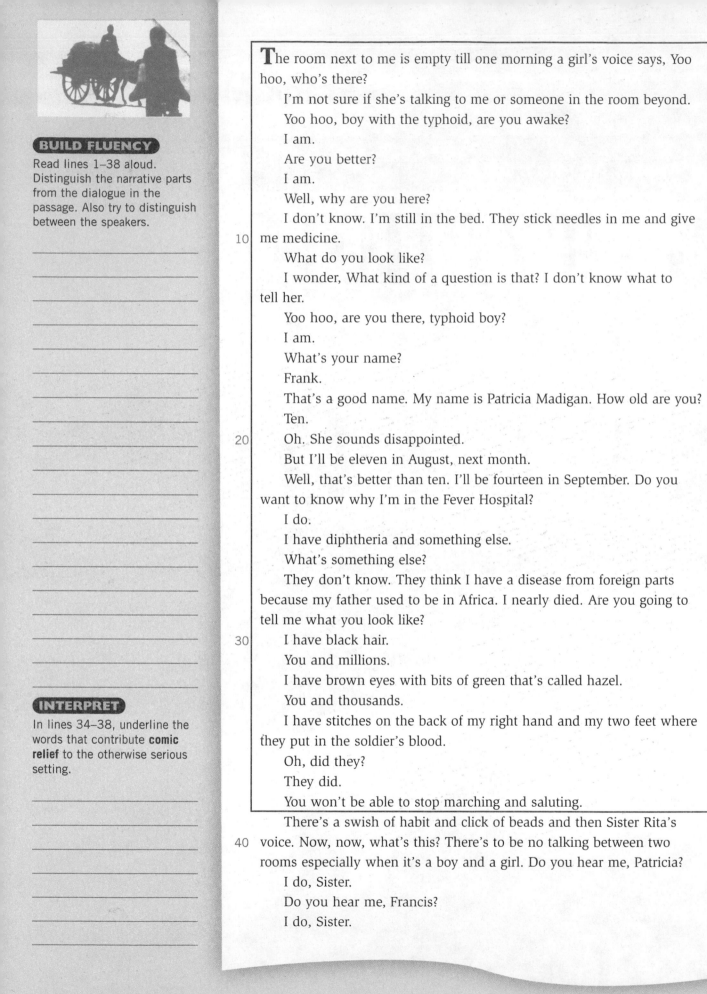

BUILD FLUENCY

Read lines 1–38 aloud. Distinguish the narrative parts from the dialogue in the passage. Also try to distinguish between the speakers.

_____

_____

_____

_____

_____

_____

_____

_____

_____

_____

_____

_____

_____

_____

_____

INTERPRET

In lines 34–38, underline the words that contribute **comic relief** to the otherwise serious setting.

_____

_____

_____

_____

_____

_____

_____

The room next to me is empty till one morning a girl's voice says, Yoo hoo, who's there?

I'm not sure if she's talking to me or someone in the room beyond.

Yoo hoo, boy with the typhoid, are you awake?

I am.

Are you better?

I am.

Well, why are you here?

I don't know. I'm still in the bed. They stick needles in me and give
10 me medicine.

What do you look like?

I wonder, What kind of a question is that? I don't know what to
tell her.

Yoo hoo, are you there, typhoid boy?

I am.

What's your name?

Frank.

That's a good name. My name is Patricia Madigan. How old are you?
Ten.
20 Oh. She sounds disappointed.

But I'll be eleven in August, next month.

Well, that's better than ten. I'll be fourteen in September. Do you
want to know why I'm in the Fever Hospital?

I do.

I have diphtheria and something else.

What's something else?

They don't know. They think I have a disease from foreign parts
because my father used to be in Africa. I nearly died. Are you going to
tell me what you look like?
30 I have black hair.

You and millions.

I have brown eyes with bits of green that's called hazel.

You and thousands.

I have stitches on the back of my right hand and my two feet where
they put in the soldier's blood.

Oh, did they?

They did.

You won't be able to stop marching and saluting.

There's a swish of habit and click of beads and then Sister Rita's
40 voice. Now, now, what's this? There's to be no talking between two
rooms especially when it's a boy and a girl. Do you hear me, Patricia?

I do, Sister.

Do you hear me, Francis?

I do, Sister.

You could be giving thanks for your two remarkable recoveries. You could be saying the rosary.[1] You could be reading *The Little Messenger of the Sacred Heart*[2] that's beside your beds. Don't let me come back and find you talking.

50 She comes into my room and wags her finger at me. Especially you, Francis, after thousands of boys prayed for you at the Confraternity.[3] Give thanks, Francis, give thanks.

She leaves and there's silence for awhile. Then Patricia whispers, Give thanks, Francis, give thanks, and say your rosary, Francis, and I laugh so hard a nurse runs in to see if I'm all right. She's a very stern nurse from the County Kerry and she frightens me. What's this, Francis? Laughing? What is there to laugh about? Are you and that Madigan girl talking? I'll report you to Sister Rita. There's to be no laughing for you could be doing serious damage to your internal apparatus.

She plods out and Patricia whispers again in a heavy Kerry accent,
60 No laughing, Francis, you could be doin' serious damage to your internal apparatus. Say your rosary, Francis, and pray for your internal apparatus.

Mam visits me on Thursdays. I'd like to see my father, too, but I'm out of danger, crisis time is over, and I'm allowed only one visitor. Besides, she says, he's back at work at Rank's Flour Mills and please God this job will last a while with the war on and the English desperate for flour. She brings me a chocolate bar and that proves Dad is working. She could never afford it on the dole.[4] He sends me notes. He tells me my brothers are all praying for me, that I should be a good boy, obey the doctors, the nuns, the nurses, and don't forget to say my prayers. He's
70 sure St. Jude pulled me through the crisis because he's the patron saint of desperate cases and I was indeed a desperate case.

Patricia says she has two books by her bed. One is a poetry book and that's the one she loves. The other is a short history of England and do I want it? She gives it to Seamus, the man who mops the floors every day, and he brings it to me. He says, I'm not supposed to be bringing anything from a dipteria room to a typhoid room with all the germs flying around and hiding between the pages and if you ever catch dipteria on top of the typhoid they'll know and I'll lose my good job and be out on the street singing patriotic songs with a tin cup in my hand,
80 which I could easily do because there isn't a song ever written about Ireland's sufferings I don't know and a few songs about the joy of whiskey too.

Oh, yes, he knows Roddy McCorley. He'll sing it for me right enough but he's barely into the first verse when the Kerry nurse rushes in. What's

---

1. **rosary:** group of prayers that Roman Catholics recite while holding a string of beads.
2. ***The Little Messenger of the Sacred Heart:*** religious publication for children.
3. **Confraternity:** here, a religious organization made up of nonclergy, or lay people.
4. **dole:** government payment to the unemployed; also, money or food given to those in need.

INTERPRET

From Sister Rita's first speech, what conclusion can you draw about her **character**?

_____
_____
_____
_____
_____

IDENTIFY

Identify an example of **comic relief** in lines 57–61 by underlining words and phrases that seem amusing to you.

_____
_____
_____
_____
_____
_____
_____
_____
_____
_____
_____
_____
_____
_____
_____
_____
_____
_____

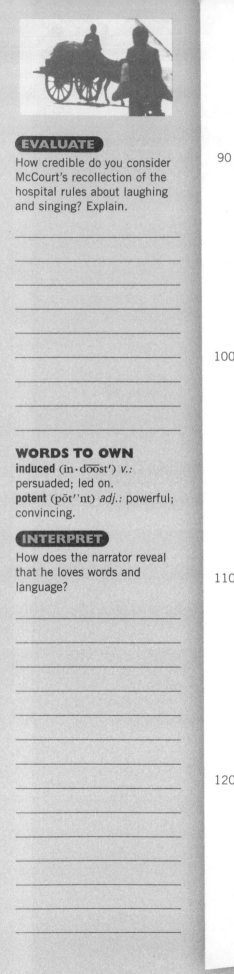

EVALUATE

How credible do you consider McCourt's recollection of the hospital rules about laughing and singing? Explain.

_____

_____

_____

_____

_____

_____

_____

_____

WORDS TO OWN
induced (in·do͞ost′) v.: persuaded; led on.
potent (pōt′′nt) adj.: powerful; convincing.

INTERPRET

How does the narrator reveal that he loves words and language?

_____

_____

_____

_____

_____

_____

_____

_____

_____

_____

_____

this, Seamus? Singing? Of all the people in this hospital you should know the rules against singing. I have a good mind to report you to Sister Rita.

Ah, don't do that, nurse.

Very well, Seamus. I'll let it go this one time. You know the singing could lead to a relapse in these patients.

90 When she leaves he whispers he'll teach me a few songs because singing is good for passing the time when you're by yourself in a typhoid room. He says Patricia is a lovely girl the way she often gives him sweets from the parcel her mother sends every fortnight. He stops mopping the floor and calls to Patricia in the next room, I was telling Frankie you're a lovely girl, Patricia, and she says, You're a lovely man, Seamus. He smiles because he's an old man of forty and he never had children but the ones he can talk to here in the Fever Hospital. He says, Here's the book, Frankie. Isn't it a great pity you have to be reading all about England after all they did to us, that there isn't a history of Ireland to
100 be had in this hospital.

The book tells me all about King Alfred and William the Conqueror and all the kings and queens down to Edward, who had to wait forever for his mother, Victoria, to die before he could be king. The book has the first bit of Shakespeare I ever read.

I do believe, induced by potent circumstances,
That thou art mine enemy.

The history writer says this is what Catherine, who is a wife of Henry the Eighth, says to Cardinal Wolsey, who is trying to have her head cut off. I don't know what it means and I don't care because it's Shakespeare
110 and it's like having jewels in my mouth when I say the words. If I had a whole book of Shakespeare they could keep me in the hospital for a year.

Patricia says she doesn't know what induced means or potent circumstances and she doesn't care about Shakespeare, she has her poetry book and she reads to me from beyond the wall a poem about an owl and a pussycat that went to sea in a green boat with honey and money and it makes no sense and when I say that Patricia gets huffy and says that's the last poem she'll ever read to me. She says I'm always reciting the lines from Shakespeare and they make no sense either. Seamus stops mopping again and tells us we shouldn't be fighting over
120 poetry because we'll have enough to fight about when we grow up and get married. Patricia says she's sorry and I'm sorry too so she reads me part of another poem[5] which I have to remember so I can say it back to

_____

5. **part . . . poem:** reference is to the poem "The Highwayman" by British poet Alfred Noyes (1880–1958). The poem is based on a true story about a highwayman who falls in love with an innkeeper's daughter in 18th-century England. Highwaymen, who robbed rich stagecoaches, were at that time popular, romantic figures.

her early in the morning or late at night when there are no nuns or nurses about,

> The wind was a <u>torrent</u> of darkness among the gusty trees,
> The moon was a ghostly galleon tossed upon cloudy seas,
> The road was a ribbon of moonlight over the purple moor,
> And the highwayman came riding—Riding—riding—
> The highwayman came riding, up to the old inn door.

130
> He'd a French cocked-hat on his forehead, a bunch of lace at his chin,
> A coat of the claret velvet, and breeches of brown doeskin,
> They fitted with never a wrinkle. His boots were up to the thigh.
> And he rode with a jeweled twinkle, His pistol butts a-twinkle,
> His rapier hilt a-twinkle, under the jeweled sky.

Every day I can't wait for the doctors and nurses to leave me alone so I can learn a new verse from Patricia and find out what's happening to the highwayman and the landlord's red-lipped daughter. I love the poem because it's exciting and almost as good as my two lines of Shakespeare. The redcoats are after the highwayman because they know he told her, I'll

140 come to thee by moonlight, though hell should bar the way.

I'd love to do that myself, come by moonlight for Patricia in the next room not giving a hoot though hell should bar the way. She's ready to read the last few verses when in comes the nurse from Kerry shouting at her, shouting at me, I told ye there was to be no talking between rooms. Dipthteria is never allowed to talk to typhoid and visa versa. I warned ye. And she calls out, Seamus, take this one. Take the by. Sister Rita said one more word out of him and upstairs with him. We gave ye a warning to stop the blathering but ye wouldn't. Take the by, Seamus, take him.

Ah, now, nurse, sure isn't he harmless. 'Tis only a bit o' poetry.

150 Take that by, Seamus, take him at once.

He bends over me and whispers, Ah, I'm sorry, Frankie. Here's your English history book. He slips the book under my shirt and lifts me from the bed. He whispers that I'm a feather. I try to see Patricia when we pass through her room but all I can make out is a blur of dark head on a pillow.

Sister Rita stops us in the hall to tell me I'm a great disappointment to her, that she expected me to be a good boy after what God had done for me, after all the prayers said by hundreds of boys at the Confraternity, after all the care from the nuns and nurses of the Fever

160 Hospital, after the way they let my mother and father in to see me, a thing rarely allowed, and this is how I repaid them lying in the bed reciting silly poetry back and forth with Patricia Madigan knowing very well there was a ban on all talk between typhoid and diphtheria. She says I'll have plenty of time to reflect on my sins in the big ward upstairs and I should beg God's forgiveness for my disobedience reciting a pagan

English poem about a thief on a horse and a maiden with red lips who commits a terrible sin when I could have been praying or reading the life of a saint. She made it her business to read that poem so she did and I'd be well advised to tell the priest in confession.

170　　The Kerry nurse follows us upstairs gasping and holding on to the banister. She tells me I better not get the notion she'll be running up to this part of the world every time I have a little pain or a twinge.

There are twenty beds in the ward, all white, all empty. The nurse tells Seamus put me at the far end of the ward against the wall to make sure I don't talk to anyone who might be passing the door, which is very unlikely since there isn't another soul on this whole floor. She tells Seamus this was the fever ward during the Great Famine[6] long ago and only God knows how many died here brought in too late for anything but a wash before they were buried and there are stories of cries and

180　moans in the far reaches of the night. She says 'twould break your heart to think of what the English did to us, that if they didn't put the blight on the potato they didn't do much to take it off. No pity. No feeling at all for the people that died in this very ward, children suffering and dying here while the English feasted on roast beef and guzzled the best of wine in their big houses, little children with their mouths all green from trying to eat the grass in the fields beyond, God bless us and save us and guard us from future famines.

Seamus says 'twas a terrible thing indeed and he wouldn't want to be walking these halls in the dark with all the little green mouths gaping

190　at him. The nurse takes my temperature, 'Tis up a bit, have a good sleep for yourself now that you're away from the chatter with Patricia Madigan below who will never know a gray hair.

She shakes her head at Seamus and he gives her a sad shake back.

Nurses and nuns never think you know what they're talking about. If you're ten going on eleven you're supposed to be simple like my uncle Pat Sheehan who was dropped on his head. You can't ask questions. You can't show you understand what the nurse said about Patricia Madigan, that she's going to die, and you can't show you want to cry over this girl who taught you a lovely poem which the nun says is bad.

200　　The nurse tells Seamus she has to go and he's to sweep the lint from under my bed and mop up a bit around the ward. Seamus tells me she's a right oul' witch for running to Sister Rita and complaining about the poem going between the two rooms, that you can't catch a disease from a poem unless it's love ha ha and that's not bloody likely when you're what? ten going on eleven? He never heard the likes of it, a little fella shifted upstairs for saying a poem and he has a good mind to go to the

---

6. **Great Famine:** refers to the great famine in Ireland in 1845–1847, when failed potato crops resulted in the starvation and death of about one million people.

INTERPRET

Which remarks in lines 173–187 ease for a moment the emotional tension of the scene? Underline two passages that provide some **comic relief.**

PREDICT

What do you think may happen to Patricia? Underline the words in the text that support your prediction.

IDENTIFY

Underline three words and phrases that give an idea of Seamus's **voice,** or characteristic way of speaking.

Limerick Leader and tell them print the whole thing except he has this job and he'd lose it if ever Sister Rita found out. Anyway, Frankie, you'll be outa here one of these fine days and you can read all the poetry you
210 want though I don't know about Patricia below, I don't know about Patricia, God help us.

He knows about Patricia in two days because she got out of the bed to go to the lavatory when she was supposed to use a bedpan and collapsed and died in the lavatory. Seamus is mopping the floor and there are tears on his cheeks and he's saying, 'Tis a dirty rotten thing to die in a lavatory when you're lovely in yourself. She told me she was sorry she had you reciting that poem and getting you shifted from the room, Frankie. She said 'twas all her fault.

It wasn't, Seamus.
220 I know and didn't I tell her that.

Patricia is gone and I'll never know what happened to the highwayman and Bess, the landlord's daughter. I ask Seamus but he doesn't know any poetry at all especially English poetry. He knew an Irish poem once but it was about fairies and had no sign of a highwayman in it. Still he'll ask the men in his local pub where there's always someone reciting something and he'll bring it back to me. Won't I be busy meanwhile reading my short history of England and finding out all about their perfidy.[7] That's what Seamus says, perfidy, and I don't know what it means and he doesn't know what it means but if it's
230 something the English do it must be terrible.

He comes three times a week to mop the floor and the nurse is there every morning to take my temperature and pulse. The doctor listens to my chest with the thing hanging from his neck. They all say, And how's our little soldier today? A girl with a blue dress brings meals three times a day and never talks to me. Seamus says she's not right in the head so don't say a word to her.

The July days are long and I fear the dark. There are only two ceiling lights in the ward and they're switched off when the tea tray is taken away and the nurse gives me pills. The nurse tells me go to sleep but I
240 can't because I see people in the nineteen beds in the ward all dying and green around their mouths where they tried to eat grass and moaning for soup Protestant soup any soup and I cover my face with the pillow hoping they won't come and stand around the bed clawing at me and howling for bits of the chocolate bar my mother brought last week.

No, she didn't bring it. She had to send it in because I can't have any more visitors. Sister Rita tells me a visit to the Fever Hospital is a privilege and after my bad behavior with Patricia Madigan and that poem I can't have the privilege anymore. She says I'll be going home in a few

---

7. **perfidy** (pur'fǝ·dē): treachery; betrayal.

INFER

Does young Frank really see "people in the nineteen beds"? How does his punishment affect him?

INTERPRET

Children can respond to adversity by becoming resentful, mistrustful, withdrawn, compassionate, courageous, or resilient. Which, if any, of these personality traits do you see in young Frank?

_____

_____

_____

_____

_____

_____

WORDS TO OWN

clamoring (klam'ər·iŋ) v.: crying out, asking.

_____

_____

_____

_____

_____

_____

_____

EVALUATE

Are you satisfied with this ending to the memoir? Why or why not?

_____

_____

_____

_____

_____

_____

weeks and my job is to concentrate on getting better and learn to walk
250 again after being in bed for six weeks and I can get out of bed tomorrow
after breakfast. I don't know why she says I have to learn how to walk
when I've been walking since I was a baby but when the nurse stands
me by the side of the bed I fall to the floor and the nurse laughs, See,
you're a baby again.

I practice walking from bed to bed back and forth back and forth. I
don't want to be a baby. I don't want to be in this empty ward with no
Patricia and no highwayman and no red-lipped landlord's daughter. I
don't want the ghosts of children with green mouths pointing bony
fingers at me and clamoring for bits of my chocolate bar.
260 Seamus says a man in his pub knew all the verses of the
highwayman poem and it has a very sad end. Would I like him to say it
because he never learned how to read and he had to carry the poem in
his head? He stands in the middle of the ward leaning on his mop and
recites,

> Tlot-tlot, _in the frosty silence! Tlot-tlot in the echoing night!_
> _Nearer he came and nearer! Her face was like a light!_
> _Her eyes grew wide for a moment; she drew one last deep breath,_
> _Then her fingers moved in the moonlight,_
> > _Her musket shattered the moonlight,_
> 270 _Shattered her breast in the moonlight and warned him—with her_
> > _death._

He hears the shot and escapes but when he learns at dawn how Bess
died he goes into a rage and returns for revenge only to be shot down by
the redcoats.

> _Blood-red were his spurs in the golden noon; wine-red was his_
> > _velvet coat,_
> _When they shot him down on the highway,_
> > _Down like a dog on the highway,_
> _And he lay in his blood on the highway, with a bunch of lace at_
> 280 > _his throat._

Seamus wipes his sleeve across his face and sniffles. He says, There
was no call at all to shift you up here away from Patricia when you
didn't even know what happened to the highwayman and Bess. 'Tis a
very sad story and when I said it to my wife she wouldn't stop crying
the whole night till we went to bed. She said there was no call for them
redcoats to shoot that highwayman, they are responsible for half the
troubles of the world and they never had any pity on the Irish, either.
Now if you want to know any more poems, Frankie, tell me and I'll get
them from the pub and bring 'em back in my head.

Comic Relief

Comic relief consists of a humorous incident or speech in a literary work that is otherwise serious in tone. Comic relief functions to ease emotional tension, add variety to a work, and keep serious or tragic elements from becoming overwhelming. Mixing comedy with sadness also helps to make a work credible, because in the cycle of real life laughter and joy often alternate with sadness or disappointment.

On the lines provided below, identify at least two examples of comic relief in "Typhoid Fever." Then, comment briefly on how you feel about the use of comedy in such a sad story.

Example 1:

_____

_____

_____

_____

Example 2:

_____

_____

_____

_____

Comment:

_____

_____

_____

_____

_____

_____

_____

_____

_____

Vocabulary: How to Own a Word

Related Meanings

Word Bank
induced
potent
torrent
clamoring

In each of the following word groups, the Word to Own is in boldface type. Cross out the word whose meaning or part of speech is different from the meanings or parts of speech of the other words in the group. Then, write a sentence or two explaining your choice.

EXAMPLE: persuasive **potent** ~~feeble~~ effective

Although all the words are adjectives, feeble means "weak," and the other words mean "strong," "powerful," and "compelling."

1. influenced discouraged convinced **induced**

2. hostility **torrent** stream flood

3. **clamoring** juggle portray fragile

Selection: _____

Evaluating Nonfiction

Record the title of the selection you are evaluating. Then, write the answers to the following questions.

Subject

1. What is the subject of the selection?

Purpose

2. What do you think is the author's purpose? Does he or she intend to inform, persuade or entertain? Is there more than one purpose?

Main Idea

3. What is the major message that the writer communicates about the subject?

Effect

4. How well does the author achieve his or her purpose? Is he or she able to make you care about the subject?

   Check the comment that best expresses your opinion.

   _____   _____   _____   _____
   Not very well   Fairly well   Very well   Extremely well

R.M.S. Titanic

Make the Connection

Facing Disaster

As you read Hanson Baldwin's account of the sinking of the *Titanic*, you feel as if you are there because the writer takes the facts and gives them life. By turning what could be a dry account of the facts of the disaster into a drama—and without sensationalizing or emphasizing the horrors of the event—Baldwin brings his readers into the action.

Jot down questions you have about the sinking of the *Titanic*. Note which of these questions are answered by the article and which still need to be researched.

Questions

_____

_____

_____

_____

_____

_____

_____

_____

_____

_____

_____

_____

_____

_____

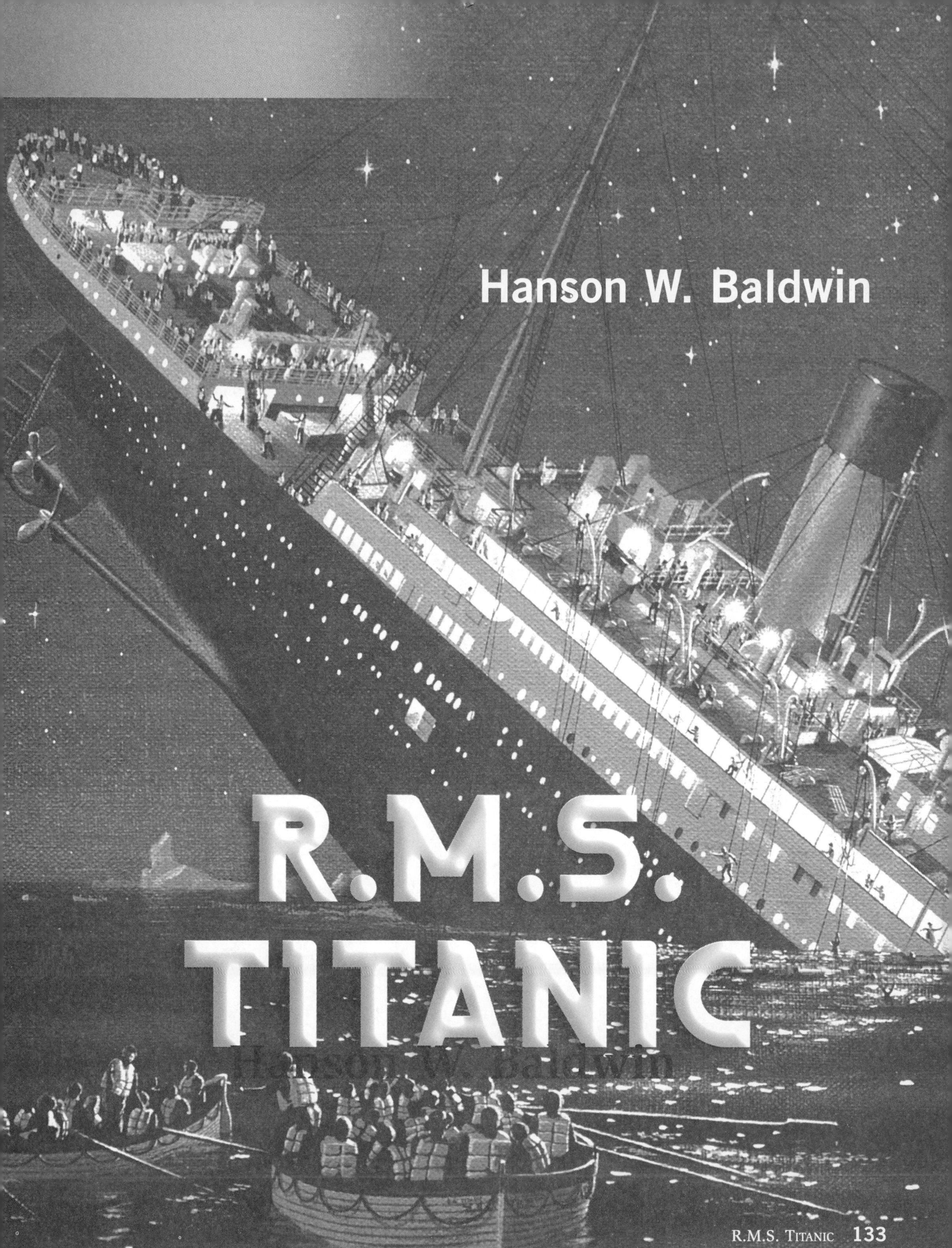

Hanson W. Baldwin

R.M.S. TITANIC

Hanson W. Baldwin

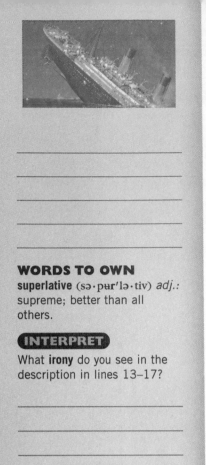

WORDS TO OWN
superlative (sə·pur′lə·tiv) *adj.:* supreme; better than all others.

INTERPRET

What **irony** do you see in the description in lines 13–17?

_____

_____

_____

_____

_____

_____

INTERPRET

How does the near collision suggest the tragedy to come?

_____

_____

_____

_____

_____

_____

_____

_____

_____

_____

I

The White Star liner *Titanic*, largest ship the world had ever known, sailed from Southampton on her maiden voyage to New York on April 10, 1912. The paint on her strakes[1] was fair and bright; she was fresh from Harland and Wolff's Belfast yards, strong in the strength of her forty-six thousand tons of steel, bent, hammered, shaped, and riveted through the three years of her slow birth.

There was little fuss and fanfare at her sailing; her sister ship, the *Olympic*—slightly smaller than the *Titanic*—had been in service for some months and to her had gone the thunder of the cheers.

10   But the *Titanic* needed no whistling steamers or shouting crowds to call attention to her <u>superlative</u> qualities. Her bulk dwarfed the ships near her as longshoremen singled up her mooring lines and cast off the turns of heavy rope from the dock bollards.[2] She was not only the largest ship afloat, but was believed to be the safest. Carlisle, her builder, had given her double bottoms and had divided her hull into sixteen watertight compartments, which made her, men thought, unsinkable. She had been built to be and had been described as a gigantic lifeboat. Her designers' dreams of a triple-screw[3] giant, a luxurious, floating hotel, which could speed to New York at twenty-three knots, had been carefully translated

20   from blueprints and mold loft lines at the Belfast yards into a living reality.

The *Titanic*'s sailing from Southampton, though quiet, was not wholly uneventful. As the liner moved slowly toward the end of her dock that April day, the surge of her passing sucked away from the quay[4] the steamer *New York*, moored just to seaward of the *Titanic*'s berth. There were sharp cracks as the manila mooring lines of the New York parted under the strain. The frayed ropes writhed and whistled through the air and snapped down among the waving crowd on the pier; the *New York* swung toward the *Titanic*'s bow, was checked and dragged back to the dock barely in time to avert a collision. Seamen muttered, thought it an

30   ominous start.

Past Spithead and the Isle of Wight the *Titanic* steamed. She called at Cherbourg at dusk and then laid her course for Queenstown. At 1:30 P.M. on Thursday, April 11, she stood out of Queenstown harbor, screaming gulls soaring in her wake, with 2,201 persons—men, women, and children—aboard.

Occupying the Empire bedrooms and Georgian suites of the first-class accommodations were many well-known men and women—Colonel John Jacob Astor and his young bride; Major Archibald Butt, military aide to President Taft, and his friend Frank D. Millet, the painter;

---

1. **strakes:** single lines of metal plating extending the whole length of a ship.
2. **bollards** (bäl′ərdz): strong posts on a pier or wharf for holding a ship's mooring ropes.
3. **triple-screw:** three-propellered.
4. **quay** (kē): dock.

40 John B. Thayer, vice president of the Pennsylvania Railroad, and Charles M. Hays, president of the Grand Trunk Railway of Canada; W. T. Stead, the English journalist; Jacques Futrelle, French novelist; H. B. Harris, theatrical manager, and Mrs. Harris; Mr. and Mrs. Isidor Straus; and J. Bruce Ismay, chairman and managing director of the White Star Line.

Down in the plain wooden cabins of the steerage class were 706 immigrants to the land of promise, and trimly stowed in the great holds was a cargo valued at $420,000: oak beams, sponges, wine, calabashes,[5] and an odd miscellany of the common and the rare.

The *Titanic* took her departure on Fastnet Light[6] and, heading into 50 the night, laid her course for New York. She was due at quarantine[7] the following Wednesday morning.

Sunday dawned fair and clear. The *Titanic* steamed smoothly toward the west, faint streamers of brownish smoke trailing from her funnels. The purser held services in the saloon in the morning; on the steerage deck aft[8] the immigrants were playing games and a Scotsman was puffing "The Campbells Are Coming" on his bagpipes in the midst of the uproar.

At 9:00 A.M. a message from the steamer *Caronia* sputtered into the wireless shack:

Captain, *Titanic*—Westbound steamers report bergs growlers and 60 field ice 42 degrees N. from 49 degrees to 51 degrees W. 12th April.

Compliments—Barr.

It was cold in the afternoon; the sun was brilliant, but the *Titanic*, her screws turning over at seventy-five revolutions per minute, was approaching the Banks.[9]

In the Marconi cabin[10] Second Operator Harold Bride, earphones clamped on his head, was figuring accounts; he did not stop to answer when he heard *MWL*, Continental Morse for the nearby Leyland liner, *Californian*, calling the *Titanic*. The *Californian* had some message about three icebergs; he didn't bother then to take it down. About 1:42 P.M. the 70 rasping spark of those days spoke again across the water. It was the *Baltic*, calling the *Titanic*, warning her of ice on the steamer track. Bride took the message down and sent it up to the bridge.[11] The officer-of-the-deck glanced at it; sent it to the bearded master of the *Titanic*, Captain E. C. Smith, a veteran of the White Star service. It was lunchtime then;

---

5. **calabashes** (kal′ə·bash′əz): large smoking pipes made from the necks of gourds.
6. **Fastnet Light:** lighthouse at the southwestern tip of Ireland. After the Fastnet Light, there is only open sea until the coast of North America.
7. **quarantine** (kwôr′ən·tēn): place where a ship is held in port after arrival to determine that its passengers and cargo are free of communicable diseases. *Quarantine* can also be used for the length of time a ship is held.
8. **aft:** in the rear of a ship.
9. **Banks:** Grand Banks, shallow waters near the southeast coast of Newfoundland.
10. **Marconi cabin:** room where messages were received and sent by radio.
11. **bridge:** raised structure on a ship. The ship is controlled from the bridge.

IDENTIFY
What range of accommodations was available to passengers?

IDENTIFY
How many warnings of icebergs were ignored? Underline each instance.

the captain, walking along the promenade deck, saw Mr. Ismay, stopped, and handed him the message without comment. Ismay read it, stuffed it in his pocket, told two ladies about the icebergs, and resumed his walk. Later, about 7:15 P.M., the captain requested the return of the message in order to post it in the chart room for the information of officers.

80   Dinner that night in the Jacobean dining room was gay. It was bitter on deck, but the night was calm and fine; the sky was moonless but studded with stars twinkling coldly in the clear air.

After dinner some of the second-class passengers gathered in the saloon, where the Reverend Mr. Carter conducted a "hymn singsong." It was almost ten o'clock and the stewards were waiting with biscuits and coffee as the group sang:

> O, hear us when we cry to Thee
> For those in peril on the sea.

INTERPRET

How does the group's choice of song create **dramatic irony**?

On the bridge Second Officer Lightoller—short, stocky, efficient—
90 was relieved at ten o'clock by First Officer Murdoch. Lightoller had talked with other officers about the proximity of ice; at least five wireless ice warnings had reached the ship; lookouts had been cautioned to be alert; captains and officers expected to reach the field at any time after 9:30 P.M. At twenty-two knots, its speed unslackened, the *Titanic* plowed on through the night.

Lightoller left the darkened bridge to his relief and turned in. Captain Smith went to his cabin. The steerage was long since quiet; in the first and second cabins lights were going out; voices were growing still; people were asleep. Murdoch paced back and forth on the bridge,
100 peering out over the dark water, glancing now and then at the compass in front of Quartermaster Hichens at the wheel.

In the crow's-nest, lookout Frederick Fleet and his partner, Leigh, gazed down at the water, still and unruffled in the dim, starlit darkness. Behind and below them the ship, a white shadow with here and there a last winking light; ahead of them a dark and silent and cold ocean.

There was a sudden clang. "Dong-dong. Dong-dong. Dong-dong. Dong!" The metal clapper of the great ship's bell struck out 11:30. Mindful of the warnings, Fleet strained his eyes, searching the darkness for the dreaded ice. But there were only the stars and the sea.
110   In the wireless room, where Phillips, first operator, had relieved Bride, the buzz of the *Californian*'s set again crackled into the earphones:

Californian: "Say, old man, we are stuck here, surrounded by ice."

Titanic: "Shut up, shut up; keep out. I am talking to Cape Race; you are jamming my signals."

Then, a few minutes later—about 11:40 . . .

II

Out of the dark she came, a vast, dim, white, monstrous shape, directly in the *Titanic*'s path. For a moment Fleet doubted his eyes. But she was a deadly reality, this ghastly *thing*. Frantically, Fleet struck three bells—*something dead ahead*. He snatched the telephone and called the
120 bridge:

"Iceberg! Right ahead!"

The first officer heard but did not stop to acknowledge the message. "Hard-a-starboard!"

Hichens strained at the wheel; the bow swung slowly to port. The monster was almost upon them now.

Murdoch leaped to the engine-room telegraph. Bells clanged. Far below in the engine room those bells struck the first warning. Danger! The indicators on the dial faces swung round to "Stop!" Then "Full speed astern!" Frantically the engineers turned great valve wheels;
130 answered the bridge bells . . .

There was a slight shock, a brief scraping, a small list to port. Shell ice—slabs and chunks of it—fell on the foredeck. Slowly the *Titanic* stopped.

Captain Smith hurried out of his cabin.

"What has the ship struck?"

Murdoch answered, "An iceberg, sir. I hard-a-starboarded and reversed the engines, and I was going to hard-a-port around it, but she was too close. I could not do any more. I have closed the watertight doors."

Fourth Officer Boxhall, other officers, the carpenter, came to the
140 bridge. The captain sent Boxhall and the carpenter below to ascertain the damage.

A few lights switched on in the first and second cabins; sleepy passengers peered through porthole glass; some casually asked the stewards:

"Why have we stopped?"

"I don't know, sir, but I don't suppose it is anything much."

In the smoking room a quorum[12] of gamblers and their prey were still sitting round a poker table; the usual crowd of kibitzers[13] looked on. They had felt the slight jar of the collision and had seen an eighty-foot
150 ice mountain glide by the smoking-room windows, but the night was calm and clear, the *Titanic* was "unsinkable"; they hadn't bothered to go on deck.

---

12. **quorum** (kwôr′əm): the number of people required for a particular activity—in this case, for a game.
13. **kibitzers** (kib′its·ərz): talkative onlookers who often give unwanted advice.

IDENTIFY
Baldwin includes sensory **images** that provide vividness and immediacy. Underline two eerie images in lines 116–118.

_____

_____

_____

_____

_____

INTERPRET
Underline the sentence that tells you of the fatal collision. What **irony** do you find in the description?

_____

_____

_____

_____

WORDS TO OWN
ascertain (as′ər·tān′) *v.*: find out with certainty; determine.

INTERPRET
Crew members and passengers respond with complacency. Why are they not worried?

_____

_____

_____

_____

_____

_____

_____

_____

IDENTIFY

Who are the first crew members to recognize the damage to the *Titanic*?

_____

_____

_____

_____

_____

IDENTIFY

Underline the **metaphor** the writer uses in lines 166–167. What is being compared to what?

_____

_____

_____

_____

_____

_____

_____

WORDS TO OWN

corroborated (kə·răb′ə·rāt′id) *v.*: supported; upheld the truth of.

_____

_____

_____

_____

_____

_____

_____

But far below, in the warren of passages on the starboard side forward, in the forward holds and boiler rooms, men could see that the *Titanic*'s hurt was mortal. In No. 6 boiler room, where the red glow from the furnaces lighted up the naked, sweaty chests of coal-blackened firemen, water was pouring through a great gash about two feet above the floor plates. This was no slow leak; the ship was open to the sea; in ten minutes there were eight feet of water in No. 6. Long before then

160 the stokers had raked the flaming fires out of the furnaces and had scrambled through the watertight doors in No. 5 or had climbed up the long steel ladders to safety. When Boxhall looked at the mailroom in No. 3 hold, twenty-four feet above the keel, the mailbags were already floating about in the slushing water. In No. 5 boiler room a stream of water spurted into an empty bunker. All six compartments forward of No. 4 were open to the sea; in ten seconds the iceberg's jagged claw had ripped a three-hundred-foot slash in the bottom of the great *Titanic*.

Reports came to the bridge; Ismay in dressing gown ran out on deck in the cold, still, starlit night, climbed up the bridge ladder.

170 "What has happened?"

Captain Smith: "We have struck ice."

"Do you think she is seriously damaged?"

Captain Smith: "I'm afraid she is."

Ismay went below and passed Chief Engineer William Bell, fresh from an inspection of the damaged compartments. Bell corroborated the captain's statement; hurried back down the glistening steel ladders to his duty. Man after man followed him—Thomas Andrews, one of the ship's designers, Archie Frost, the builder's chief engineer, and his twenty assistants—men who had no posts of duty in the engine room but whose

180 traditions called them there.

On deck, in corridor and stateroom, life flowed again. Men, women, and children awoke and questioned; orders were given to uncover the lifeboats; water rose into the firemen's quarters; half-dressed stokers streamed up on deck. But the passengers—most of them—did not know that the *Titanic* was sinking. The shock of the collision had been so slight that some were not awakened by it; the *Titanic* was so huge that she must be unsinkable; the night was too calm, too beautiful, to think of death at sea.

Captain Smith half ran to the door of the radio shack. Bride, partly

190 dressed, eyes dulled with sleep, was standing behind Phillips, waiting.

"Send the call for assistance."

The blue spark danced: "CQD—CQD—CQD—CQ——"[14]

Miles away Marconi men heard. Cape Race heard it, and the steamships *La Provence* and *Mt. Temple*.

_____

14. **CQD:** call by radio operators, inviting others to communicate with them.

The sea was surging into the *Titanic*'s hold. At 12:20 the water burst into the seamen's quarters through a collapsed fore-and-aft wooden bulkhead. Pumps strained in the engine rooms—men and machinery making a futile fight against the sea. Steadily the water rose.

200 The boats were swung out—slowly, for the deckhands were late in reaching their stations; there had been no boat drill, and many of the crew did not know to what boats they were assigned. Orders were shouted; the safety valves had lifted, and steam was blowing off in a great rushing roar. In the chart house Fourth Officer Boxhall bent above a chart, working rapidly with pencil and dividers.

12:25 A.M. Boxhall's position is sent out to a fleet of vessels: "Come at once; we have struck a berg."

To the Cunarder *Carpathia* (Arthur Henry Rostron, Master, New York to Liverpool, fifty-eight miles away): "It's a CQD, old man. Position 41–46N.; 50–14 W."

210 The blue spark dancing: "Sinking; cannot hear for noise of steam."

12:30 A.M. The word is passed: "Women and children in the boats." Stewards finish waking their passengers below; life preservers are tied on; some men smile at the precaution. "The *Titanic* is unsinkable." The *Mt. Temple* starts for the *Titanic*; the *Carpathia*, with a double watch in her stokeholds, radios, "Coming hard." The CQD changes the course of many ships—but not of one; the operator of the *Californian*, nearby, has just put down his earphones and turned in.

The CQD flashes over land and sea from Cape Race to New York; newspaper city rooms leap to life and presses whir.

220 On the *Titanic*, water creeps over the bulkhead between Nos. 5 and 6 firerooms. She is going down by the head; the engineers—fighting a losing battle—are forced back foot by foot by the rising water. Down the promenade deck, Happy Jock Hume, the bandsman, runs with his instrument.

12:45 A.M. Murdoch, in charge on the starboard side, eyes tragic, but calm and cool, orders boat No. 7 lowered. The women hang back; they want no boat ride on an ice-strewn sea; the *Titanic* is unsinkable. The men encourage them, explain that this is just a precautionary measure: "We'll see you again at breakfast." There is little confusion; passengers stream slowly to the boat deck. In the steerage the immigrants chatter excitedly.

230 A sudden sharp hiss—a streaked flare against the night; Boxhall sends a rocket toward the sky. It explodes, and a parachute of white stars lights up the icy sea. "God! Rockets!" The band plays ragtime.

No. 8 is lowered, and No. 5. Ismay, still in dressing gown, calls for women and children, handles lines, stumbles in the way of an officer, is told to "get the hell out of here." Third Officer Pitman takes charge of

INTERPRET

Lifeboat drills were standard procedure. Why do you suppose none were held on the *Titanic*?

_____

_____

_____

_____

_____

INTERPRET

Time notations now open many paragraphs. How do these notations clarify the narrative for readers?

_____

_____

_____

_____

_____

_____

BUILD FLUENCY

Read these two paragraphs aloud as expressively as you can. Then, explain at least two **ironic** details in the passage.

_____

_____

_____

_____

_____

_____

_____

IDENTIFY

Underline the **repetition** that Baldwin uses here to reinforce the **mood**.

WORDS TO OWN

quelled (kweld) *v.*: quieted; subdued.

PREDICT

What would happen to the ship's radiotelegraph if the steam boilers stopped functioning?

No. 5; as he swings into the boat, Murdoch grasps his hand. "Goodbye and good luck, old man."

240   No. 6 goes over the side. There are only twenty-eight people in a lifeboat with a capacity of sixty-five.

A light stabs from the bridge; Boxhall is calling in Morse flashes, again and again, to a strange ship stopped in the ice jam five to ten miles away. Another rocket drops its shower of sparks above the ice-strewn sea and the dying ship.

1:00 A.M. Slowly the water creeps higher; the fore ports of the *Titanic* are dipping into the sea. Rope squeaks through blocks; lifeboats drop jerkily seaward. Through the shouting on the decks comes the sound of the band playing ragtime.

250   The "Millionaires' Special" leaves the ship—boat No. 1, with a capacity of forty people, carries only Sir Cosmo and Lady Duff Gordon and ten others. Aft, the frightened immigrants mill and jostle and rush for a boat. An officer's fist flies out; three shots are fired in the air, and the panic is <u>quelled</u>. . . . Four Chinese sneak unseen into a boat and hide in the bottom.

1:20 A.M. Water is coming into No. 4 boiler room. Stokers slice and shovel as water laps about their ankles—steam for the dynamos, steam for the dancing spark! As the water rises, great ash hoes rake the flaming coals from the furnaces. Safety valves pop; the stokers retreat aft, and the
260   watertight doors clang shut behind them.

The rockets fling their splendor toward the stars. The boats are more heavily loaded now, for the passengers know the *Titanic* is sinking. Women cling and sob. The great screws aft are rising clear of the sea. Half-filled boats are ordered to come alongside the cargo ports and take on more passengers, but the ports are never opened—and the boats are never filled. Others pull for the steamer's light miles away but never reach it; the lights disappear; the unknown ship steams off.

The water rises and the band plays ragtime.

1:30 A.M. Lightoller is getting the port boats off; Murdoch, the
270   starboard. As one boat is lowered into the sea, a boat officer fires his gun along the ship's side to stop a rush from the lower decks. A woman tries to take her Great Dane into a boat with her; she is refused and steps out of the boat to die with her dog. Millet's "little smile which played on his lips all through the voyage" plays no more; his lips are grim, but he waves goodbye and brings wraps for the women.

Benjamin Guggenheim, in evening clothes, smiles and says, "We've dressed up in our best and are prepared to go down like gentlemen."

1:40 A.M. Boat 14 is clear, and then 13, 16, 15, and C. The lights still shine, but the *Baltic* hears the blue spark say, "Engine room getting
280   flooded."

The *Olympia* signals, "Am lighting up all possible boilers as fast as can."

Major Butt helps women into the last boats and waves goodbye to them. Mrs. Straus puts her foot on the gunwale of a lifeboat; then she draws back and goes to her husband: "We have been together many years; where you go, I will go." Colonel John Jacob Astor puts his young wife in a lifeboat, steps back, taps cigarette on fingernail: "Goodbye, dearie; I'll join you later."

1:45 A.M. The foredeck is under water; the fo'c'sle[15] head almost 290 awash; the great stern is lifted high toward the bright stars; and still the band plays. Mr. and Mrs. Harris approach a lifeboat arm in arm.

Officer: "Ladies first, please."

Harris bows, smiles, steps back: "Of course, certainly; ladies first."

Boxhall fires the last rocket, then leaves in charge of boat No. 2.

2:00 A.M. She is dying now; her bow goes deeper, her stern higher. But there must be steam. Below in the stokeholds the sweaty firemen keep steam up for the flaring lights and the dancing spark. The glowing coals slide and tumble over the slanted grate bars; the sea pounds behind that yielding bulkhead. But the spark dances on.

300 The *Asian* hears Phillips try the new signal—SOS.

Boat No. 4 has left now; boat D leaves ten minutes later. Jacques Futrelle clasps his wife: "For God's sake, go! It's your last chance; go!" Madame Futrelle is half forced into the boat. It clears the side.

There are about 660 people in the boats and 1,500 still on the sinking *Titanic*.

On top of the officers' quarters, men work frantically to get the two collapsibles stowed there over the side. Water is over the forward part of A deck now; it surges up the companionways toward the boat deck. In the radio shack, Bride has slipped a coat and life jacket about Phillips 310 as the first operator sits hunched over his key, sending—still sending— "41–46 N.; 50–14 W. CQD—CQD—SOS—SOS——"

The captain's tired white face appears at the radio-room door. "Men, you have done your full duty. You can do no more. Now, it's every man for himself." The captain disappears—back to his sinking bridge, where Painter, his personal steward, stands quietly waiting for orders. The spark dances on. Bride turns his back and goes into the inner cabin. As he does so, a stoker, grimed with coal, mad with fear, steals into the shack and reaches for the life jacket on Phillips's back. Bride wheels about and brains him with a wrench.

320 2:10 A.M. Below decks the steam is still holding, though the pressure is falling—rapidly. In the gymnasium on the boat deck, the athletic instructor watches quietly as two gentlemen ride the bicycles and another swings casually at the punching bag. Mail clerks stagger up the

---

15. fo'c'sle (fōk´s'l): forecastle, front upper deck of a ship.

INTERPRET

Underline the words that illustrate **personification**. What **mood** does this personification of the ship evoke?

IDENTIFY

Which details in lines 321–324 show that some people still expect to be rescued? Underline the words giving the answer.

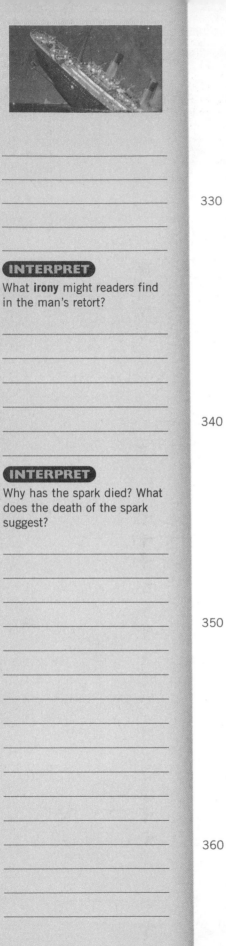

INTERPRET

What **irony** might readers find in the man's retort?

INTERPRET

Why has the spark died? What does the death of the spark suggest?

boatdeck stairways, dragging soaked mail sacks. The spark still dances. The band still plays—but not ragtime:

Nearer my God to Thee.
Nearer to Thee . . .

A few men take up the refrain; others kneel on the slanting decks to pray. Many run and scramble aft, where hundreds are clinging above the
330 silent screws on the great uptilted stern. The spark still dances and the lights still flare; the engineers are on the job. The hymn comes to its close. Bandmaster Hartley, Yorkshireman violinist, taps his bow against a bulkhead, calls for "Autumn" as the water curls about his feet, and the eight musicians brace themselves against the ship's slant. People are leaping from the decks into the nearby water—the icy water. A woman cries, "Oh, save me, save me!" A man answers, "Good lady, save yourself. Only God can save you now." The band plays "Autumn":

God of Mercy and Compassion!
Look with pity on my pain . . .

340 The water creeps over the bridge where the *Titanic*'s master stands; heavily he steps out to meet it.

2:17 A.M. "CQ——" The *Virginian* hears a ragged, blurred CQ, then an abrupt stop. The blue spark dances no more. The lights flicker out; the engineers have lost their battle.

2:18 A.M. Men run about blackened decks; leap into the night; are swept into the sea by the curling wave that licks up the *Titanic*'s length. Lightoller does not leave the ship; the ship leaves him; there are hundreds like him, but only a few who live to tell of it. The funnels still swim above the water, but the ship is climbing to the perpendicular; the
350 bridge is under and most of the foremast; the great stern rises like a squat leviathan.[16] Men swim away from the sinking ship; others drop from the stern.

The band plays in the darkness, the water lapping upward:

Hold me up in mighty waters,
Keep my eyes on things above,
Righteousness, divine atonement,
Peace and everlas . . .

The forward funnel snaps and crashes into the sea; its steel tons hammer out of existence swimmers struggling in the freezing water.
360 Streams of sparks, of smoke and steam, burst from the after funnels. The ship upends to 50—to 60 degrees.

Down in the black abyss of the stokeholds, of the engine rooms, where the dynamos have whirred at long last to a stop, the stokers and

---

16. **leviathan** (lə·vī′ə·thən): Biblical sea monster, perhaps a whale.

the engineers are reeling against the hot metal, the rising water clutching at their knees. The boilers, the engine cylinders, rip from their bed plates; crash through bulkheads; rumble—steel against steel.

The *Titanic* stands on end, <u>poised</u> briefly for the plunge. Slowly she slides to her grave—slowly at first, and then more quickly—quickly—quickly.

370   2:20 A.M. The greatest ship in the world has sunk. From the calm, dark waters, where the floating lifeboats move, there goes up, in the white wake of her passing, "one long continuous moan."

III

The boats that the *Titanic* had launched pulled safely away from the slight suction of the sinking ship, pulled away from the screams that came from the lips of the freezing men and women in the water. The boats were poorly manned and badly equipped, and they had been unevenly loaded. Some carried so few seamen that women bent to the oars. Mrs. Astor tugged at an oar handle; the Countess of Rothes took a tiller. Shivering stokers in sweaty, coal-blackened singlets and light

380   trousers steered in some boats; stewards in white coats rowed in others. Ismay was in the last boat that left the ship from the starboard side; with Mr. Carter of Philadelphia and two seamen he tugged at the oars. In one of the lifeboats an Italian with a broken wrist—disguised in a woman's shawl and hat—huddled on the floorboards, ashamed now that fear had left him. In another rode the only baggage saved from the *Titanic*—the carryall of Samuel L. Goldenberg, one of the rescued passengers.

There were only a few boats that were heavily loaded; most of those that were half empty made but <u>perfunctory</u> efforts to pick up the moaning swimmers, their officers and crew fearing they would endanger

390   the living if they pulled back into the midst of the dying. Some boats beat off the freezing victims; fear-crazed men and women struck with oars at the heads of swimmers. One woman drove her fist into the face of a half-dead man as he tried feebly to climb over the gunwale. Two other women helped him in and staunched the flow of blood from the ring cuts on his face.

One of the collapsible boats, which had floated off the top of the officers' quarters when the *Titanic* sank, was an icy haven for thirty or forty men. The boat had capsized as the ship sank; men swam to it, clung to it, climbed upon its slippery bottom, stood knee-deep in water

400   in the freezing air. Chunks of ice swirled about their legs; their soaked clothing clutched their bodies in icy folds. Colonel Archibald Gracie was cast up there, Gracie who had leaped from the stern as the *Titanic* sank; young Thayer who had seen his father die; Lightoller who had twice been sucked down with the ship and twice blown to the surface by a belch of air; Bride, the second operator, and Phillips, the first. There were

IDENTIFY

How long has it been since the *Titanic* hit the iceberg? Scan the time notations on pages 136–143 to find out.

_____

_____

_____

_____

_____

_____

_____

_____

_____

IDENTIFY

Underline the parts of this paragraph that seem objective (fact-based). Circle the parts that seem subjective (emotion-based).

_____

_____

_____

_____

_____

_____

_____

_____

many stokers, half naked; it was a shivering company. They stood there in the icy sea, under the far stars, and sang and prayed—the Lord's Prayer. After a while a lifeboat came and picked them off, but Phillips was dead then or died soon afterward in the boat.

410   Only a few of the boats had lights; only one—No. 2—had a light that was of any use to the *Carpathia*, twisting through the ice field to the rescue. Other ships were "coming hard" too; one, the *Californian*, was still dead to opportunity.

The blue sparks still danced, but not the *Titanic*'s. *La Provence* to *Celtic*: "Nobody has heard the *Titanic* for about two hours."

It was 2:40 when the *Carpathia* first sighted the green light from No. 2 boat; it was 4:10 when she picked up the first boat and learned that the *Titanic* had foundered.[17] The last of the moaning cries had just died away then.

420   Captain Rostron took the survivors aboard, boatload by boatload. He was ready for them, but only a small minority of them required much medical attention. Bride's feet were twisted and frozen; others were suffering from exposure; one died, and seven were dead when taken from the boats, and were buried at sea.

It was then that the fleet of racing ships learned they were too late; the *Parisian* heard the weak signals of *MPA*, the *Carpathia*, report the death of the *Titanic*. It was then—or soon afterward, when her radio operator put on his earphones—that the *Californian*, the ship that had been within sight as the *Titanic* was sinking, first learned of the disaster.

430   And it was then, in all its white-green majesty, that the *Titanic*'s survivors saw the iceberg, tinted with the sunrise, floating idly, pack ice jammed about its base, other bergs heaving slowly nearby on the blue breast of the sea.

IV

But it was not until later that the world knew, for wireless then was not what wireless is today, and <u>garbled</u> messages had nourished a hope that all of the *Titanic*'s company were safe. Not until Monday evening, when P.A.S. Franklin, vice president of the International Mercantile Marine Company, received relayed messages in New York that left little hope, did the full extent of the disaster begin to be known. Partial and

440   garbled lists of the survivors; rumors of heroism and cowardice; stories spun out of newspaper imagination, based on a few bare facts and many false reports, misled the world, terrified and frightened it. It was not until Thursday night, when the *Carpathia* steamed into the North River, that the full truth was pieced together.

Flashlights flared on the black river when the *Carpathia* stood up to her dock. Tugs nosed about her, shunted her toward Pier 54. Thirty

---

17. **foundered:** filled with water, so that it sank; generally, collapsed or failed.

PREDICT

Section III deals with the rescue of the survivors. What does it seem likely that Section IV will deal with?

WORDS TO OWN
garbled (gär′bəld) *v.* used as *adj.:* confused; mixed up.

thousand people jammed the streets; ambulances and stretchers stood on the pier; coroners and physicians waited.

450   In midstream the Cunarder dropped over the *Titanic*'s lifeboats; then she headed toward the dock. Beneath the customs letters on the pier stood relatives of the 711 survivors, relatives of the missing—hoping against hope. The *Carpathia* cast her lines ashore; stevedores[18] looped them over bollards. The dense throngs stood quiet as the first survivor stepped down the gangway. The woman half staggered—led by customs guards—beneath her letter. A "low wailing" moan came from the crowd; fell, grew in volume, and dropped again.

    Thus ended the maiden voyage of the *Titanic*. The lifeboats brought to New York by the *Carpathia*, a few deck chairs and gratings awash in the ice field off the Grand Bank eight hundred miles from shore, were all 460 that was left of the world's greatest ship.

V

    The aftermath of weeping and regret, of <u>recriminations</u> and investigations, dragged on for weeks. Charges and countercharges were hurled about; the White Star Line was bitterly criticized; Ismay was denounced on the floor of the Senate as a coward but was defended by those who had been with him on the sinking *Titanic* and by the Board of Trade investigation in England.

    It was not until weeks later, when the hastily convened Senate investigation in the United States and the Board of Trade report in England had been completed, that the whole story was told. The Senate 470 investigating committee, under the chairmanship of Senator Smith, who was attacked in both the American and the British press as a "backwoods politician," brought out numerous <u>pertinent</u> facts, though its proceedings verged at times on the farcical.[19] Senator Smith was ridiculed for his lack of knowledge of the sea when he asked witnesses, "Of what is an iceberg composed?" and "Did any of the passengers take refuge in the watertight compartments?" The senator seemed particularly interested in the marital status of Fleet, the lookout, who was saved. Fleet, puzzled, growled aside, "Wot questions they're arskin' me!"

    The report of Lord Mersey, wreck commissioner in the British Board 480 of Trade's investigation, was tersely damning.

    The *Titanic* had carried boats enough for 1,178 persons, only one third of her capacity. Her sixteen boats and four collapsibles had saved but 711 persons; 400 people had needlessly lost their lives. The boats had been but partly loaded; officers in charge of launching them had been afraid the falls[20] would break or the boats buckle under their rated loads; boat crews had been slow in reaching their stations; launching

---

18. stevedores (stē′və·dôrz′): persons who load and unload ships.
19. farcical (fär′si·kəl): absurd; ridiculous; like a farce (an exaggerated comedy).
20. falls: chains used for hoisting.

VISUALIZE

Underline three factual details in lines 445–448 that help you visualize the scene.

WORDS TO OWN
recriminations (ri·krim′ə·nā′shənz) *n.*: accusations leveled against an accuser; countercharges.
pertinent (purt′′n·ənt) *adj.*: having some connection with the subject.

RETELL

Briefly summarize the results of the inquiry stated in lines 481–489.

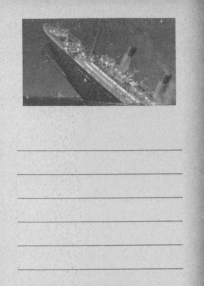

WORDS TO OWN
vainly (vān'lē) *adv.:* without
success; fruitlessly.

EVALUATE

Do you consider Lord Mersey's
condemnation of the
Californian objective (based on
fact), or subjective (based on
emotion)? Tell why.

arrangements were confused because no boat drill had been held;
passengers were loaded into the boats haphazardly because no boat
assignments had been made.

490   But that was not all. Lord Mersey found that sufficient warnings of
ice on the steamer track had reached the *Titanic*, that her speed of
twenty-two knots was "excessive under the circumstances," that "in view
of the high speed at which the vessel was running it is not considered
that the lookout was sufficient," and that her master made "a very
grievous mistake"—but should not be blamed for negligence. Captain
Rostron of the *Carpathia* was highly praised. "He did the very best that
could be done." The *Californian* was damned. The testimony of her
master, officers, and crew showed that she was not, at the most, more
than nineteen miles away from the sinking *Titanic* and probably no more
500 than five to ten miles distant. She had seen the *Titanic*'s lights; she had
seen the rockets; she had not received the CQD calls because her radio
operator was asleep. She had attempted to get in communication with
the ship she had sighted by flashing a light, but <u>vainly</u>.

"The night was clear," reported Lord Mersey, "and the sea was
smooth. When she first saw the rockets, the *Californian* could have
pushed through the ice to the open water without any serious risk and
so have come to the assistance of the *Titanic*. Had she done so she
might have saved many if not all of the lives that were lost.

"She made no attempt."

Dramatic and Situational Irony

In **dramatic irony,** the reader knows something important that the characters don't know. In **situational irony,** what happens is the opposite of what is expected to happen or what should have happened.

Use the spaces provided to classify each incident from the narrative listed below as either **D** (for dramatic irony) or **S** (for situational irony). Then, briefly explain why each incident is ironic.

_____ **1.** Ismay's pocketing the iceberg warnings

_____

_____

_____

_____ **2.** Phillips's telling the *Californian* to "shut up" when it warned of ice

_____

_____

_____

_____ **3.** the *Californian*'s operator removing his headphones only minutes before the *Titanic* radioed for help

_____

_____

_____

_____ **4.** the band playing ragtime

_____

_____

_____

_____ **5.** the lifeboats being launched half empty

_____

_____

_____

Vocabulary: How to Own a Word

Analogies

A **word analogy** shows the relationship between two pairs of words. The relationship may be stated in a sentence, or it may be expressed by using symbols (: and :: meaning "is to" and "as," respectively). There are many ways in which two words in a given pair can be related. Five ways are presented in the following chart.

Word Bank	
superlative	perfunctory
ascertain	garbled
corroborated	recriminations
quelled	pertinent
poised	vainly

Relationship	Example	Explanation	Analogy	Translation
Similarity	potato : yam	A *potato* is similar to a *yam*.	potato : yam :: middle : halfway	*Potato* is to *yam* as *middle* is to *halfway*.
Antonym	cold : hot	*Cold* is the opposite of *hot*.	cold : hot :: liquid : solid	*Cold* is to *hot* as *liquid* is to *solid*.
Synonym	gentle : calm	*Gentle* is a synonym of *calm*.	gentle : calm :: smooth : even	*Gentle* is to *calm* as *smooth* is to *even*.
Related Action	write : author	An *author* writes.	write : author :: swim : fish	*Write* is to *author* as *swim* is to *fish*.
Cause	gift : joy	A *gift* causes *joy*.	gift : joy :: joke : laughter	*Gift* is to *joy* as *joke* is to *laughter*.

On the line after each colon, write a word that correctly completes the analogy. On the line between the parentheses, write the relationship between the word pairs. You may use a dictionary or a thesaurus. The boldface words are the Words to Own.

EXAMPLE: musician : perform :: athlete : _____ run _____ (related action)

1. agile : lithe :: **perfunctory** : _____ ( )

2. **superlative** : best :: joyous : _____ ( )

3. **pertinent** : applicable :: irrelevant : _____ ( )

4. aimed : hunter :: **poised** : _____ ( )

5. effectively : successfully :: **vainly** : _____ ( )

6. raised : lowered :: **corroborated** : _____ ( )

7. **garbled** : clear :: hurried : _____ ( )

8. **recrimination** : accused :: congratulations : _____ ( )

9. **quelled** : storm :: baked : _____ ( )

10. disruption : interference :: **ascertain** : _____ ( )

The Man in the Water

Make the Connection

Who's a Hero?

In the central circle of the word web below, write the name of someone (real or ficti-
tious) whom you consider a hero. Then, in each of the four outer circles, write a word
or phrase identifying an important characteristic of your hero—a quality that makes
the person admirable in your eyes. Alongside each of the circles, jot down something
your hero has done that illustrates the characteristic written in each circle. Finally,
answer the questions that follow the diagram.

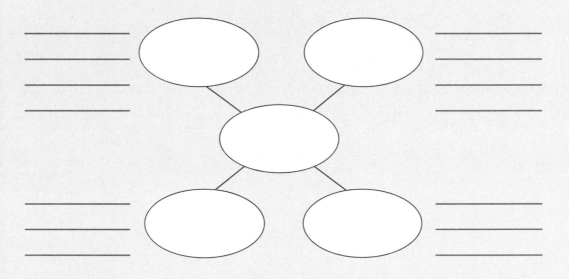

1. Which of the characteristics that you included above do you think is most important
    for a hero to have? Why?

    _____

    _____

2. Which characteristic would be most needed if the hero were involved in a life-or-death
    situation? Why?

    _____

    _____

    _____

Roger Rosenblatt

The Man in the Water

INTERPRET

A **rhetorical question** is one to which the writer or speaker does not really expect an answer. What, then, is the purpose of the question in line 15?

_____

_____

_____

_____

_____

_____

INTERPRET

How does Rosenblatt answer his own question in the second paragraph?

_____

_____

_____

_____

_____

_____

IDENTIFY

Underline the sentence that states the **main idea** of the essay.

WORDS TO OWN
flailing (flāl′iŋ) v.: waving wildly.

_____

_____

_____

_____

_____

As disasters go, this one was terrible but not unique, certainly not among the worst on the roster of U.S. air crashes. There was the unusual element of the bridge, of course, and the fact that the plane clipped it at a moment of high traffic, one routine thus intersecting another and disrupting both. Then, too, there was the location of the event. Washington, the city of form and regulations, turned chaotic, deregulated, by a blast of real winter and a single slap of metal on metal. The jets from Washington National Airport that normally swoop around the presidential monuments like famished gulls were, for the moment,

10 emblemized[1] by the one that fell; so there was that detail. And there was the aesthetic clash[2] as well—blue-and-green Air Florida, the name a flying garden, sunk down among gray chunks in a black river. All that was worth noticing, to be sure. Still, there was nothing very special in any of it, except death, which, while always special, does not necessarily bring millions to tears or to attention. Why, then, the shock here?

Perhaps because the nation saw in this disaster something more than a mechanical failure. Perhaps because people saw in it no failure at all, but rather something successful about their makeup. Here, after all, were two forms of nature in collision: the elements and human character. Last

20 Wednesday, the elements, indifferent as ever, brought down Flight 90. And on that same afternoon, human nature—groping and <u>flailing</u> in mysteries of its own—rose to the occasion.

Of the four acknowledged heroes of the event, three are able to account for their behavior. Donald Usher and Eugene Windsor, a park-police helicopter team, risked their lives every time they dipped the skids[3] into the water to pick up survivors. On television, side by side in bright blue jumpsuits, they described their courage as all in the line of duty. Lenny Skutnik, a 28-year-old employee of the Congressional Budget Office, said: "It's something I never thought I would do"—referring to

30 his jumping into the water to drag an injured woman to shore. Skutnik added that "somebody had to go in the water," delivering every hero's line that is no less admirable for its repetitions. In fact, nobody had to go into the water. That somebody actually did so is part of the reason this particular tragedy sticks in the mind.

But the person most responsible for the emotional impact of the disaster is the one known at first simply as "the man in the water." (Balding, probably in his 50s, an extravagant moustache.) He was seen clinging with five other survivors to the tail section of the airplane. This man was described by Usher and Windsor as appearing alert and in

40 control. Every time they lowered a lifeline and flotation ring to him, he

---

1. **emblemized** (em′bləm·īzd′): represented; symbolized.
2. **aesthetic** (es·thet′ik) **clash:** unpleasant visual contrast.
3. **skids:** long, narrow pieces used in place of wheels for aircraft landing gear.

passed it on to another of the passengers. "In a mass casualty, you'll find people like him," said Windsor. "But I've never seen one with that commitment." When the helicopter came back for him, the man had gone under. His selflessness was one reason the story held national attention; his anonymity another. The fact that he went unidentified invested him with a universal character. For a while he was Everyman, and thus proof (as if one needed it) that no man is ordinary.

Still, he could never have imagined such a capacity in himself. Only minutes before his character was tested, he was sitting in the ordinary
50 plane among the ordinary passengers, dutifully listening to the stewardess telling him to fasten his seat belt and saying something about the "No Smoking" sign. So our man relaxed with the others, some of whom would owe their lives to him. Perhaps he started to read, or to doze, or to regret some harsh remark made in the office that morning. Then suddenly he knew that the trip would not be ordinary. Like every other person on that flight, he was desperate to live, which makes his final act so stunning.

For at some moment in the water he must have realized that he would not live if he continued to hand over the rope and ring to others.
60 He *had* to know it, no matter how gradual the effect of the cold. In his judgment he had no choice. When the helicopter took off with what was to be the last survivor, he watched everything in the world move away from him, and he deliberately let it happen.

Yet there was something else about our man that kept our thoughts on him, and which keeps our thoughts on him still. He was *there*, in the essential, classic circumstance. Man in nature. The man in the water. For its part, nature cared nothing about the five passengers. Our man, on the other hand, cared totally. So the timeless battle commenced in the Potomac. For as long as that man could last, they went at each other,
70 nature and man; the one making no distinctions of good and evil, acting on no principles, offering no lifelines; the other acting wholly on distinctions, principles, and, one supposes, on faith.

Since it was he who lost the fight, we ought to come again to the conclusion that people are powerless in the world. In reality, we believe the reverse, and it takes the act of the man in the water to remind us of our true feelings in this matter. It is not to say that everyone would have acted as he did, or as Usher, Windsor, and Skutnik. Yet whatever moved these men to challenge death on behalf of their fellows is not peculiar to them. Everyone feels the possibility in himself. That is the abiding
80 wonder of the story. That is why we would not let go of it. If the man in the water gave a lifeline to the people gasping for survival, he was likewise giving a lifeline to those who observed him.

RETELL

Restate the meaning of lines 45–47 in your own words.

_____

_____

_____

_____

_____

_____

_____

_____

_____

_____

IDENTIFY

List the two forces Rosenblatt is contrasting in lines 64–72.

_____

_____

_____

_____

_____

_____

_____

_____

_____

_____

WORDS TO OWN
abiding (ə·bīd′iŋ) *adj.*: continuing; lasting.

_____

_____

EVALUATE

Do you agree that the man in the water really won his fight? Why or why not?

_____

_____

_____

_____

_____

_____

_____

_____

_____

WORDS TO OWN

pitted (pit′id) _v._: placed in competition.
implacable (im·plak′ə·bəl) _adj._: relentless; not affected by attempts at change.

EVALUATE

Think about the last sentence. Is it an effective closing for the essay, in your opinion? Why or why not?

_____

_____

_____

_____

_____

_____

_____

_____

_____

_____

_____

The odd thing is that we do not even really believe that the man in the water lost his fight. "Everything in Nature contains all the powers of Nature," said Emerson. Exactly. So the man in the water had his own natural powers. He could not make ice storms, or freeze the water until it froze the blood. But he could hand life over to a stranger, and that is a power of nature too. The man in the water <u>pitted</u> himself against an <u>implacable</u>, impersonal enemy; he fought it with charity; and he held
90 it to a standoff. He was the best we can do.

Main Idea

The **main idea** of a text is the central insight or message that the writer wishes to communicate. In a well-written, factual news article, events are reported with accuracy and objectivity. In an essay, however, the writer provides an opinion, a message, an insight, or a lesson that he or she has drawn from these events. Some essayists directly state their main idea, while others let us infer the idea for ourselves.

Use the diagram below to summarize Roger Rosenblatt's main idea in "The Man in the Water." In the central circle, write the main idea in your own words. In the outer spaces, indicate the details that most directly support this idea.

Vocabulary: How to Own a Word

Making Word Connections

Word Bank
flailing
abiding
pitted
implacable

1. Look up the noun *flail* in a dictionary. Describe a flail.

   _____

   _____

   _____

   Now explain how the verb *to flail* is related to the noun.

   _____

   _____

   _____

2. *Abiding* comes from a Middle English word meaning "to remain." Look up the noun *abode*, which is related to the same Middle English word. Explain how the noun *abode* and the adjective *abiding* are related.

   _____

   _____

   _____

3. One meaning of the noun *pit* is "a place where animals are put to fight." (You might think of a lion pit or a snake pit.) How are the noun *pit* and the past tense verb *pitted* related?

   _____

   _____

   _____

4. Use an unabridged dictionary to find the meanings of the three word parts that make up *implacable* and write the meaning of each part below.

   im– _____ *placare* _____ *–able* _____

Selection: _____

The Personal Essay

1. What is the central image, metaphor, or occasion around which the essay is organized?	
2. What is the tone of the essay? What is the author's attitude toward the subject?	
3. What are the different uses or meanings of the central image, metaphor, or occasion in the essay?	
4. What is the author's purpose, or aim? To inform? To speculate? To remember? To persuade?	

Summary Statement:

Mother to Son;
The Moon was but a Chin of Gold

Make the Connection

Challenging Words

In "Mother to Son" by Langston Hughes, stairs are a figure of speech used to describe life. On each step of the diagram below, a figurative word or phrase from the poem is shown. Below the step, give a specific example of something in your own life or in the life of someone you know that reflects each word or phrase. (If you prefer, use a character from a book or movie as an example.) One step has been filled in as an example.

the dark
_____

no carpet
_____

boards torn up
_____

splinters
_____

tacks
_____

broken arm
being teased

Mother to Son

Langston Hughes

The Moon was but a Chin of Gold

Emily Dickinson

Mother to Son

Langston Hughes

INTERPRET

What **connotations** or associations are suggested by the image of a crystal stairway?

_____

_____

_____

_____

_____

_____

_____

INTERPRET

In lines 15–19, how does the speaker **extend** the **metaphor** of the staircase to encourage her son?

Well, son, I'll tell you:
Life for me ain't been no crystal stair.
It's had tacks in it,
And splinters,
And boards torn up,
And places with no carpet on the floor—
Bare.
But all the time
I'se been a-climbin' on,
10 And reachin' landin's,
And turnin' corners,
And sometimes goin' in the dark
Where there ain't been no light.
So boy, don't you turn back.
Don't you set down on the steps
'Cause you finds it's kinder hard.
Don't you fall now—
For I'se still goin', honey,
I'se still climbin',
20 And life for me ain't been no crystal stair.

The Moon was but a Chin of Gold

Emily Dickinson

The Moon was but a Chin of Gold
A Night or two ago—
And now she turns Her perfect Face
Upon the World below—

Her Forehead is of Amplest Blonde—
Her Cheek—a Beryl[1] hewn—
Her Eye unto the Summer Dew
The likest I have known—

Her Lips of Amber never part—
10 But what must be the smile
Upon Her Friend she could confer
Were such Her Silver Will—

And what a privilege to be
But the remotest Star—
For Certainty She takes Her Way
Beside Your Palace Door—

Her Bonnet is the Firmament[2]—
The Universe—Her Shoe—
The Stars—the Trinkets at Her Belt—
20 Her Dimities[3]—of Blue—

1. **beryl:** mineral that usually occurs in crystals of blue, green, pink, or yellow.
2. **firmament:** sky.
3. **dimities:** dresses made of dimity, a sheer, cool, cotton material.

Extended Metaphor

An **extended metaphor** is a metaphor that develops its comparison over several lines of a poem or even throughout a whole poem. In "Mother to Son," the poem's speaker compares the process of living life to a challenging climb up a staircase. In "The Moon was but a Chin of Gold," the poet's extended metaphor compares the moon to the face of a beautiful woman.

Write a pair of extended metaphors of your own. Flesh out each comparison shown below with specific details and additional similarities. If you prefer, make up your own comparisons and substitute them for the ones given below. Remember that a metaphor directly compares one thing to another, without the use of such words as *like, as,* or *resembles.*

1. Life is a tennis match.

   _____

   _____

   _____

   _____

   _____

   _____

   _____

   _____

2. A tiger is fire in motion.

   _____

   _____

   _____

   _____

   _____

   _____

   _____

   _____

Vocabulary: How to Own a Word

Column Match

For each word in Column A, write the letter of the correct definition shown in Column B.

Column A

_____ **1.** hewn

_____ **2.** confer

_____ **3.** remotest

_____ **4.** firmament

_____ **5.** trinkets

Column B

a. most distant

b. trifling ornaments

c. carved into shape

d. bestow on; grant

e. sky

Shall I Compare Thee to a Summer's Day?

Make the Connection

Eloquent Comparisons

Think about someone you care for, or even someone you admire from afar. Choose three things to compare this person to, and write them in the boxes below. For each thing you name, write two similarities between the person you admire and the thing to which you are comparing the person. For example, you might compare the person you admire to a piece of music; both are intriguing and beautiful. Sum up your feelings in two words and write them at the bottom of the chart.

Things

_____

_____

Similarities

_____

_____

Things

_____

_____

Similarities

_____

_____

Things

_____

_____

Similarities

_____

_____

Summary: _____

Shall I Compare Thee to a Summer's Day?

William Shakespeare

RETELL

In lines 3–4, Shakespeare gives two reasons to support his claim in lines 1–2 about the beloved. Summarize these reasons in your own words.

_____

_____

_____

_____

_____

_____

INTERPRET

What change occurs in the third quatrain (lines 9–12) of the **sonnet**?

_____

_____

_____

_____

_____

_____

INTERPRET

What do you think the poet means by the word *this* in line 14?

_____

_____

_____

_____

_____

BUILD FLUENCY

Read the sonnet aloud, expressing the passionate feelings of the speaker.

Shall I compare thee to a summer's day?
Thou art more lovely and more temperate.
Rough winds do shake the darling buds of May,
And summer's lease hath all too short a date.
Sometime too hot the eye of heaven shines,
And often is his gold complexion dimmed;
And every fair from fair sometime declines,
By chance, or nature's changing course, untrimmed;[1]
But thy eternal summer shall not fade,
10 Nor lose possession of that fair thou ow'st,[2]
Nor shall Death brag thou wand'rest in his shade,
When in eternal lines to time thou grow'st:
    So long as men can breathe or eyes can see,
    So long lives this, and this gives life to thee.

1. **untrimmed**: without trimmings (decorations).
2. **thou ow'st**: you own.

Sonnet

A **sonnet** is a fourteen-line poem written within very strict rules. In a **Shakespearean,** or **English, sonnet** the poem's fourteen lines are divided into three **quatrains** (rhyming groups of four lines each) and a concluding **couplet** (pair of rhyming lines). Each quatrain makes a point or gives an example. The couplet usually sums up the poem's main idea or points to the writer's theme.

Use the diagram below to chart the thoughts in each part of Shakespeare's "Shall I Compare Thee to a Summer's Day?"

Passage	Main Idea/Point/Example
Quatrain 1 (lines 1–4):	
Quatrain 2 (lines 5–8):	
Quatrain 3 (lines 9–12):	
Couplet (lines 13–14):	

Vocabulary: How to Own a Word

Developing Vocabulary

Carefully read each word's definition, explanation, and sample sentence. Then, write a sentence of your own using that word.

1. **temperate** (tĕm′pər·it) *adj.:* moderate, restrained.
   - *Temperate* is often applied to both the weather and human behavior.

   The climate in Florida was unusually <u>temperate</u> for August.

   _____

   _____

   _____

   _____

2. **lease** (lēs) *n.:* duration or continuation (archaic); a contract involving real estate.
   - The root of the word is the Old French *laissier*, meaning "to let go."

   The philosopher lamented that the <u>lease</u> of human life, which lasts several decades at the most, always comes to an end.

   _____

   _____

   _____

   _____

3. **fair** (fer) *n.:* beauty; something or someone who is beautiful.
   - The noun *fair*, meaning "beauty," is now obsolete. More common is the adjective *fair*, which means "beautiful, pure, or clear."

   Respect goes to the virtuous, but admiration to the <u>fair</u>.

   _____

   _____

   _____

   _____

Selection: _____

Imagery: Seeing Things Freshly

Imagery

Language that appeals to the senses of sight, hearing, taste, smell, or touch.

Sight

Examples: _____
_____
_____

Hearing

Examples: _____
_____
_____

Taste

Examples: _____
_____
_____

Smell

Examples: _____
_____
_____

Touch

Examples: _____
_____
_____

Ex-Basketball Player;
We Real Cool

Make the Connection

Past Dreams

People sometimes get stuck in dreams of their past. Sports heroes whose careers have ended abruptly often try to relive their past glories. What other things in life besides early sports success can cause people to "live in the past"? Name some experiences that might cause people to stop maturing, to cease dreaming, or to focus only on the past. For examples, think of the lives of characters in movies, books, and TV shows.

What can people do in order to avoid getting caught in the past? Offer at least two suggestions.

_____

_____

_____

_____

_____

_____

_____

_____

_____

_____

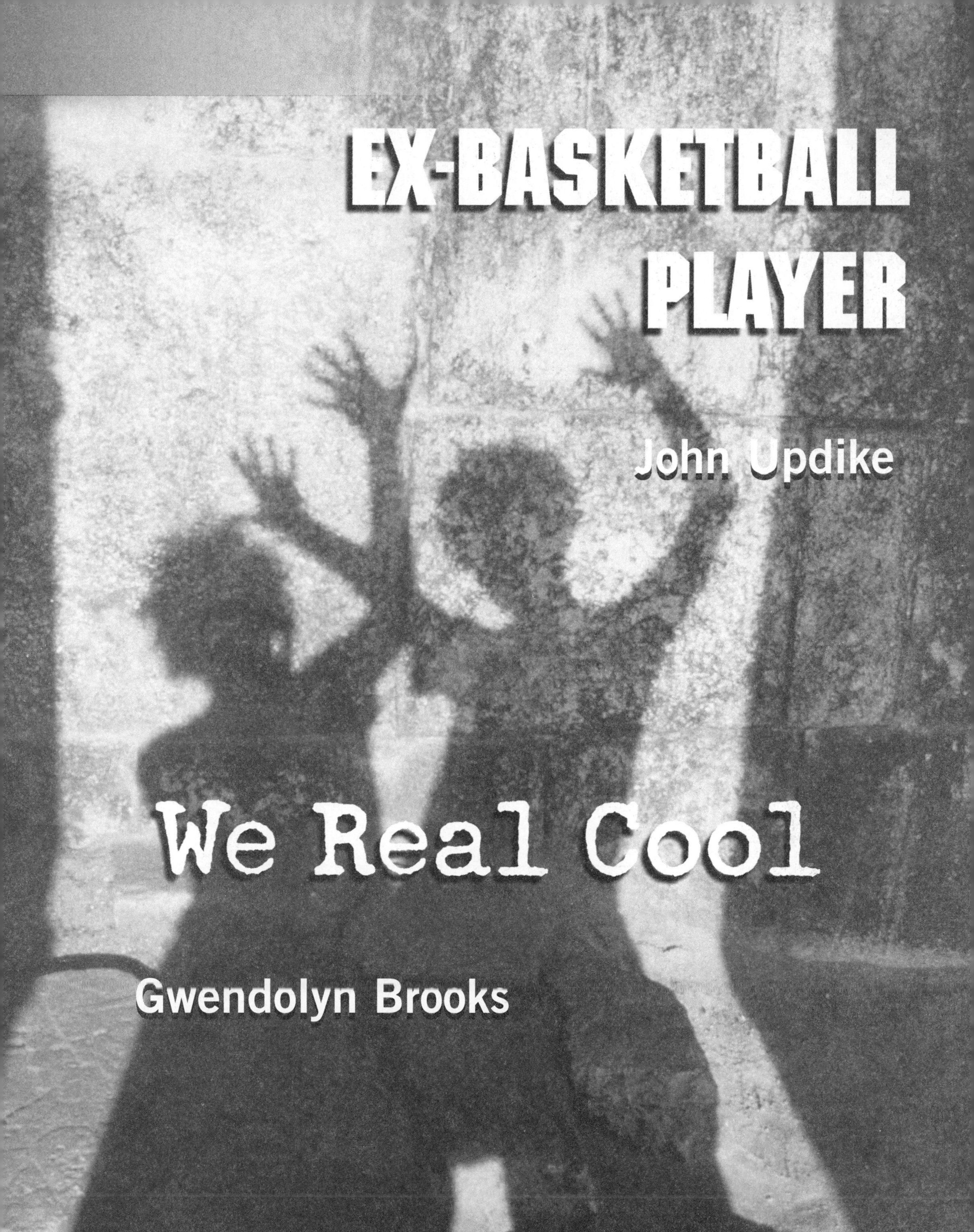

EX-BASKETBALL PLAYER

John Updike

We Real Cool

Gwendolyn Brooks

IDENTIFY

The basic beat in this poem is **iambic pentameter**—five iambs (˘ ′) to a line. Draw a line under the lines in the first stanza that do not follow this metrical pattern.

_____

_____

_____

IDENTIFY

In lines 11–12, what is the last gas pump compared to? Underline the words giving the answer.

INTERPRET

In context, what do the verbs *bucketed* (line 15) and *rack up* (line 17) mean?

_____

_____

_____

_____

INTERPRET

What is **ironic** about the poem's last three lines?

_____

_____

_____

_____

_____

_____

_____

BUILD FLUENCY

Read the last stanza aloud. Try to capture the speaker's **tone.**

Ex-Basketball Player

John Updike

Pearl Avenue runs past the high-school lot,
Bends with the trolley tracks, and stops, cut off
Before it has a chance to go two blocks,
At Colonel McComsky Plaza. Berth's Garage
Is on the corner facing west, and there,
Most days, you'll find Flick Webb, who helps Berth out.

Flick stands tall among the idiot pumps—
Five on a side, the old bubble-head style,
Their rubber elbows hanging loose and low.
10 One's nostrils are two S's, and his eyes
An E and O. And one is squat, without
A head at all—more of a football type.

Once Flick played for the high-school team, the Wizards.
He was good: in fact, the best. In '46
He bucketed three hundred ninety points,
A county record still. The ball loved Flick.
I saw him rack up thirty-eight or forty
In one home game. His hands were like wild birds.

He never learned a trade, he just sells gas,
20 Checks oil, and changes flats. Once in a while,
As a gag, he dribbles an inner tube,
But most of us remember anyway.
His hands are fine and nervous on the lug wrench.
It makes no difference to the lug wrench, though.

Off work, he hangs around Mae's luncheonette.
Grease-gray and kind of coiled, he plays pinball,
Smokes thin cigars, and nurses lemon phosphates.
Flick seldom says a word to Mae, just nods
Beyond her face toward bright applauding tiers
30 Of Necco Wafers, Nibs, and Juju Beads.

We Real Cool

Gwendolyn Brooks

The Pool Players.
Seven at The Golden Shovel.

We real cool. We
Left school. We

Lurk late. We
Strike straight. We

Sing sin. We
Thin gin. We

Jazz June. We
Die soon.

IDENTIFY

What is the **internal rhyme** in lines 3–4?

_____

_____

_____

_____

_____

_____

INTERPRET

What message is Brooks sending to young people in this poem?

_____

_____

_____

_____

_____

_____

_____

_____

_____

_____

_____

_____

_____

_____

_____

_____

Sound Effects

Poets use many different types of **sound effects,** including rhythm, end rhyme, internal rhyme, and alliteration. Such sound effects lend verbal music to poems.

In John Updike's "Ex-Basketball Player," for example, the basic rhythmical beat is **iambic pentameter**—five iambs (˘ ´) to a line. An iamb contains one unstressed syllable followed by a stressed syllable. This meter is closest to the pattern of everyday English speech, and its use gives the poem an informal, conversational sound. You'll find the same meter in Shakespeare's sonnets and plays.

Alliteration is repetition of the same or similar consonant sounds in words that are close together. **End rhyme** is repetition of accented vowel sounds and all sounds following them at the ends of lines of verse. **Internal rhyme** occurs within lines.

1. Where does alliteration occur in line 26 of "Ex-Basketball Player"?

_____

_____

2. In lines 5–6 of "We Real Cool," identify one example of alliteration and one example of internal rhyme.

_____

_____

Vocabulary: How to Own a Word

Developing Vocabulary

Carefully read each word's definition, explanation, and sample sentence. Then, write a sentence of your own using that word.

1. **squat** (skwät) *adj.:* low to the ground; short and stocky.
 • "To squat" means "to crouch or sit on one's haunches."

The catcher on the baseball team was short and squat.

_____

_____

_____

_____

2. **phosphates** (fäs′fāts′) *n. pl.:* soft drinks made of soda water, syrup, and a few drops of phosphoric acid.
 • Phosphoric acid has many and varied uses, including rustproofing metals and preparing fertilizers.

The old man fondly recalled drinking phosphates at the soda fountain of the general store.

_____

_____

_____

_____

3. **lurk** (lurk) *v.:* to lie in wait; to behave furtively.
 • Some synonyms of *lurk* include *skulk*, *slink*, and *sneak*.

Pickpockets will sometimes lurk in bus stations and other public places, looking for potential victims.

_____

_____

_____

_____

From The Tragedy of Julius Caesar

Make the Connection

The Context of Shakespeare's Play

In Shakespeare's day, the Elizabethans believed that the universe was essentially good and orderly. All order stemmed from divine authority, as did the monarch's right to rule. Therefore, opposition to the anointed ruler was considered a grave offense against God's law. If the chain of authority were broken, the Heavens would be offended, and a whole society could be plunged into disorder. Thus, the story of the assassination of Julius Caesar in ancient Rome had immediate connections for the Elizabethans—it tapped into their own desire for stability in government and into their dread of civil war.

Think about some of the similarities and differences between the Elizabethan view of the universe and our modern ideas about government. On the lines provided, write your responses to each of the following statements.

1. Chaos results when the lawful social order is broken.

   _____

   _____

2. The best intentions of good, noble people can lead to tragedy.

   _____

   _____

3. Language is a powerful weapon, and in the hands of a skilled person it can be used to manipulate others.

   _____

   _____

4. Violence and bloodshed can never have morally good results.

   _____

   _____

5. Orderliness and stable rule, even though dictatorial, are preferable to chaos.

   _____

   _____

FROM

The Tragedy of
JULIUS CAESAR

IDENTIFY

Who is Calphurnia?

INTERPRET

What does line 10 reveal about Antony's devotion and loyalty to Caesar?

IDENTIFY

In the modern calendar, what date corresponds to the ides of March?

Act I, Scene 2

A number of Romans fear CAESAR'S *growing power and favor with the people. In this scene, we learn of the conspiracy to assassinate him.*

Scene 2. *A public place.*

Enter CAESAR, ANTONY (*dressed for the race*), CALPHURNIA,
    PORTIA, DECIUS, CICERO, BRUTUS, CASSIUS, CASCA, *a* SOOTHSAYER;
    after them, MARULLUS *and* FLAVIUS.

Caesar.
    Calphurnia!

Casca.   Peace, ho! Caesar speaks.

Caesar.   Calphurnia!

Calphurnia. Here, my lord.

Caesar.
    Stand you directly in Antonius' way
    When he doth run his course. Antonius!

Antony. Caesar, my lord?

Caesar.
    Forget not in your speed, Antonius,
    To touch Calphurnia; for our elders say
    The barren, touchèd in this holy chase,
    Shake off their sterile curse.

Antony.   I shall remember:

10   When Caesar says "Do this," it is performed.

Caesar.
    Set on, and leave no ceremony out.

Soothsayer. Caesar!

Caesar. Ha! Who calls?

Casca.
    Bid every noise be still; peace yet again!

Caesar.
    Who is it in the press[1] that calls on me?
    I hear a tongue, shriller than all the music,
    Cry "Caesar." Speak; Caesar is turned to hear.

Soothsayer.
    Beware the ides of March.[2]

Caesar.   What man is that?

Brutus.
    A soothsayer bids you beware the ides of March.

---

1. **press:** crowd.
2. **ides of March:** March 15.

Caesar.

20   Set him before me; let me see his face.

Cassius.

Fellow, come from the throng; look upon Caesar.

Caesar.

What say'st thou to me now? Speak once again.

Soothsayer.

Beware the ides of March.

Caesar.

He is a dreamer, let us leave him. Pass.

[*Sennet.*³ *Exeunt all except* BRUTUS *and* CASSIUS.]

Cassius.

Will you go see the order of the course?

Brutus. Not I.

Cassius. I pray you do.

Brutus.

I am not gamesome: I do lack some part

Of that quick spirit that is in Antony.

30   Let me not hinder, Cassius, your desires;

I'll leave you.

Cassius.

Brutus, I do observe you now of late;

I have not from your eyes that gentleness

And show of love as I was wont to have;

You bear too stubborn and too strange a hand⁴

Over your friend that loves you.

Brutus.   Cassius,

Be not deceived: if I have veiled my look,

I turn the trouble of my countenance

Merely⁵ upon myself. Vexèd I am

40   Of late with passions of some difference,⁶

Conceptions only proper to myself,

Which give some soil,⁷ perhaps, to my behaviors;

But let not therefore my good friends be grieved

(Among which number, Cassius, be you one)

Nor construe⁸ any further my neglect

Than that poor Brutus, with himself at war,

Forgets the shows of love to other men.

---

3. Sennet: flourish, or fanfare of trumpets announcing a ceremonial entrance or exit.
4. You . . . hand: Cassius is comparing Brutus's treatment of him with the way a
trainer treats a horse.
5. Merely: wholly.
6. passions of some difference: conflicting feelings or emotions.
7. give some soil: stain or mar.
8. construe: interpret.

INTERPRET

Why do you think Caesar dismisses the soothsayer's warning so quickly?

Cassius.

 Then, Brutus, I have much mistook your passion,[9]

 By means whereof this breast of mine hath buried

50 Thoughts of great value, worthy cogitations.[10]

 Tell me, good Brutus, can you see your face?

Brutus.

 No, Cassius; for the eye sees not itself

 But by reflection, by some other things.

Cassius.

 'Tis just:[11]

 And it is very much lamented, Brutus,

 That you have no such mirrors as will turn

 Your hidden worthiness into your eye,

 That you might see your shadow.[12] I have heard

 Where many of the best respect[13] in Rome

60 (Except immortal Caesar), speaking of Brutus,

 And groaning underneath this age's yoke,

 Have wished that noble Brutus had his eyes.

Brutus.

 Into what dangers would you lead me, Cassius,

 That you would have me seek into myself

 For that which is not in me?

Cassius.

 Therefore, good Brutus, be prepared to hear;

 And since you know you cannot see yourself

 So well as by reflection, I, your glass[14]

 Will modestly discover to yourself

70 That of yourself which you yet know not of.

 And be not jealous on[15] me, gentle Brutus:

 Were I a common laughter,[16] or did use

 To stale with ordinary oaths my love

 To every new protester,[17] if you know

 That I do fawn on men and hug them hard,

 And after scandal them;[18] or if you know

 That I profess myself in banqueting

EVALUATE

Re-read lines 55–62. Are these lines meant sincerely or are they flattery? Explain.

IDENTIFY

To what does Cassius indirectly compare himself in line 68?

---

 9. passion: feeling.

10. worthy cogitations: reflections of great value.

11. just: true.

12. shadow: reflection (of what others think of him).

13. respect: reputation.

14. glass: mirror.

15. jealous on: suspicious of.

16. common laughter: butt of a joke; object of mockery.

17. To stale . . . new protestor: In other words, if he swore to love everyone who came along.

18. scandal them: ruin them by gossip.

To all the rout,[19] then hold me dangerous.

[*Flourish*[20] *and shout.*]

Brutus.

What means this shouting? I do fear the people
Choose Caesar for their king.

80 **Cassius.**   Ay, do you fear it?
Then must I think you would not have it so.

Brutus.

I would not, Cassius, yet I love him well.
But wherefore do you hold me here so long?
What is it that you would impart to me?
If it be aught toward the general good,
Set honor in one eye and death i' th' other,
And I will look on both indifferently;[21]
For let the gods so speed me, as I love
The name of honor more than I fear death.

Cassius.

90
I know that virtue to be in you, Brutus,
As well as I do know your outward favor.[22]
Well, honor is the subject of my story.
I cannot tell what you and other men
Think of this life, but for my single self,
I had as lief[23] not be, as live to be
In awe of such a thing as I myself.
I was born free as Caesar; so were you:
We both have fed as well, and we can both
Endure the winter's cold as well as he:
100
For once, upon a raw and gusty day,
The troubled Tiber chafing with[24] her shores,
Caesar said to me "Dar'st thou, Cassius, now
Leap in with me into this angry flood,
And swim to yonder point?" Upon the word,
Accout'red as I was, I plungèd in
And bade him follow: so indeed he did.
The torrent roared, and we did buffet it
With lusty sinews, throwing it aside
And stemming it with hearts of controversy.[25]

---

19. **rout:** common people, the mob.
20. **Flourish:** brief, elaborate music of trumpets.
21. **indifferently:** impartially; fairly.
22. **outward favor:** appearance.
23. **as lief:** just as soon.
24. **chafing with:** raging against (the river was rough with waves and currents).
25. **hearts of controversy:** hearts full of aggressive feelings, or fighting spirit.

INTERPRET

Why do you think the scene of Caesar being acclaimed by the Roman people occurs offstage, while the drama focuses on the interaction between Brutus and Cassius?

_____
_____
_____
_____
_____

EVALUATE

According to line 89, what seems to be Brutus's most cherished value?

_____
_____
_____
_____

INTERPRET

In lines 93–96, what value does Cassius champion?

_____
_____
_____

BUILD FLUENCY

Read Cassius's speech aloud, using the punctuation as a guide to units of meaning.

_____
_____
_____
_____
_____
_____
_____

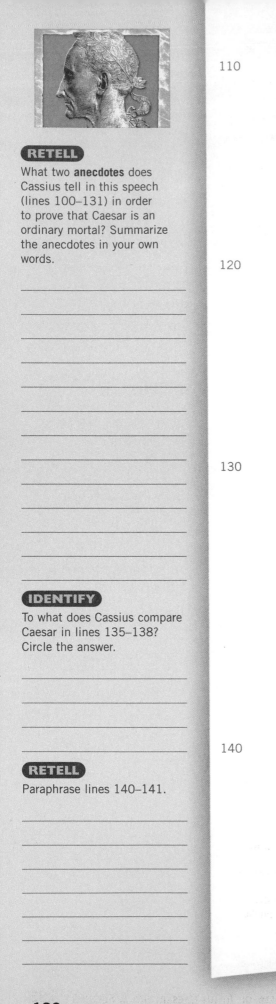

RETELL

What two **anecdotes** does Cassius tell in this speech (lines 100–131) in order to prove that Caesar is an ordinary mortal? Summarize the anecdotes in your own words.

_____

_____

_____

_____

_____

_____

_____

_____

_____

_____

_____

IDENTIFY

To what does Cassius compare Caesar in lines 135–138? Circle the answer.

_____

_____

_____

_____

RETELL

Paraphrase lines 140–141.

_____

_____

_____

_____

_____

_____

_____

_____

110
> But ere we could arrive the point proposed,
> Caesar cried "Help me, Cassius, or I sink!"
> I, as Aeneas,[26] our great ancestor,
> Did from the flames of Troy upon his shoulder
> The old Anchises bear, so from the waves of Tiber
> Did I the tired Caesar. And this man
> Is now become a god, and Cassius is
> A wretched creature, and must bend his body
> If Caesar carelessly but nod on him.
> He had a fever when he was in Spain,
120
> And when the fit was on him, I did mark
> How he did shake; 'tis true, this god did shake.
> His coward lips did from their color fly,
> And that same eye whose bend doth awe the world
> Did lose his luster; I did hear him groan;
> Ay, and that tongue of his, that bade the Romans
> Mark him and write his speeches in their books,
> Alas, it cried, "Give me some drink, Titinius,"
> As a sick girl. Ye gods! It doth amaze me,
> A man of such a feeble temper should
130
> So get the start of the majestic world,
> And bear the palm[27] alone.

[*Shout. Flourish.*]

Brutus.
> Another general shout?
> I do believe that these applauses are
> For some new honors that are heaped on Caesar.

Cassius.
> Why, man, he doth bestride the narrow world
> Like a Colossus,[28] and we petty men
> Walk under his huge legs and peep about
> To find ourselves dishonorable graves.
> Men at some time are masters of their fates:
140
> The fault, dear Brutus, is not in our stars,[29]
> But in ourselves, that we are underlings.

---

26. **Aeneas** (i·nē'əs): legendary forefather of the Roman people who, in Virgil's *Aeneid,* fled from the burning city of Troy carrying his old father on his back. (In many accounts of the legend, Romulus and Remus were descendants of Aeneas.)
27. **bear the palm:** hold the palm branch, an award given to a victorious general.
28. **Colossus:** huge statue of Helios that was said to straddle the entrance to the harbor at Rhodes, an island in the Aegean Sea. The statue, so huge that ships passed under its legs, was one of the Seven Wonders of the Ancient World. It was destroyed by an earthquake in 224 B.C.
29. **stars:** Elizabethans believed that one's life was governed by the stars or constellation one was born under.

Brutus and Caesar: what should be in that "Caesar"?
Why should that name be sounded more than yours?
Write them together, yours is as fair a name;
Sound them, it doth become the mouth as well;
Weigh them, it is as heavy; conjure with 'em,
"Brutus" will start a spirit as soon as "Caesar."
Now, in the names of all the gods at once,
Upon what meat doth this our Caesar feed,

150 That he is grown so great? Age, thou art shamed!
Rome, thou hast lost the breed of noble bloods!
When went there by an age, since the great flood,[30]
But it was famed with more than with one man?
When could they say (till now) that talked of Rome,
That her wide walks encompassed but one man?
Now is it Rome indeed, and room[31] enough,
When there is in it but one only man.
O, you and I have heard our fathers say,
There was a Brutus once that would have brooked[32]

160 Th' eternal devil to keep his state in Rome
As easily as a king.[33]

Brutus.

> That you do love me, I am nothing jealous;
> What you would work me to, I have some aim;[34]
> How I have thought of this, and of these times,
> I shall recount hereafter. For this present,
> I would not so (with love I might entreat you)
> Be any further moved. What you have said
> I will consider; what you have to say
> I will with patience hear, and find a time
> 170 Both meet[35] to hear and answer such high things.
> Till then, my noble friend, chew upon this:
> Brutus had rather be a villager
> Than to repute himself a son of Rome
> Under these hard conditions as this time
> Is like to lay upon us.

Cassius.   I am glad
That my weak words have struck but thus much show
Of fire from Brutus.

---

30. **the great flood:** flood sent by Zeus to drown all the wicked people on Earth.
    Only the faithful couple Deucalion and Pyrrha were saved.
31. **Rome . . . room:** a pun; both words were pronounced room in Shakespeare's day.
32. **brooked:** put up with.
33. **Th' eternal . . . king:** This refers to the ancestor of Brutus who, in the sixth
    century B.C., helped to expel the last king from Rome and set up the Republic.
34. **aim:** idea.
35. **meet:** appropriate.

IDENTIFY

What words in line 156 contain a **pun,** or play on words?

BUILD FLUENCY

Read lines 162–175 aloud as expressively as you can. Note the inverted word order in several sentences. Shakespeare uses this device either for emphasis or to preserve the rhythm of **iambic pentameter.**

INFER

Is Brutus aware that Cassius is hinting at a conspiracy against Caesar? Does Brutus understand that Cassius is trying to flatter and manipulate him? Explain.

[*Enter* CAESAR *and his* TRAIN.]

Brutus.

The games are done, and Caesar is returning.

Cassius.

180　As they pass by, pluck Casca by the sleeve,

And he will (after his sour fashion) tell you

What hath proceeded worthy note today.

Brutus.

I will do so. But look you, Cassius,

The angry spot doth glow on Caesar's brow,

And all the rest look like a chidden³⁶ train:

Calphurnia's cheek is pale, and Cicero

Looks with such ferret³⁷ and such fiery eyes

As we have seen him in the Capitol,

Being crossed in conference by some senators.

Cassius.

Casca will tell us what the matter is.

190　**Caesar.** Antonius.

Antony. Caesar?

Caesar.

Let me have men about me that are fat,

Sleek-headed men, and such as sleep a-nights.

Yond Cassius has a lean and hungry look;

He thinks too much: such men are dangerous.

Antony.

Fear him not, Caesar, he's not dangerous;

He is a noble Roman, and well given.³⁸

Caesar.

Would he were fatter! But I fear him not.

Yet if my name were liable to fear,

200　I do not know the man I should avoid

So soon as that spare Cassius. He reads much,

He is a great observer, and he looks

Quite through the deeds of men.³⁹ He loves no plays,

As thou dost, Antony; he hears no music;

Seldom he smiles, and smiles in such a sort⁴⁰

As if he mocked himself, and scorned his spirit

That could be moved to smile at anything.

---

36. chidden: rebuked; corrected.

37. ferret: weasellike animal, usually considered crafty.

38. well given: well disposed to support Caesar.

39. he looks . . . of men: In other words, he looks through what men do to search out their feelings and motives.

40. sort: manner.

IDENTIFY

Underline the lines that reveal Caesar's suspicion of Cassius.

INTERPRET

Caesar's first observation about Cassius reveals impressive insight. What less favorable side of Caesar's character do lines 198–212 show?

Such men as he be never at heart's ease
Whiles they behold a greater than themselves,
210   And therefore are they very dangerous.
I rather tell thee what is to be feared
Than what I fear; for always I am Caesar.
Come on my right hand, for this ear is deaf,
And tell me truly what thou think'st of him.

[*Sennet. Exeunt* CAESAR *and his* TRAIN.]

Casca.
You pulled me by the cloak; would you speak with me?
Brutus.
Ay, Casca; tell us what hath chanced today,
That Caesar looks so sad.[41]
Casca.
Why, you were with him, were you not?
Brutus.
I should not then ask Casca what had chanced.
220   **Casca.** Why, there was a crown offered him; and being
offered him, he put it by[42] with the back of his hand,
thus; and then the people fell a-shouting.
Brutus. What was the second noise for?
Casca. Why, for that too.
Cassius.
They shouted thrice; what was the last cry for?
Casca. Why, for that too.
Brutus. Was the crown offered him thrice?
Casca. Ay, marry,[43] was't, and he put it by thrice, every
time gentler than other; and at every putting-by mine
230   honest neighbors shouted.
Cassius.
Who offered him the crown?
Casca. Why, Antony.
Brutus.
Tell us the manner of it, gentle Casca.
Casca. I can as well be hanged as tell the manner of it:
it was mere foolery; I did not mark it. I saw Mark
Antony offer him a crown—yet 'twas not a crown
neither, 'twas one of these coronets[44]—and, as I told
you, he put it by once; but for all that, to my thinking,

---

41. **sad:** serious.
42. **put it by:** pushed it aside.
43. **marry:** a mild oath meaning "by the Virgin Mary."
44. **coronets:** small crowns.

INFER

The real Caesar was not deaf in one ear, as he says in line 213. Why do you think Shakespeare invented this detail about the Roman leader?

_____

_____

_____

_____

_____

_____

INTERPRET

Why do you think Shakespeare has Casca speak in prose, rather than blank verse?

_____

_____

_____

_____

_____

_____

_____

_____

_____

_____

_____

_____

_____

IDENTIFY

After the serious speeches of Cassius and Brutus, Shakespeare provides some **humor** with Casca's lively description. Circle colorful details in Casca's delivery and speech that would appeal to the audience.

_____

_____

_____

_____

_____

_____

_____

_____

_____

_____

_____

_____

_____

_____

_____

IDENTIFY

An **anachronism** is an event or detail in a literary work that is chronologically out of place. What anachronism appears in line 265? Circle the answer.

_____

_____

_____

_____

_____

240 he would fain[45] have had it. Then he offered it to him again; then he put it by again; but to my thinking, he was very loath to lay his fingers off it. And then he offered it the third time. He put it the third time by; and still as he refused it, the rabblement hooted, and clapped their chopt[46] hands, and threw up their sweaty nightcaps,[47] and uttered such a deal of stinking breath because Caesar refused the crown, that it had, almost, choked Caesar; for he swounded[48] and fell down at it. And for mine own part, I durst not laugh, for fear of opening my lips and receiving the

250 bad air.

Cassius.

But, soft,[49] I pray you; what, did Caesar swound?

Casca. He fell down in the market place, and foamed at mouth, and was speechless.

Brutus.

'Tis very like he hath the falling-sickness.[50]

Cassius.

No, Caesar hath it not; but you, and I,
And honest Casca, we have the falling-sickness.

Casca. I know not what you mean by that, but I am sure Caesar fell down. If the tag-rag people[51] did not clap him and hiss him, according as he pleased and displeased them, as they use to do the players in the

260 theater, I am no true man.

Brutus.

What said he when he came unto himself?

Casca. Marry, before he fell down, when he perceived the common herd was glad he refused the crown, he plucked me ope[52] his doublet[53] and offered them his throat to cut. An[54] I had been a man of any occupation,[55] if I would not have taken him at a word, I would I might go to hell among the rogues. And so he fell. When he came to himself again, he

---

45. **fain:** happily.
46. **chopt:** chapped (raw and rough from hard work and the weather).
47. **nightcaps:** Casca is mockingly referring to the hats of the workingmen.
48. **swounded:** swooned or fainted.
49. **soft:** wait a minute.
50. **falling-sickness:** old term for the disease we now call epilepsy, which is marked by seizures and momentary loss of consciousness.
51. **tag-rag people:** contemptuous reference to the commoners in the crowd.
52. **plucked me ope:** plucked open.
53. **doublet:** close-fitting jacket.
54. **An:** if.
55. **man of any occupation:** working man.

270 said, if he had done or said anything amiss, he desired
their worships to think it was his infirmity. Three or
four wenches,[56] where I stood, cried "Alas, good
soul!" and forgave him with all their hearts; but
there's no heed to be taken of them; if Caesar had
stabbed their mothers, they would have done no less.

Brutus.

And after that, he came thus sad away?

Casca. Ay.

Cassius.

Did Cicero say anything?

Casca. Ay, he spoke Greek.

280 **Cassius.** To what effect?

Casca. Nay, an I tell you that, I'll ne'er look you i' th'
face again. But those that understood him smiled at
one another and shook their heads; but for mine own
part, it was Greek to me. I could tell you more news
too: Marullus and Flavius, for pulling scarfs off
Caesar's images, are put to silence.[57] Fare you well.
There was more foolery yet, if I could remember it.

Cassius. Will you sup with me tonight, Casca?

Casca. No, I am promised forth.[58]

290 **Cassius.** Will you dine with me tomorrow?

Casca. Ay, if I be alive, and your mind hold, and your
dinner worth the eating.

Cassius. Good; I will expect you.

Casca. Do so. Farewell, both.   [*Exit.*]

Brutus.

What a blunt fellow is this grown to be!
He was quick mettle[59] when he went to school.

Cassius.

So is he now in execution
Of any bold or noble enterprise,
However he puts on this tardy form.[60]

300 This rudeness[61] is a sauce to his good wit,[62]
Which gives men stomach to disgest[63] his words
With better appetite.

---

56. **wenches:** girls or young women.
57. **put to silence:** silenced, perhaps being dismissed from their positions as
tribunes or by being exiled.
58. **forth:** previously (he has other plans).
59. **quick mettle:** lively of disposition.
60. **tardy form:** sluggish appearance.
61. **rudeness:** rough manner.
62. **wit:** intelligence.
63. **disgest:** digest.

INFER

How is Casca's sarcasm shown
in lines 271–275?

INTERPRET

Why are Marullus and Flavius
silenced? What does this
development tell you about
Caesar?

Brutus.

    And so it is. For this time I will leave you.

    Tomorrow, if you please to speak with me,

    I will come home to you; or if you will,

    Come home to me, and I will wait for you.

Cassius.

    I will do so. Till then, think of the world.[64]

                                    [*Exit* BRUTUS.]

    Well, Brutus, thou art noble; yet I see

    Thy honorable mettle may be wrought

310   From that it is disposed;[65] therefore it is meet

    That noble minds keep ever with their likes;

    For who so firm that cannot be seduced?

    Caesar doth bear me hard,[66] but he loves Brutus.

    If I were Brutus now and he were Cassius,

    He should not humor[67] me. I will this night,

    In several hands,[68] in at his windows throw,

    As if they came from several citizens,

    Writings, all tending to the great opinion

    That Rome holds of his name; wherein obscurely

320   Caesar's ambition shall be glancèd at.[69]

    And after this, let Caesar seat him sure;[70]

    For we will shake him, or worse days endure.   [*Exit.*]

INTERPRET

Why do you think Cassius uses the respectful *you* when talking to Brutus and then uses the familiar *thou* here?

INTERPRET

Cassius's speech is a **soliloquy,** a long speech by a character who is alone on stage. What do you learn about Cassius's motives from this speech?

---

64. **the world:** the state of affairs in Rome.
65. **Thy honorable . . . disposed:** In other words, he may be persuaded against his better nature to join the conspirators.
66. **bear me hard:** has a grudge (hard feelings) against me.
67. **humor:** influence by flattery.
68. **hands:** varieties of handwriting.
69. **glancèd at:** touched on.
70. **seat him sure:** make his position secure.

Figurative Language

Figurative language is language that is not intended to be understood literally. Two of the most important figures of speech are simile and metaphor.

- A **simile** uses words such as *like, as, than,* or *resembles* to compare two unlike things.
  EXAMPLE: I hear a tongue, shriller than all the music,/Cry "Caesar." (lines 16–17)

- A **metaphor** directly compares two unlike things without using a comparative word such as *like* or *as*.
  EXAMPLE: I, your glass/Will modestly discover to yourself/That of yourself which you yet know not of. (lines 68–70)

Re-read Act I, Scene 2 of *Julius Caesar* and write down in the left column three similes or metaphors the playwright uses. In the right column, describe the two things each simile or metaphor compares.

Simile/Metaphor	Explanation
a. _____	_____
_____	_____
_____	_____
_____	_____
_____	_____
b. _____	_____
_____	_____
_____	_____
_____	_____
_____	_____
c. _____	_____
_____	_____
_____	_____
_____	_____
_____	_____

Vocabulary: How to Own a Word

Developing Vocabulary

Carefully read each word's definition, explanation, and sample sentence. Then, write a sentence of your own using that word.

1. **barren** (bar′ən) *adj.:* unable to bear children. *Barren* can also refer to land that will not produce crops or that lacks vegetation.

   The woman thought she was barren, but then she happily discovered that she was going to have a baby.

   Original sentence: _____

   _____

2. **countenance** (koun′tə·nəns) *n.:* face. This word comes from a Latin word meaning "the way one holds oneself."

   Russ was relieved to see his father's smiling countenance as he awoke from the operation.

   Original sentence: _____

   _____

3. **aught** (ôt) *n.:* anything. This archaic word is from the Old English word *awiht*.

   Michael was confused by the question on the Shakespeare test, and he jokingly told his teacher, "The answer could be aught."

   Original sentence: _____

   _____

4. **torrent** (tôr′ənt) *n.:* a swift, violent stream. This word was borrowed from French in its present form.

   The water came down the mountainside in a rushing torrent.

   Original sentence: _____

   _____

5. **blunt** (blunt) *adj.:* abrupt; frank; outspoken. This word can also mean "dull; slow to understand."

   Sometimes it is kinder to be blunt with someone than to hide the truth in order to protect his or her feelings.

   Original sentence: _____

   _____

Act III, Scene 2

CASSIUS *succeeds in persuading* BRUTUS *to join the conspiracy, and the assassination of* CAESAR *is carried out on the ides of March in the senate house. After* CAESAR *falls dead at the base of the statue of his old rival,* POMPEY, MARK ANTONY *enters. Over* CASSIUS'S *objections,* BRUTUS *gives* ANTONY *permission to address the crowd at* CAESAR'S *funeral, but he makes* ANTONY *promise to say nothing critical of the conspirators.*

Scene 2. *The Forum.*

Enter BRUTUS *and goes into the pulpit, and* CASSIUS, *with the* PLEBEIANS.[1]

Plebeians.
We will be satisfied! Let us be satisfied!

Brutus.
Then follow me, and give me audience, friends.
Cassius, go you into the other street
And part the numbers.
Those that will hear me speak, let 'em stay here;
Those that will follow Cassius, go with him;
And public reasons shall be renderèd
Of Caesar's death.

First Plebeian.　　I will hear Brutus speak.

Second Plebeian.
I will hear Cassius, and compare their reasons,
When severally we hear them renderèd.

[*Exit* CASSIUS, *with some of the* PLEBEIANS.]

Third Plebeian.
The noble Brutus is ascended. Silence!

Brutus. Be patient till the last.

> Romans, countrymen, and lovers, hear me for my
> cause, and be silent, that you may hear. Believe me
> for mine honor, and have respect to mine honor, that
> you may believe. Censure[2] me in your wisdom, and
> awake your senses,[3] that you may the better judge.
> If there be any in this assembly, any dear friend of
> Caesar's, to him I say that Brutus' love to Caesar
> was no less than his. If then that friend demand why
> Brutus rose against Caesar, this is my answer: Not

10

20

---

1. **Plebeians:** the common people.
2. **Censure:** judge.
3. **senses:** reasoning powers.

INTERPRET

This scene is wild and noisy. What is Brutus's mood as he fights free of the people and goes up to the pulpit to speak?

INFER

Why do you think Shakespeare has Brutus deliver his speech in **prose,** rather than in **blank verse**?

BUILD FLUENCY

Read lines 13–35 aloud as expressively as you can, focusing on **rhythm, repetition, balance,** and **parallel structure.**

_____

_____

_____

_____

_____

_____

PREDICT

Why might it have been a mistake for Brutus to allow Antony to bear Caesar's body into the Forum?

_____

_____

_____

_____

_____

INTERPRET

What does the Third Plebeian's remark "Let him be Caesar" suggest about the mob?

_____

_____

_____

_____

_____

_____

_____

that I loved Caesar less, but that I loved Rome more. Had you rather Caesar were living, and die all slaves, than that Caesar were dead, to live all free men? As Caesar loved me, I weep for him; as he was fortunate, I rejoice at it; as he was valiant, I honor him; but, as he was ambitious, I slew him. There is tears, for his love; joy, for his fortune; honor, for his valor; and death, for his ambition. Who is here so base, that would be a bondman?[4] If any, speak; for him have I offended. Who is here so rude,[5] that would not be a Roman? If any, speak; for him have I offended. Who is here so vile, that will not love his country? If any, speak; for him have I offended. I pause for a reply.

All. None, Brutus, none!

Brutus.

Then none have I offended. I have done no more to Caesar than you shall do to Brutus. The question of his death is enrolled[6] in the Capitol; his glory not extenuated,[7] wherein he was worthy, nor his offenses enforced,[8] for which he suffered death.

[*Enter* MARK ANTONY, *with Caesar's body.*]

Here comes his body, mourned by Mark Antony, who, though he had no hand in his death, shall receive the benefit of his dying, a place in the commonwealth, as which of you shall not? With this I depart, that, as I slew my best lover for the good of Rome, I have the same dagger for myself, when it shall please my country to need my death.

All. Live, Brutus! Live, live!

First Plebeian.

Bring him with triumph home unto his house.

Second Plebeian.

Give him a statue with his ancestors.

Third Plebeian.

Let him be Caesar.

Fourth Plebeian. Caesar's better parts[9]

Shall be crowned in Brutus.

30

40

50

---

4. **bondman:** slave.
5. **rude:** rough and uncivilized.
6. In other words, there is a record of the reasons he was killed.
7. **extenuated:** lessened.
8. **enforced:** exaggerated.
9. **better parts:** better qualities.

First Plebeian.

We'll bring him to his house with shouts and clamors.

Brutus. My countrymen—

Second Plebeian.   Peace! Silence! Brutus speaks.

First Plebeian. Peace, ho!

Brutus.

Good countrymen, let me depart alone,

And, for my sake, stay here with Antony.

60   Do grace to Caesar's corpse, and grace his speech[10]

Tending to Caesar's glories, which Mark Antony

By our permission, is allowed to make.

I do entreat you, not a man depart,

Save I alone, till Antony have spoke.   [*Exit.*]

First Plebeian.

Stay, ho! And let us hear Mark Antony.

Third Plebeian.

Let him go up into the public chair;[11]

We'll hear him. Noble Antony, go up.

Antony.

For Brutus' sake, I am beholding to you.

Fourth Plebeian.

What does he say of Brutus?

Third Plebeian.   He says, for Brutus' sake,

70   He finds himself beholding to us all.

Fourth Plebeian.

'Twere best he speak no harm of Brutus here!

First Plebeian.

This Caesar was a tyrant.

Third Plebeian.   Nay, that's certain.

We are blest that Rome is rid of him.

Second Plebeian.

Peace! Let us hear what Antony can say.

Antony.

You gentle Romans—

All.   Peace, ho! Let us hear him.

Antony.

> Friends, Romans, countrymen, lend me your ears;
> I come to bury Caesar, not to praise him.
> The evil that men do lives after them,
> The good is oft interrèd with their bones;
80 > So let it be with Caesar. The noble Brutus
> Hath told you Caesar was ambitious.

---

10. **grace his speech:** listen respectfully to Antony's funeral oration.
11. **public chair:** pulpit or rostrum.

IDENTIFY

Antony's speech is one of literature's most famous examples of **verbal irony**— the use of words to suggest the opposite of their usual meaning. Underline examples of verbal irony in the speech.

IDENTIFY

Where does Antony use **repetition** effectively in this speech? Circle the words.

BUILD FLUENCY

Read lines 76–110 aloud as expressively as you can, using techniques that would be appropriate for a public speech to a large crowd.

INTERPRET

Why do you think Antony picks Brutus, not Cassius or the other conspirators, as the target of his attack?

_____

_____

_____

_____

_____

_____

_____

_____

_____

PREDICT

What do the plebeians' initial comments about Antony's speech **foreshadow**?

_____

_____

_____

_____

_____

_____

_____

_____

_____

If it were so, it was a grievous fault,
And grievously hath Caesar answered[12] it.
Here, under leave of Brutus and the rest
(For Brutus is an honorable man,
So are they all, all honorable men),
Come I to speak in Caesar's funeral.
He was my friend, faithful and just to me;
But Brutus says he was ambitious,
90   And Brutus is an honorable man.
He hath brought many captives home to Rome,
Whose ransoms did the general coffers[13] fill;
Did this in Caesar seem ambitious?
When that the poor have cried, Caesar hath wept;
Ambition should be made of sterner stuff.
Yet Brutus says he was ambitious;
And Brutus is an honorable man.
You all did see that on the Lupercal
I thrice presented him a kingly crown,
100   Which he did thrice refuse. Was this ambition?
Yet Brutus says he was ambitious;
And sure he is an honorable man.
I speak not to disprove what Brutus spoke,
But here I am to speak what I do know.
You all did love him once, not without cause;
What cause withholds you then to mourn for him?
O judgment, thou art fled to brutish beasts,
And men have lost their reason! Bear with me;
My heart is in the coffin there with Caesar,
110   And I must pause till it come back to me.

First Plebeian.
    Methinks there is much reason in his sayings.
Second Plebeian.
    If thou consider rightly of the matter,
    Caesar has had great wrong.
Third Plebeian.   Has he, masters?
    I fear there will a worse come in his place.
Fourth Plebeian.
    Marked ye his words? He would not take the crown,
    Therefore 'tis certain he was not ambitious.
First Plebeian.
    If it be found so, some will dear abide it.[14]

---

12. **answered:** paid the penalty for.
13. **general coffers:** public funds.
14. **dear abide it:** pay dearly for it.

Second Plebeian.

Poor soul, his eyes are red as fire with weeping.

Third Plebeian.

There's not a nobler man in Rome than Antony.

Fourth Plebeian.

120 Now mark him, he begins again to speak.

Antony.

But yesterday the word of Caesar might

Have stood against the world; now lies he there,

And none so poor to¹⁵ do him reverence.

O masters! If I were disposed to stir

Your hearts and minds to mutiny and rage,

I should do Brutus wrong and Cassius wrong,

Who, you all know, are honorable men.

I will not do them wrong; I rather choose

To wrong the dead, to wrong myself and you,

130 Than I will wrong such honorable men.

But here's a parchment with the seal of Caesar;

I found it in his closet; 'tis his will.

Let but the commons hear this testament,

Which, pardon me, I do not mean to read,

And they would go and kiss dead Caesar's wounds,

And dip their napkins¹⁶ in his sacred blood;

Yea, beg a hair of him for memory,

And dying, mention it within their wills,

Bequeathing it as a rich legacy

140 Unto their issue.¹⁷

Fourth Plebeian.

We'll hear the will; read it, Mark Antony.

All. The will, the will! We will hear Caesar's will!

Antony.

Have patience, gentle friends, I must not read it.

It is not meet you know how Caesar loved you.

You are not wood, you are not stones, but men;

And being men, hearing the will of Caesar,

It will inflame you, it will make you mad.

'Tis good you know not that you are his heirs;

For if you should, O, what would come of it?

Fourth Plebeian.

150 Read the will! We'll hear it, Antony!

You shall read us the will, Caesar's will!

---

15. **so poor to:** so low in rank as to.
16. **napkins:** handkerchiefs.
17. **issue:** children; heirs.

EVALUATE

Do you think a crowd could really be swayed as easily as the plebeians are? Explain.

VISUALIZE

How do you visualize the placement of the actors at this point? Where is Caesar's body?

INFER

How do you know that Antony is making up this information about the assassination?

Antony.

Will you be patient? Will you stay awhile?

I have o'ershot myself[18] to tell you of it.

I fear I wrong the honorable men

Whose daggers have stabbed Caesar; I do fear it.

Fourth Plebeian.

They were traitors. Honorable men!

All. The will! The testament!

Second Plebeian. They were villains, murderers! The

will! Read the will!

Antony.

160   You will compel me then to read the will?

Then make a ring about the corpse of Caesar,

And let me show you him that made the will.

Shall I descend? And will you give me leave?

All. Come down.

Second Plebeian. Descend.

[ANTONY *comes down.*]

Third Plebeian. You shall have leave.

Fourth Plebeian. A ring! Stand round.

First Plebeian.

Stand from the hearse, stand from the body!

Second Plebeian.

Room for Antony, most noble Antony!

Antony.

Nay, press not so upon me; stand far off.

170   **All.** Stand back! Room! Bear back.

Antony.

If you have tears, prepare to shed them now.

You all do know this mantle; I remember

The first time ever Caesar put it on:

'Twas on a summer's evening, in his tent,

That day he overcame the Nervii.[19]

Look, in this place ran Cassius' dagger through;

See what a rent the envious[20] Casca made;

Through this the well-belovèd Brutus stabbed,

And as he plucked his cursèd steel away,

180   Mark how the blood of Caesar followed it,

As rushing out of doors, to be resolved

If Brutus so unkindly knocked, or no;

---

18. **o'ershot myself:** gone farther than I intended.
19. **Nervii:** one of the tribes conquered by Caesar, in 57 B.C.
20. **envious:** spiteful.

For Brutus, as you know, was Caesar's angel.
Judge, O you gods, how dearly Caesar loved him!
This was the most unkindest cut of all;
For when the noble Caesar saw him stab,
Ingratitude, more strong than traitors' arms,
Quite vanquished him. Then burst his mighty heart;
And, in his mantle muffling up his face,
190 Even at the base of Pompey's statue[21]
(Which all the while ran blood) great Caesar fell.
O, what a fall was there, my countrymen!
Then I, and you, and all of us fell down,
Whilst bloody treason flourished over us.
O, now you weep, and I perceive you feel
The dint[22] of pity; these are gracious drops.
Kind souls, what weep you when you but behold
Our Caesar's vesture[23] wounded? Look you here,
Here is himself, marred as you see with traitors.

200 **First Plebeian.** O piteous spectacle!

Second Plebeian. O noble Caesar!

Third Plebeian. O woeful day!

Fourth Plebeian. O traitors, villains!

First Plebeian. O most bloody sight!

Second Plebeian. We will be revenged.

All. Revenge! About! Seek! Burn! Fire! Kill! Slay! Let not
a traitor live!

Antony. Stay, countrymen.

First Plebeian. Peace there! Hear the noble Antony.

210 **Second Plebeian.** We'll hear him, we'll follow him, we'll
die with him!

Antony.
Good friends, sweet friends, let me not stir you up
To such a sudden flood of mutiny.
They that have done this deed are honorable.
What private griefs[24] they have, alas, I know not,
That made them do it. They are wise and honorable,
And will, no doubt, with reasons answer you.
I come not, friends, to steal away your hearts;
I am no orator, as Brutus is;
220 But (as you know me all) a plain blunt man
That love my friend, and that they know full well
That gave me public leave to speak of him.

---

21. **statue:** pronounced in three syllables.
22. **dint:** stroke.
23. **vesture:** clothing.
24. **griefs:** grievances.

PREDICT

Why might the end of Antony's address be the **turning point** of the play as a whole?

INTERPRET

Why does Antony say he does not know what "private griefs" motivated the conspirators?

EVALUATE

Would you agree with Antony's assessment of himself as someone who does not have "the power of speech/To stir men's blood"? Explain.

_____

_____

_____

_____

_____

_____

_____

_____

_____

INFER

Why does Antony remind the crowd about the will?

_____

_____

_____

_____

_____

_____

_____

_____

_____

_____

For I have neither writ, nor words, nor worth,
Action, nor utterance, nor the power of speech
To stir men's blood; I only speak right on.
I tell you that which you yourselves do know,
Show you sweet Caesar's wounds, poor poor dumb
    mouths,
And bid them speak for me. But were I Brutus,
And Brutus Antony, there were an Antony
230   Would ruffle up your spirits, and put a tongue
In every wound of Caesar that would move
The stones of Rome to rise and mutiny.

All.
We'll mutiny.

First Plebeian. We'll burn the house of Brutus.

Third Plebeian.
Away, then! Come, seek the conspirators.

Antony.
Yet hear me, countrymen. Yet hear me speak.

All.
Peace, ho! Hear Antony, most noble Antony!

Antony.
Why, friends, you go to do you know not what:
Wherein hath Caesar thus deserved your loves?
Alas, you know not; I must tell you then:
240   You have forgot the will I told you of.

All.
Most true, the will! Let's stay and hear the will.

Antony.
Here is the will, and under Caesar's seal.
To every Roman citizen he gives,
To every several[25] man, seventy-five drachmas.[26]

Second Plebeian.
Most noble Caesar! We'll revenge his death!

Third Plebeian. O royal Caesar!

Antony. Hear me with patience.

All. Peace, ho!

Antony.
Moreover, he hath left you all his walks,
250   His private arbors, and new-planted orchards,
On this side Tiber; he hath left them you,
And to your heirs forever: common pleasures,[27]

---

25. **several:** individual.
26. **drachmas:** silver coins (Greek currency).
27. **common pleasures:** public recreation areas.

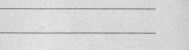

To walk abroad and recreate yourselves.

Here was a Caesar! When comes such another?

First Plebeian.

Never, never! Come, away, away!

We'll burn his body in the holy place,

And with the brands fire the traitors' houses.

Take up the body.

Second Plebeian. Go fetch fire.

Third Plebeian. Pluck down benches.

260 **Fourth Plebeian.** Pluck down forms, windows,[28] anything!

[*Exeunt* PLEBEIANS *with the body*.]

Antony.

Now let it work: Mischief, thou art afoot,

Take thou what course thou wilt.

[*Enter* SERVANT.]

How now, fellow?

Servant.

Sir, Octavius is already come to Rome.

Antony. Where is he?

Servant.

He and Lepidus are at Caesar's house.

Antony.

And thither will I straight to visit him;

He comes upon a wish. Fortune is merry,

And in this mood will give us anything.

Servant.

I heard him say, Brutus and Cassius

270 Are rid[29] like madmen through the gates of Rome.

Antony.

Belike[30] they had some notice of the people,

How I had moved them. Bring me to Octavius.

[*Exeunt*.]

EVALUATE

Do you think that the oratorical methods Mark Antony uses to "move" the people are unscrupulous? Why or why not?

---

28. forms, windows: long benches and shutters.
29. Are rid: have ridden.
30. Belike: probably.

The Tragedy of Julius Caesar, Act III, Scene 2

Persuasion

Persuasion is a type of writing or speaking designed to change the way a reader or listener thinks or acts. Persuasive writing can be found in speeches, newspaper editorials, essays, articles, and advertisements.

In *Julius Caesar,* Mark Antony plays a relatively minor role in the play until Act III, when he becomes the major force driving the action. This transformation occurs largely because of Antony's skill as an orator. Carefully re-read his speech to the crowd, which is divided into five major parts or movements: lines 76–110, 121–140, 143–149, 171–199, and 212–232. Then, explain how each element shown in the left-hand chart below contributes to Antony's persuasive purpose.

Elements/Stage Directions	Persuasive Function
1. blank verse (rather than prose)	
2. verbal irony	
3. repetition	
4. the presence of Caesar's body	
5. the references to Caesar's will	

Vocabulary: How to Own a Word

Developing Vocabulary

Carefully read each word's definition, explanation, and sample sentence. Then, write a sentence of your own using that word.

1. **censure** (sen'shər) *v.:* to express strong disapproval of. In modern times this word has taken on the meaning "to blame or criticize."

The state legislature passed a resolution to censure the governor for misconduct.

Original sentence: _____

_____

2. **interred** (in·turd') *adj.:* a form of the verb *inter,* which means "to bury." This word combines the prefix *in-,* here meaning "into," with the Latin word *terra,* meaning "earth."

The dog quickly located the interred beef bone and dug it up.

Original sentence: _____

_____

3. **bequeathing** (bē·kwēth'iŋ) *v.:* a form of *bequeath,* which means "to give by will" or "to hand down." This word is from the Old English word *becwethan,* having the same definition.

The king declared, "When I die, I am bequeathing my gold to my oldest daughter."

Original sentence: _____

_____

4. **legacy** (leg'ə·sē) *n.:* an inheritance; anything handed down from an ancestor. This word derives from a Latin word meaning "to send as an ambassador."

Sharon's only legacy from her father was a gold watch.

Original sentence: _____

_____

The Parable of the Prodigal Son; The Prodigal

Make the Connection

Forgive and Forget

The parable of the prodigal son is one of the most famous stories in world literature about the theme of forgiveness—a value that is championed by many of the major world religions and ethical systems.

What is your view of forgiveness? Are there both advantages and disadvantages to the action of forgiving? What features of human nature sometimes make it hard for us to forgive certain actions by other people? In the space below, write a few sentences in which you state and discuss your opinions.

_____
_____
_____
_____
_____
_____
_____
_____
_____
_____
_____
_____
_____
_____
_____
_____
_____
_____

The Parable of the Prodigal Son

New English Bible

The Prodigal

Elizabeth Bishop

IDENTIFY

The word *prodigal* means "extravagant" or "recklessly wasteful." What is the prodigal son forced to do after he squanders his inheritance?

_____

_____

_____

_____

PREDICT

How do you think the father will react to the homecoming of the younger son?

_____

_____

_____

_____

IDENTIFY

Underline the two comparisons the father uses for his son in this speech.

_____

_____

_____

_____

INTERPRET

What is the moral lesson of this **parable** in your view? Explain your answer.

_____

_____

_____

_____

_____

The Parable of the Prodigal Son
New English Bible

There was once a man who had two sons, and the younger said to his father, "Father, give me my share of the property." So he divided his estate between them. A few days later the younger son turned the whole of his share into cash and left home for a distant country, where he squandered it in reckless living. He had spent it all, when a severe famine fell upon that country and he began to feel the pinch.

So he went and attached himself to one of the local landowners, who sent him on to his farm to mind the pigs. He would have been glad to fill his belly with the pods that the pigs were eating; and no one gave him 10 anything. Then he came to his senses and said, "How many of my father's paid servants have more food than they can eat, and here am I, starving to death! I will set off and go to my father and say to him, 'Father, I have sinned, against God and against you; I am no longer fit to be called your son; treat me as one of your paid servants.'"

So he set out for his father's house. But while he was still a long way off, his father saw him, and his heart went out to him. He ran to meet him, flung his arms round him, and kissed him. The son said, "Father, I have sinned, against God and against you; I am no longer fit to be called your son."

20 But the father said to his servants, "Quick! fetch a robe, my best one, and put it on him; put a ring on his finger and shoes on his feet. Bring the fatted calf and kill it, and let us have a feast to celebrate the day. For this son of mine was dead and has come back to life; he was lost and is found." And the festivities began.

Now the elder son was out on the farm; and on his way back, as he approached the house, he heard music and dancing. He called one of the servants and asked what it meant. The servant told him, "Your brother has come home, and your father has killed the fatted calf because he has him back safe and sound."

30 But he was angry and refused to go in. His father came out and pleaded with him; but he retorted, "You know how I have slaved for you all these years; I never once disobeyed your orders; and you never gave me so much as a kid,[1] for a feast with my friends. But now that this son of yours turns up, after running through your money with his women, you kill the fatted calf for him."

"My boy," said the father, "you are always with me, and everything I have is yours. How could we help celebrating this happy day? Your brother here was dead and has come back to life, was lost and is found."

—Luke 15:11–32

---

1. **kid:** young goat.

The Prodigal

Elizabeth Bishop

The brown enormous odor he lived by
was too close, with its breathing and thick hair,
for him to judge. The floor was rotten; the sty[1]
was plastered halfway up with glass-smooth dung.
Light-lashed, self-righteous, above moving snouts,
the pigs' eyes followed him, a cheerful stare—
even to the sow[2] that always ate her young—
till, sickening, he leaned to scratch her head.
But sometimes mornings after drinking bouts
10 (he hid the pints behind a two-by-four),
the sunrise glazed the barnyard mud with red;
the burning puddles seemed to reassure.
And then he thought he almost might endure
his exile yet another year or more.

But evenings the first star came to warn.
The farmer whom he worked for came at dark
to shut the cows and horses in the barn
beneath their overhanging clouds of hay,
with pitchforks, faint forked lightnings, catching light,
20 safe and companionable as in the Ark.[3]
The pigs stuck out their little feet and snored.
The lantern—like the sun, going away—
laid on the mud a pacing aureole.[4]
Carrying a bucket along a slimy board,
he felt the bats' uncertain staggering flight,
his shuddering insights, beyond his control,
touching him. But it took him a long time
finally to make his mind up to go home.

---

1. **sty:** pen for pigs.
2. **sow:** adult female pig.
3. **Ark:** In the story of the flood in the Bible, the ark was a boat in which Noah, his family, and two of every kind of creature survived.
4. **aureole:** illuminated area around the sun or a light when seen in a mist; also, the halo or radiance encircling the head or body of a holy person in religious paintings.

INTERPRET

What is the meaning of the poem's first sentence (lines 1–3)?

INTERPRET

What details from the Biblical parable have been elaborated in the poem?

INTERPRET

Why do you think it takes so long for him to make up his mind?

Parable and Allegory

A **parable** is a short, simple story about ordinary events and human characters that teaches a moral lesson about life. A parable may contain elements of **allegory,** or a narrative in which the characters, settings, and events stand for certain other people, events, or ideas.

The parable of the prodigal son is often interpreted allegorically. Match each of the features in the first column below with one of the allegorical interpretations from the following list. Write the letter of the allegorical meaning in the second column, and in the third column give at least one reason for your choice.

Allegorical Interpretations

a. a righteous person   **e.** hell

b. forgiveness of sin   **f.** sinful actions

c. God the father   **g.** a sinner

d. heaven   **h.** repentance for sin

Feature	Allegorical Meaning	Reason(s) for Your Choice
1. a father who had two sons		
2. the younger son		
3. the older son		
4. riotous living		
5. the father's welcome		
6. the youngest son's apology		
7. the pigsty		
8. the father's house		

Vocabulary: How to Own a Word

Word Maps

Below are four word maps, partially filled out. At the center of each map is a word from one of the selections. To the north is a space for the definition of the word as it is used in the selection; to the west is a space for a synonym; to the east is a space for an antonym; and to the south is a space for images or feelings you might associate with the word. Complete each map.

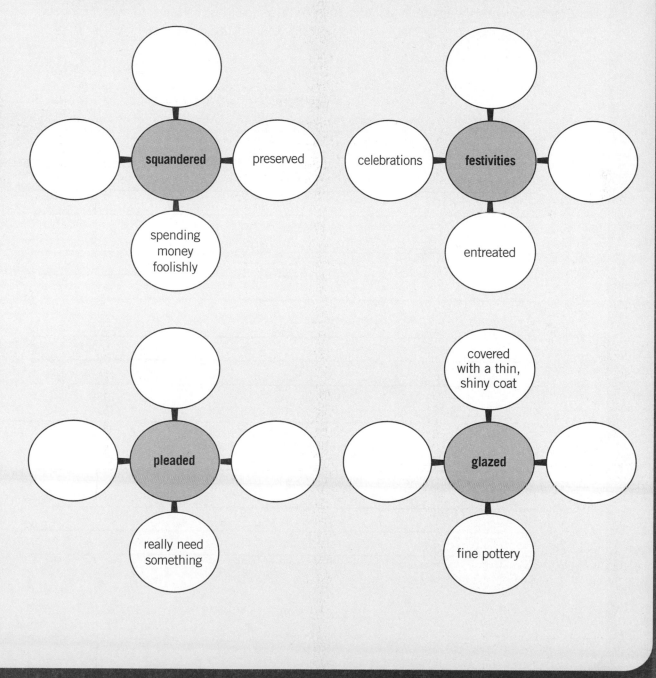

The Sword in the Stone

Make the Connection

What Makes a Hero?

Who are your real heroes, and why do you regard them as heroic? In the space below, name a person you admire. Your hero can be living or dead, a character from literature or mythology, or a person from real life. Then, list five qualities, personality traits, or accomplishments that you associate with the word *hero*. Briefly explain the significance of each item on your list.

My Hero:

_____

1. _____
   _____
   _____

2. _____
   _____
   _____

3. _____
   _____
   _____

4. _____
   _____
   _____

5. _____
   _____
   _____

IDENTIFY

What is the **setting** of this story? Underline the words that give the time and place where the events unfold.

_____

_____

_____

_____

_____

_____

INFER

What might "RIGHTWYS KYNGE BORNE" mean?

_____

_____

_____

_____

_____

_____

_____

_____

_____

_____

_____

INTERPRET

Why is Arthur able to free the sword from the stone without effort or forethought?

_____

_____

_____

_____

_____

_____

_____

During the years that followed the death of King Uther, while Arthur was still a child, the ambitious barons fought one another for the throne, and the whole of Britain stood in jeopardy. Finally the day came when the Archbishop of Canterbury, on the advice of Merlin, summoned the nobility to London for Christmas morning. In his message the archbishop promised that the true succession to the British throne would be miraculously revealed. Many of the nobles purified themselves during their journey, in the hope that it would be to them that the succession would fall.

10   The archbishop held his service in the city's greatest church (St. Paul's), and when matins[1] were done, the congregation filed out to the yard. They were confronted by a marble block into which had been thrust a beautiful sword. The block was four feet square, and the sword passed through a steel anvil which had been struck in the stone and which projected a foot from it. The anvil had been inscribed with letters of gold:

> WHOSO PULLETH OUTE THIS SWERD OF THIS STONE AND ANVYLD IS RIGHTWYS KYNGE BORNE OF ALL BRYTAYGNE

The congregation was awed by this miraculous sight, but the
20 archbishop forbade anyone to touch the sword before Mass had been heard. After Mass, many of the nobles tried to pull the sword out of the stone, but none was able to, so a watch of ten knights was set over the sword, and a tournament proclaimed for New Year's Day, to provide men of noble blood with the opportunity of proving their right to the succession.

Sir Ector, who had been living on an estate near London, rode to the tournament with Arthur and his own son Sir Kay, who had been recently knighted. When they arrived at the tournament, Sir Kay found to his annoyance that his sword was missing from its sheath, so he begged
30 Arthur to ride back and fetch it from their lodging.

Arthur found the door of the lodging locked and bolted, the landlord and his wife having left for the tournament. In order not to disappoint his brother, he rode on to St. Paul's, determined to get for him the sword which was lodged in the stone. The yard was empty, the guard also having slipped off to see the tournament, so Arthur strode up to the sword and, without troubling to read the inscription, tugged it free. He then rode straight back to Sir Kay and presented him with it.

Sir Kay recognized the sword and, taking it to Sir Ector, said, "Father, the succession falls to me, for I have here the sword that was lodged
40 in the stone." But Sir Ector insisted that they should all ride to the churchyard, and once there, bound Sir Kay by oath to tell how he had

---

1. **matins** (mat′′nz): morning prayers.

come by the sword. Sir Kay then admitted that Arthur had given it to him. Sir Ector turned to Arthur and said, "Was the sword not guarded?"

"It was not," Arthur replied.

"Would you please thrust it into the stone again?" said Sir Ector. Arthur did so, and first Sir Ector and then Sir Kay tried to remove it, but both were unable to. Then Arthur, for the second time, pulled it out. Sir Ector and Sir Kay both knelt before him.

"Why," said Arthur, "do you both kneel before me?"

50 "My lord," Sir Ector replied, "there is only one man living who can draw the sword from the stone, and he is the true-born king of Britain." Sir Ector then told Arthur the story of his birth and upbringing.

"My dear father," said Arthur, "for so I shall always think of you—if, as you say, I am to be king, please know that any request you have to make is already granted."

Sir Ector asked that Sir Kay should be made royal seneschal,[2] and Arthur declared that while they both lived it should be so. Then the three of them visited the archbishop and told him what had taken place.

All those dukes and barons with ambitions to rule were present at 60 the tournament on New Year's Day. But when all of them had failed, and Arthur alone had succeeded in drawing the sword from the stone, they protested against one so young, and of ignoble blood, succeeding to the throne.

The secret of Arthur's birth was known to only a few of the nobles surviving from the days of King Uther. The archbishop urged them to make Arthur's cause their own; but their support proved ineffective. The tournament was repeated at Candlemas[3] and at Easter, with the same outcome as before.

Finally, at Pentecost,[4] when once more Arthur alone had been able 70 to remove the sword, the commoners arose with a tumultuous cry and demanded that Arthur should at once be made king. The nobles, knowing in their hearts that the commoners were right, all knelt before Arthur and begged forgiveness for having delayed his succession for so long. Arthur forgave them and then, offering his sword at the high altar, was dubbed first knight of the realm. The coronation took place a few days later, when Arthur swore to rule justly, and the nobles swore him their allegiance.

---

2. **royal seneschal** (sɛn′ə·shəl): person in charge of the king's household. This was a powerful and respected position.

3. **Candlemas:** Christian festival that honors the purification of the Virgin Mary after the birth of Jesus. It falls on February 2.

4. **Pentecost:** Christian festival celebrated on the seventh Sunday after Easter, commemorating the descent of the Holy Spirit upon the Apostles.

INTERPRET

A **character foil** highlights another character's personality by displaying contrasting traits. How is Sir Kay a foil to Arthur?

_____
_____
_____
_____
_____
_____

RETELL

Why wasn't Arthur allowed to become king immediately after pulling the sword from the stone?

_____
_____
_____
_____
_____
_____

INTERPRET

What is the significance of Arthur offering his sword at the high altar?

_____
_____
_____
_____
_____
_____
_____
_____

Romance

A romance is a story, usually in verse, about the adventures of a **hero** who undertakes a quest to achieve some goal. Romances were one of the most popular literary forms in medieval times, especially in England and France.

The critic Northrop Frye wrote that the hero of a romance exists "in a world in which the ordinary laws of nature are slightly suspended." What elements of magic separate romance from more ordinary?

_____

_____

_____

_____

_____

_____

_____

_____

The hero is usually mysterious. He is often raised in obscurity before coming into his own. His quest is often a model for society as a whole. How does the hero embody the values of his society? Why do you think people so enjoy these stories about a character who starts out as an underdog but who then turns out to be a real hero?

_____

_____

_____

_____

_____

_____

_____

_____

Vocabulary: How to Own a Word

Column Match

For each word in Column A, write the letter of the correct definition shown in Column B.

Column A

_____ **1.** jeopardy

_____ **2.** congregation

_____ **3.** lodging

_____ **4.** ignoble

_____ **5.** tumultuous

Column B

a. temporary accommodation

b. noisy; turbulent

c. danger; peril

d. gathering of people for religious worship

e. dishonorable; of low birth

PART 2 READING INFORMATIONAL MATERIALS

Taste—the Final Frontier

Make the Connection

Generating Research Questions

When you set out to do a research project, your first step is to generate research questions that will yield specific, relevant information. Here are some guidelines for generating productive research questions:

- **Stay focused.** Don't write a long list of questions that cover everything about a broad, general subject. Instead, focus on one aspect of your subject, and stick to questions about your narrowed topic. Try to identify the **main idea** of your topic to better focus your questions.
- **Check the subheads.** In an informational article, subheads indicate smaller divisions of the article's subject. They may give you ideas for a limited topic to research.
- **Do what reporters do.** Research questions that can be answered with "yes" or "no" will get you nowhere. When reporters investigate a story, their questions begin with *Who, What, Where, When, Why,* and *How?* Asking these **"5W and How questions"** will lead you to specific information.
- **Be realistic.** Ask questions that you think you can answer with the resources available to you. For example:

Will future space travelers be able to eat fresh foods cultivated in space?

The following article discusses this very question. Before you read it, though, use the prompts below to generate six questions about this topic that might lead to productive research later.

Who?	
What?	
Where?	
When?	
Why?	
How?	

FROM *The Guardian*, April 21, 2000

Esther Addley

Final Frontier

WORDS TO OWN

breached (brēcht) *v.* used as an *adj.*: broken through.

INFER

Lines 9–15 provide specific, relevant information about the topic. Reconstruct the **research question** that likely led the reporter to seek this information.

_____

_____

_____

_____

_____

WORDS TO OWN

palatable (pal'it·ə·bəl) *adj.*: tasty; fit to be eaten or drunk.
rancid (ran'sid) *adj.*: stale or spoiled.

_____

_____

WORDS TO OWN

mutiny (myōōt''n·ē) *n.*: rebellion or revolt against authority.
impoverished (im·päv'ər·isht) *v.* used as an *adj.*: poor; without funds.
habitat (hab'i·tat') *n.*: a person's environment or living space.

_____

_____

_____

_____

_____

Yuri Gagarin's first trip into space on April 12, 1961, was a brief one, which is perhaps just as well. If he'd stayed up any longer than his brief 108-minute orbit, he might have started getting peckish.[1] And since no one had any idea whether humans could swallow in zero gravity, he hadn't been allowed to take any food. The Soviets were ignoring the recommendations of the British interplanetary society in 1939, which advised that astronauts should be fattened up in advance, then given a daily pound of butter while on board to fulfill their calorific needs.

10   Space nutrition has completed several missions of its own in the four decades since the final frontier was breached, and the popular image of high-protein slop that tastes like liquidized cardboard is now largely outdated. But while the presentation may have improved, astronauts broadly agree that food in space has remained pretty awful since John Glenn returned from his mission in 1962 demanding a real sandwich instead of mush in a tube.

The way we feed ourselves in space has actually changed very little. Foods are freeze-dried and vacuum-packed to weigh next to nothing; when you feel like lunch you select a sachet,[2] add water, stir, and suck it out of the carton. Delicious.

20   The main challenge in cooking for long-haul astronauts, as anyone who has taken a transatlantic flight will know, is making the food palatable. NASA is careful to supply every vitamin, mineral, and calorie an astronaut requires, calculated to the minutest scale. But that doesn't mean it tastes nice. French astronaut Jean-Loup Chrétien described the Russian prepacked pot noodles on Mir as tasting like "rancid almonds"; his countryman Richard Filippi was so appalled at the menus that he devised a culinary art he called "gastronautics" to cater to the space station's final missions. "It was clearly unacceptable that a Frenchman should eat poorly in space," said Filippi. "Something had to be done."

30   Astronauts, he figured, are like armies; they march—or spacewalk—on their stomachs.

It's not just that astronauts are fussy eaters. Russian cosmonauts were rumoured at one point to be close to mutiny, so bad was the food provided by their impoverished space agency. "It is extremely important that you have a varied diet in space," says Jean Hunter, associate professor of agricultural and biological engineering at Cornell University. "Food assumes an especially large role in psychological support of the crew. The astronauts are living in a habitat that doesn't change from day to day, so the most reliable source of variety in those conditions comes

40   from the food."

The main gripe, unsurprisingly, is that nothing is fresh. Despite the introduction of refrigeration facilities, a locker of fresh apples and

_____

1. **peckish** *adj.*: (chiefly British) slightly hungry.
2. **sachet** (sa·shā') *n.*: (chiefly British) small bag.

oranges will last only 48 hours. Then it's back to cartons, cans, and hot water, at least until a considerate shuttle drops by.

The solution? Grow the crops yourself. As well as providing variety, space crops would allow a future colony to be more self-sufficient. And it's not such a distant prospect. NASA has been investigating for some years the possibility of growing crops in space—artificially lit, watered, and temperature-controlled, of course. The atmosphere of Mars, 95%

50 carbon dioxide, could be relatively easily managed for grain or vegetable production, the byproduct oxygen being used to produce water combined with imported hydrogen. And if the claims of ice having been discovered on the moon prove true, agriculture galactic-style could really be in business.

Enter Hunter and her colleagues at Cornell. Raw grain or potato, after all, is unlikely to prove any more popular than in freeze-dried form. What astronauts will need is recipes, culinary tips, a cookbook. And this month 16 volunteers completed the first extended trial of moon food, for 30 days eating nothing but food that could, in theory, be grown and

60 harvested on the moon or Mars.

"We developed more than 200 recipes using plants that could be grown in a lunar colony, in hydroponic cultures (i.e., using nutrient-enriched fluid instead of soil) with artificial lighting, and looked at the ways they would have to be processed to turn them into food that people would want to eat," says Hunter.

Considering the restrictions on which plants can be cultivated—they need to be short, high yielding, and require little maintenance—the potential variety of diet is impressive. Rice, wheat, potato, sweet potato, tomato, and other vegetables are all seen as prime candidates. Soy beans

70 would give oil and milk; meat substitute could be made from wheat. With <u>judicious</u> use of flavoring, believe the researchers, the food produced could be extremely tasty. Sweet potato pancakes, lentil loaf sandwiches, or chocolate soy candy, anyone?

Rupert Spies, senior lecturer at the university's school of hotel administration and developer of most of the recipes, admits to being frustrated that all Mars menus must be low in salt, but says he got round it by adding "a lot of herbs." "The lack of salt is very important because it affects the <u>metabolism</u> in space. Salt and bone loss is a very specific issue if you are in microgravity."

80 At this stage, of course, all the recipes are necessarily vegan[3]—tethering a cow to a star-spangled banner on the surface of the moon is not yet a viable option. But not all animal protein will eventually need to be imported. "It is a very, very long way off until we will be farming animals in space," says Hunter. "But it does seem likely that the first

---

3. vegan (vē′gən) *adj.:* vegetarian and not using any animal protein.

90

Research Question Chart

Background information—information a writer uses to support a main idea or to describe an aspect of the topic—can often spark questions that lead to further research. Below is a list of facts or statements from the article you've just read. In the column to the right, try to come up with a question or two about the statement that might lead to further research.

Facts	Research Questions
The British interplanetary society in 1939 advised astronauts to fatten up before space travel and consume a pound of butter a day to fulfill their calorific needs.	
Richard Filippi devised a culinary art called "gastronautics" to cater to the space station Mir's final missions.	
Astronauts' most reliable source of variety during space travel is their food.	
Plants need to be short, high yielding, and require low maintenance to be cultivated in space.	
Salt and bone loss is a concern in microgravity.	

Analyzing Informational Materials

Reading Check

1. What is the astronauts' main complaint about food in space?

_____

_____

2. Why do astronauts use freeze-dried food instead of fresh vegetables and fruits?

_____

_____

Test Practice

Circle the letter of the correct answer.

1. Which sentence states this article's main idea?

   A Astronauts' meals are freeze-dried and vacuum packed.

   B Fresh vegetables may someday be grown aboard spaceships—but not yet.

   C Nutritionists are trying to solve the problem of unappetizing food in space.

   D A new recipe book has been compiled for astronauts who are vegetarians.

2. If you were researching the latest developments in food for American astronauts, which question would provide the most relevant information?

   F How is food freeze-dried?

   G What is the history of hydroponic agriculture?

   H Do U.S. astronauts still complain about food on extended space missions?

   J What foods did U.S. astronauts eat during their last three space missions?

3. "What input have astronauts had in the most recent experiments on space food?" is a more useful first research question than "Has space food changed since the 1960s?" because —

   A it is a broad, general question about growing food on the moon or Mars

   B it will yield specific, detailed information

   C it can be answered with "yes" or "no"

   D it is about future, not past, events

4. Which of the following research questions does *not* arise from issues covered in this article?

   F How might grains and vegetables be grown on Mars?

   G What would be needed for astronauts to grow fresh vegetables aboard a space flight?

   H Who would pay for constructing and maintaining lunar and Martian colonies?

   J In a Martian or lunar colony, how might residents get their food?

Vocabulary: How to Own a Word

Word Mapping

Sometimes you can figure out a word's meaning from its context, but sometimes you can't. In lines 20–24, the writer gives context clues—spread over three sentences—to help you understand what the word *palatable* means:

> The main challenge in cooking for long-haul astronauts, as anyone who has taken a transatlantic flight will know, is making the food <u>palatable</u>. NASA is careful to supply every vitamin, mineral, and calorie an astronaut requires, calculated to the minutest scale. But that doesn't mean it tastes nice.

Making a **semantic map,** or **meaning map,** can help you pin down the meaning of a new word. Here is a sample map for the word *palatable*. Note how the questions, answers, and examples show the word in action and help to clarify its meaning.

Word Bank
breached
palatable
rancid
mutiny
impoverished
habitat
judicious
metabolism
arresting

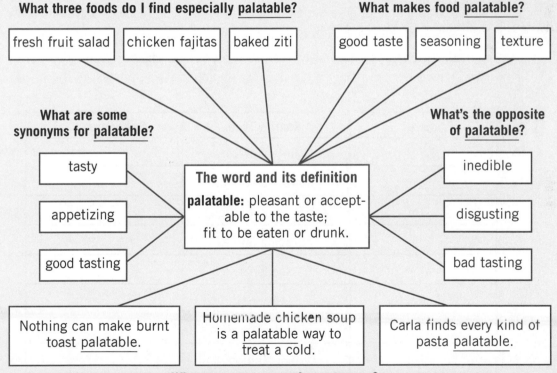

What three foods do I find especially <u>palatable</u>?
fresh fruit salad | chicken fajitas | baked ziti

What makes food <u>palatable</u>?
good taste | seasoning | texture

What are some synonyms for <u>palatable</u>?
tasty
appetizing
good tasting

The word and its definition
palatable: pleasant or acceptable to the taste; fit to be eaten or drunk.

What's the opposite of <u>palatable</u>?
inedible
disgusting
bad tasting

Nothing can make burnt toast <u>palatable</u>.

Homemade chicken soup is a <u>palatable</u> way to treat a cold.

Carla finds every kind of pasta <u>palatable</u>.

What are some example sentences?

Practice

Make a semantic map for each remaining word in the Word Bank. You may need to create some of your own questions and answers. In class, compare your maps with those of your classmates.

From A Communion of the Spirits: African American Quilters, Preservers, and Their Stories

Make the Connection

Using Primary and Secondary Sources

The materials found when researching historical information can be classified into two categories: primary sources and secondary sources.

- A **primary source** is an eyewitness account of an event or an opinion that has not been interpreted or edited by others.
- A **secondary source** contains information that is at least one step removed from an event and is usually retold, interpreted, or summarized by the writer. Secondary sources are often based on primary sources. Unless they are firsthand accounts written at the time of an event or are editorial or opinion pieces, most sources are considered secondary.

The following chart lists several types of sources. Decide whether each type of source is primary or secondary and place a check in the appropriate column next to it.

Primary	Source Type	Secondary
	interviews	
	literary criticism	
	encyclopedia articles	
	autobiographies	
	speeches	
	textbooks	
	literary works	
	biographies	
	editorials	
	journal articles	
	oral histories	
	letters	

FROM

A Communion of the Spirits:

African American Quilters,

Preservers, and Their Stories

INTERVIEW WITH ALICE WALKER

INTERVIEW WITH NIKKI GIOVANNI

Roland L. Freeman

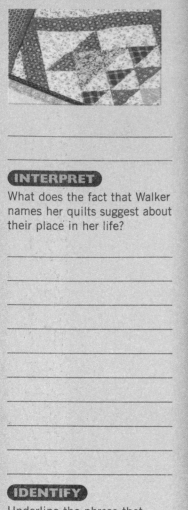

Interview with Alice Walker

I asked Alice to talk first about the tradition of quilting in her family.

Well, my mother was a quilter, and I remember many, many afternoons of my mother and the neighborhood women sitting on the porch around the quilting frame, quilting and talking, you know; getting up to stir something on the stove and coming back and sitting down.

The first quilt I worked on was the *In Love and Trouble* quilt. And I did that one when I was living in Mississippi. It was during a period when we were wearing African-inspired dresses. So all of the pieces are from dresses that I actually wore. This yellow and black fabric I bought
10 when I was in Uganda, and I had a beautiful dress made of it that I wore and wore and wore and eventually I couldn't wear it anymore; partly I had worn it out and also I was pregnant, so it didn't fit, and I used that and I used the red and white and black, which was a long, floor-length dress that I had when I was pregnant with my daughter, Rebecca, who is now twenty-three. I took these things apart or I used scraps. I put them together in this quilt, because it just seemed perfect. Mississippi was full of political and social struggle, and regular quilts were all African American with emphasis on being here in the United States. But because of the African consciousness that was being raised[1] and the way that we
20 were all wearing our hair in naturals[2] and wearing all of these African dresses, I felt the need to blend these two traditions. So it's a quilt of great memory and importance to me. I use it a lot and that's why it's so worn.

I asked her what happens when she sleeps under that quilt.

Oh . . . I am warm and I am secure and I am safe. I feel that I know how to create my own environment, and I know how to protect it. And I know how to choose it. I realize that my quilts are really simple, and yet, they give me so much pleasure, because even in their extreme simplicity they are just as useful as the most complex. And in their own way, they are beautiful because they do express what I was feeling and they clearly
30 mark a particular time for me.

I asked her if she had made a quilt for her daughter.

No. I'm sure that she will make her own quilt. I'll be happy to leave her these if they are not worn out, which they will probably be, but I hope that she will make quilts for her own grounding and her own connection to me and to her grandmother and to her great-grandmother. I've seen quilts that my grandmother made. They tended to be very serviceable, very heavy and really for warmth, and, well of course,

---

1. **the African . . . raised:** reference to the increased pride that many African Americans were taking in their African ethnic heritage in the early 1970s.
2. **naturals** *n.:* African American hairstyles that don't involve chemical straightening.

INTERPRET
What does the fact that Walker names her quilts suggest about their place in her life?

IDENTIFY
Underline the phrase that reveals Walker's quilts are a record of her personal history.

RETELL
Restate the meaning of lines 24–25.

beautiful. My daughter has a quilt that she travels with. It's just a beautiful simple quilt that she loves. I gave it to her because she

40 just feels like you can't sleep under just any old thing. It's got to be something that is congenial with your dreams—your dream sense, your dreamtime. I'm trying to think of where I got it. I think that I just bought it somewhere. I believe it is from Texas.

I asked Alice what she'd like to say to people in general about quilting.

That they should learn to do it. That they should think less about collecting quilts and give more thought to making them. Because, really, that is the power. It may do all kinds of good things, too, to collect what others have made, but I think it is essential that we know how to

50 express, you know, our own sense of connection. And there is no better sense of understanding our own creation than to create, and so we should do that.

Interview with Nikki Giovanni

I asked Nikki whether she had ever written about quilts.

I have used quilts as a metaphor. That's because I have a line in a poem called "Hands," which is a poem I wrote for Mother's Day. It says, "Quilts are the way our lives are lived. We survive on the scraps, the leftovers from a materially richer society." Quilts are such a—what's the word I'm looking for—banner to black women. Because what they ended up taking was that which nobody wanted, and making something totally

60 beautiful out of it. Making something in fact quite valuable. At least to this day. But that's like the spirituals. We took a bad situation and found a way to make a song. So it's a definite part of the heritage.

EVALUATE

Do you agree with Walker's opinion that the power of making and creating transcends generations? Explain.

_____
_____
_____
_____
_____
_____
_____
_____
_____
_____
_____

EVALUATE

Explain Giovanni's use of quilts as a **metaphor.** Do you think the metaphor is effective? Why or why not?

_____
_____
_____
_____
_____
_____
_____
_____
_____
_____
_____

Primary and Secondary Source Quilt

A quilt is comprised of scraps of cloth that, when sewn together, create something useful and beautiful. Similarly, a report or article is comprised of bits of information that, when brought together into an account, inform or entertain us.

Use the following "source quilt" to spark ideas for an article you might write about a local event from your town's recent or distant past. Fill in each box with a source that you'd explore for the article. Then, circle what kind of source it is, primary or secondary. The first box has been filled in as a sample.

EVENT: _____

Source: _history of town written by local historian_ primary or (secondary)	**Source:** _____ primary or secondary	**Source:** _____ primary or secondary
Source: _____ primary or secondary	**Source:** _____ primary or secondary	**Source:** _____ primary or secondary
Source: _____ primary or secondary	**Source:** _____ primary or secondary	**Source:** _____ primary or secondary

Analyzing Informational Materials

Reading Check

1. What was the name of Alice Walker's first quilt, and what was it made from?

   _____

2. What do quilts represent for Nikki Giovanni?

   _____

   _____

Test Practice

Circle the letter of the best answer to each question.

1. Which statement best summarizes Nikki Giovanni's **main idea**?

   A Quilts are beautiful.

   B Quilts remind us of family and of our heritage.

   C African Americans created beauty with quilts and spirituals despite their bad situations.

   D African Americans created quilts as a form of political and moral protest.

2. Walker and Giovanni agree that quilting is —

   F tedious

   G difficult

   H rewarding

   J expensive

3. If you were writing a report on quilting and needed a secondary source, which would you choose?

   A An autobiography of a quilter

   B A collection of a quilters' letters

   C An encyclopedia article about quilting

   D A speech about quilting

4. How can you evaluate whether the speaker in an oral history is telling the truth?

   F By asking the interviewer

   G By reading the text aloud

   H By reading the text carefully

   J By checking other sources

5. In a secondary source such as a newspaper article, you can identify a speaker's exact words by observing the —

   A italic type

   B title and author of the source

   C paragraph breaks

   D quotation marks

6. If you were trying to find out what it might feel like to sew your own quilt, which kind of source would *not* be helpful?

   F An oral history

   G An interview

   H An encyclopedia article

   J A short story

Call of the Wild—Save Us!

Make the Connection

Evaluating an Author's Argument

Persuasive writing tries to convince you to take an action or believe an idea. You'll find persuasive writing in advertisements, speeches, editorials, letters to the editor, position papers, and magazine articles. To evaluate an argument, take these steps:

1. **Follow the author's argument.** Identify the **main idea** of each paragraph. The writer has carefully ordered the argument to be persuasive, so it's important to understand each main idea in the order it's presented.
2. **Evaluate the support.** Look for logical appeals—facts, examples, statistics. Be on the lookout for emotional appeals, too. Be sure to distinguish **facts** from **opinions.** Try outlining the argument, using a chart like the one below.

Evaluating an Author's Argument	
Argument or Opinion	
Logical Appeals	
Reason 1	
Evidence	
Reason 2	
Evidence	
Emotional Appeals	
Loaded words, etc.	

3. **Identify the author's intent.** Sometimes the writer's goal is just to change your thinking, but often a **call to action** asks you to go out and *do* something.
4. **Identify the author's tone.** A writer's intent directly affects **tone,** which is created through choice of language, images, and figures of speech. Identifying the tone may help you evaluate the credibility of an argument.
5. **Evaluate the author's credentials**. Evaluate the writer's **credibility.** Identify what makes the writer an expert on the subject, and try to determine from the article if the writer knows what he or she is talking about.

Call of the Wild— Save Us!

FROM *Good Housekeeping*, April 1991

Dr. Norman Myers

PREDICT

Based on the first paragraph (lines 1–3), guess the author's **intent**.

_____

_____

_____

_____

_____

_____

WORDS TO OWN

habitats (hab′i·tats′) *n.:* native environments.
extinct (ek·stiŋkt′) *adj.:* no longer in existence.
impoverishment
(im·päv′ər·ish·mənt) *n.:* barrenness.
degradation (deg′rə·dā′shən) *n.:* decline; decay.

IDENTIFY

How does the first subhead help to set the **tone** of the rest of the section that follows?

_____

_____

_____

_____

_____

_____

_____

_____

_____

_____

_____

WORDS TO OWN

ethical (eth′i·kəl) *adj.:* moral; having to do with goodness or rightness in conduct.

Each day we lose roughly 50 to 100 wildlife species. They are crowded off the planet by human beings, who are deciding that there isn't enough room on the one Earth for them and us too.

We don't do it deliberately. We simply destroy their habitats. We chop down their forests, dig up their grasslands, drain their marshes, pollute their rivers and lakes, pave over their other habitats, and generally jump on whatever corners of the Earth they have chosen to make their last stand. We certainly don't drive them extinct with malice aforethought.[1] Very few species are eliminated through overhunting and
10 other direct forms of assault.

But effectively and increasingly, we are denying living space to thousands of fellow species, animals and plants, each year. By the time readers of this magazine climb into their rocking chairs, the total may well become millions, in fact a whopping half of *all* species. This is a holocaust[2]—a rending of the very fabric of life on Earth—because mass extinction will impose a longer-lasting impoverishment on the planetary ecosystem than any other environmental problem. All other kinds of environmental degradation are reversible. But when a species is gone, it is gone for good.

We Are All Losers

20 All too often we shall find that will be "for bad" in terms of our everyday welfare. When we visit our neighborhood drugstore, there is one chance in two that our purchase—an antibiotic, an antiviral, a diuretic, a laxative, an analgesic,[3] or a host of other items—would not be available for us without raw materials from wild plants and animals. The commercial value of all these products worldwide is more than $400 million a year. The rosy periwinkle of Madagascar provided one of the most significant breakthroughs against cancer in recent decades. It has led to the manufacture of two potent therapies against Hodgkin's disease, leukemia, and other blood cancers. Cancer specialists believe there could
30 be at least another ten tropical forest plants with capacity to generate similar superstar drugs against other forms of cancer—provided the scientist can get to them before the chainsaw devastates their habitats.

The economic argument in support of species carries weight with politicians and planners. If wildlife can pay its way in the marketplace, they will listen; if not, then they won't. But should we not consider a further argument as well—the ethical aspect? What right have we, a single species, to eliminate even a single other species, let alone to knock them off in vast numbers? Shouldn't our fellow passengers on Planet

---

1. **malice aforethought:** deliberate intention to do something unlawful.
2. **holocaust** *n.:* great or total destruction of life.
3. **antibiotic, . . . analgesic:** types of medication. An antibiotic fights infection; an analgesic relieves pain.

Earth, many of them like us, the refined outcome of evolution, enjoy as
40 much right to continued existence as we do?

Therein lies another irony. We are the sole species with the capacity
to wantonly[4] snuff out the life of other species—yet we are also the sole
species with the capacity to save other creatures. Fortunately, and at long
glorious last, we are starting to realize this fundamental truth. The U.N.
is putting together a global treaty to safeguard wildlife. This will mean an
effort on the part of nations to preserve wildlife wherever it occurs; in
practice it will entail a campaign on the part of the rich nations to
finance conservation activities in developing, mainly tropical, nations
where species are most abundant—and where conservation resources
50 are scarcest.

What Will It Cost

Probably several billions of dollars a year. But it will be a sound
investment. Suppose we save those anticancer plants: that alone would
generate health benefits worth several billions annually.

Suppose, moreover, the entire bill were to be picked up by people in
the world's rich nations. There are 1.2 billion of us. If the bill were, say,
$2.5 billion a year, we would each pay just over $2 per year. For the cost
of a beer or a hamburger, we could do it.

A rich-nation couple spends $175,000 to bring up a child from cradle
through college. For the sake of a *tiny* additional investment, that child
60 will grow up into a world deprived of millions of wildlife species and
bereft of much of what makes the world diverse and interesting,
spectacular and special. The question is not "Can we afford to do it
eventually?" It is "How can we possibly afford *not* to do it now?"

What You Can Do

I am often asked what individuals can do while waiting for political
leaders to get a move on. Lots of specific things. They can support their
conservation group of choice, perhaps bearing in mind that the longest
established is the World Wildlife Fund (1250 24th St., N.W., Washington,
D.C. 20037). After writing that check, they can write another piece of
paper, one that costs less, yet seems to cost more, given the relatively
70 small number of conservationists who do it! They can write to their
senator and congressperson, urging support for the legislative initiative in
behalf of global wildlife.

More importantly still, they can figure out ways to tread more
lightly on the planet, notably by cutting back on excessive forms of
consumerism and waste. This helps environments generally, and habitats
for wildlife specifically. There will ultimately be no healthy place for

---

4. **wantonly** *adv.*: senselessly; carelessly.

WORDS TO OWN
terminal (tur′mə·nəl) *adj.:*
disastrous; catastrophic.
veritable (ver′i·tə·bəl) *adj.:*
actual; truly.

wildlife except on a planet that is healthy all 'round. So: more recycling, fewer gas-guzzling cars, and all the other "think globally, act locally" measures.

80   Above all, remember that not only our children will look back upon this time of gathering shadows for the wildlife world. Their children and thousands of generations into the future will wonder why more was not done to tackle the terminal threat to wildlife. Alternatively, if we get our conservation act together, our successors will marvel at how we measured up to the challenge, and how we saved species in their veritable millions. We still have time, though only *just* time. Those species out there—they are waiting to hear from us.

Norman Myers is a university lecturer, an author, and an environmental consultant to many organizations, including the United Nations.

Argument Evaluation Chart

Analyze the article you've just read by completing the outline below. After you've mapped the writer's argument, evaluate how **credible**, or convincing, you find the argument. Point out any flaws you see in it.

Writer's Opinion or Claim:	
Main Idea 1:	
Supporting evidence (facts, statistics, etc.)	
Emotional appeals (loaded words, anecdotes, etc.)	
Intent (change thinking or call to action)	
Tone (formal, informal, humorous, etc.)	
Main Idea 2:	
Supporting evidence (facts, statistics, etc.)	
Emotional appeals (loaded words, anecdotes, etc.)	
Intent (change thinking or call to action)	
Tone (formal, informal, humorous, etc.)	
Main Idea 3:	
Supporting evidence (facts, statistics, etc.)	
Emotional appeals (loaded words, anecdotes, etc.)	
Intent (change thinking or call to action)	
Tone (formal, informal, humorous, etc.)	

Analyzing Informational Materials

Reading Check

1. What does the article's **title** mean?

_____

_____

2. Why does the writer mention the rosy periwinkle of Madagascar?

_____

_____

3. What three things does the writer say individuals can do to help solve the problem of species extinction?

_____

_____

Test Practice

Circle the letter of the correct answer to each question.

1. The **main idea** of this article is that something must be done *now* to—

A bring back extinct species
B prevent more species from becoming extinct
C increase the number of species on Earth
D stop the destruction of rain forests

2. The first **reason** the writer gives to support this opinion is—

F politicians and planners don't care
G tropical nations are already preserving wildlife
H rich nations must help provide aid
J wild plants and animals are the source of medications for humans

3. The second **reason** the writer gives to support his opinion is—

A humans have an ethical obligation to preserve other species
B the United Nations has ignored the problem
C every nation is already doing its best
D the United States is funding the efforts of tropical nations

4. Next, the writer considers how to cope with the—

F politicians' objections
G public's lack of interest
H cost of conservation efforts
J cost of higher education

Vocabulary: How to Own a Word

Using Contexts

Use context clues in the following sentences to help you choose the correct Word Bank word for each blank.

Word Bank
habitats
extinct
impoverishment
degradation
ethical
conservation
bereft
consumerism
terminal
veritable

1. There are no dinosaurs on earth today because they are

   _____.

2. He was very concerned about the _____ of standards and values.

3. Her illness had grown very severe and was now in a(n)

   _____ stage.

4. Law and religion both deal with _____ questions and issues.

5. The charity was completely _____ of the funds it needed to keep operating.

6. The _____ of many exotic animals can be found in the rain forest.

7. Some critics are unhappy with the amount of _____ practiced by today's free-spending public.

8. The drought had turned the countryside into a _____ desert.

9. The careful _____ of resources is vital for insuring adequate energy supplies in the future.

10. Sadly, the economic decline caused a further _____ of the country's factory workers and farmers.

The War Escalates;
From Declaration of Independence from the War in Vietnam

Make the Connection

Using Primary and Secondary Sources: Balancing Viewpoints

As you've learned, research materials can be classified according to two main groups: primary sources and secondary sources.

- A **primary source** is a firsthand account, original material that has not been interpreted or edited by any other writers. Primary sources are valuable because they include details and feelings that only an eyewitness can provide. However, they may be highly subjective.
- A **secondary source** contains information that is retold, summarized, or interpreted by a writer. A secondary source is often written about events after they have occurred and by someone who did not witness them.

Imagine that you are writing a paper on the American Civil War (1861–1865). Study the list of sources below. Which sources would you consult to obtain the most complete and credible view of the topic? Make some notes about your decisions below.

A. The diary of a soldier in the Union Army

B. The oral histories of slaves from certain Southern States

C. An 1863 newspaper article from a Boston, Massachusetts, paper about the progress of the war

D. An American history textbook published in 1954

E. An American history textbook published in 2000

F. An academic journal article on the Civil War written by a British historian

G. An 1863 newspaper article from an Atlanta, Georgia, paper about Northern casualty rates

H. The letters of a soldier in the Confederate Army

I. An academic journal article on the Civil War written by an American historian

NOTES:

_____

_____

_____

_____

The War Escalates

FROM **The American Nation,** A TEXTBOOK BY **Paul Boyer**

Declaration of Independence from the War in Vietnam

Martin Luther King, Jr.

IDENTIFY

Although history textbooks are secondary sources, they may include some primary sources. Circle the primary source on this page.

The Vietnam War (1961–1975) was a civil war between noncommunist South Vietnam and communist North Vietnam. In 1961, the United States began officially supporting the South Vietnamese in their war against the communist guerrillas. As you will read, the Gulf of Tonkin incident, in 1964, led to increased U.S. involvement in this regional conflict. By 1966, there were 90,000 U.S. troops in Vietnam; by 1968, that number topped 500,000. By the time King made his speech "Declaration of Independence from the War in Vietnam," many U.S. citizens had begun to speak out against the war. The length of the war, the high casualty rates, and disturbing reports about troop conduct led to the growth of an antiwar protest movement at home. U.S. troops withdrew in 1973. U.S. casualties totaled more than 50,000 during the period of the U.S.'s greatest involvement (1961–1972).

The War Escalates

"Renewed hostile actions against United States ships on the high seas in the Gulf of Tonkin have today required me to order the military forces of the United States to take action in reply. The initial attack on the destroyer Maddox, _on August 2, was repeated today by a number of hostile vessels attacking two U.S. destroyers with torpedoes. . . . We believe at least two of the attacking boats were sunk. There were no U.S. losses. . . . But repeated acts of violence against the Armed Forces of the United States must be met not only with alert defense, but with positive reply. That reply is being given as I speak to you tonight. Air_

10 _action is now in execution against gunboats and certain supporting facilities in North Vietnam which have been used in these hostile operations."_

—Lyndon B. Johnson, nationally televised speech, August 4, 1964

Near midnight on August 4, 1964, President Lyndon B. Johnson appeared on national television. His announcement to the American people that night marked a new stage in U.S. involvement in the war in Vietnam.

The Tonkin Gulf Resolution

In 1963 Secretary of Defense Robert S. McNamara had advised President Johnson that he would have to increase the U.S. military commitment to

20 South Vietnam to prevent a Communist victory. Before increasing the U.S. commitment, Johnson needed to get congressional backing. The events in the Gulf of Tonkin gave him the opportunity. Johnson asked Congress to authorize the use of military force "to prevent further aggression." In response, both houses of Congress overwhelmingly passed the **Tonkin Gulf Resolution**. This gave the president authority to

take "all necessary measures to repel any armed attack against forces of the United States."

Johnson claimed that the attacks in the Gulf of Tonkin were unprovoked. In reality, however, the U.S. destroyer *Maddox* had been
30 spying in support of South Vietnamese raids against North Vietnam and had fired first. The second attack, moreover, probably never occurred. Some U.S. sailors apparently misinterpreted interference on their radar and sonar as enemy ships and torpedoes. Nonetheless, Johnson and his advisers got what they wanted: authority to expand the war.

Wayne Morse of Oregon was one of just two senators who voted against the Tonkin Gulf Resolution. He warned, "I believe that history will record we have made a great mistake. . . . We are in effect giving the President war-making powers in the absence of a declaration of war."
40 In other words, by passing the resolution, Congress had essentially given up its constitutional power to declare war.

U.S. Forces in Vietnam

President Johnson soon called for an escalation, or buildup, of U.S. military forces in Vietnam. He ordered the Selective Service, the agency charged with carrying out the military draft, to begin calling up young men to serve in the armed forces. In April 1965 the Selective Service notified 13,700 draftees.

The troops. During the war more than 2 million Americans served in Vietnam. In the beginning most were professional soldiers who were already enlisted in the armed forces. As the demand for troops grew,
50 however, more and more draftees were shipped to Vietnam. The average U.S. soldier in Vietnam was younger, poorer, and less educated than those who had served in World War II or in the Korean War.

One out of four young men who registered for the draft was excused from service for health reasons. Another 30 percent received non-health-related exemptions or deferments—postponements of service. Most of these were for college enrollment. Mainly because of college deferments, young men from higher-income families were the least likely to be drafted. As a result, poor Americans served in numbers far greater than their proportion in the general population.
60 African Americans and Hispanics served in combat in very high numbers, particularly during the early years of the war. Many served in the most dangerous ground units. As a result, they experienced very high casualty rates. In 1965, for example, African Americans accounted for almost 24 percent of all battle deaths, even though they made up just 11 percent of the U.S. population.

INTERPRET

Underline the sentences suggesting that Johnson manipulated the Gulf of Tonkin events to political ends. What was his desired political goal?

_____
_____
_____
_____
_____
_____
_____
_____
_____
_____
_____
_____
_____
_____
_____
_____
_____
_____
_____
_____
_____
_____
_____

IDENTIFY

Why did a higher proportion of low-income Americans end up serving in Vietnam?

_____
_____
_____
_____
_____
_____
_____

INTERPRET

Textbooks usually aim for an objective, unbiased **tone**. What is the tone of the subsection "The troops"?

The most vivid images of the war show soldiers facing the hardships and terrors of battle. Some confronted the enemy in well-defined battles in the highlands. Others cut their way through the jungle, where they heard but seldom saw the enemy. Still others waded

70 through rice paddies and searched rural villages for guerrillas. Most Americans who went to Vietnam, however, served in support positions such as administration, communications, engineering, medical care, and supply and transportation. They were rarely safe. Enemy rockets and mortars could—and did—strike anywhere.

Some 10,000 servicewomen filled noncombat positions in Vietnam, mostly as nurses. Although they did not carry guns into battle, nurses faced the horrors of combat on a daily basis. Edie Meeks described the experience of working as a nurse at a field hospital.

"We really saw the worst of it, because the nurses never saw any of the
80 *victories. If the Army took a hill, we saw what was left over. I remember one boy who was brought in missing two legs and an arm, and his eyes were bandaged. A general came in later and pinned a Purple Heart on the boy's hospital gown, and the horror of it all was so amazing that it just took my breath away. You thought, was this supposed to be an even trade?"*

—Edie Meeks, quoted in *Newsweek,* March 8, 1999

Another 20,000 to 45,000 women worked in civilian capacities, many as volunteers for humanitarian organizations such as the Red Cross.

From Declaration of Independence from the War in Vietnam
Martin Luther King, Jr.

IDENTIFY

In the first sentence, underline the subject of King's speech.

Since I am a preacher by trade, I suppose it is not surprising that I have . . . major reasons for bringing Vietnam into the field of my moral vision. There is at the outset a very obvious and almost facile connection between the war in Vietnam and the struggle I, and others, have been waging in America. A few years ago there was a shining moment in that struggle. It seemed as if there was a real promise of hope for the poor—both black and white—through the Poverty Program.[1] Then came the

---

1. **Poverty Program:** In May 1964, President Lyndon B. Johnson declared a nationwide war on poverty. He announced a number of federal programs to aid the nation's poor and to create what he called the Great Society.

WORDS TO OWN
facile (fas′il) *adj.:* easy.

buildup in Vietnam, and I watched the program broken and eviscerated[2]
as if it were some idle political plaything or a society gone mad on war,
10 and I knew that America would never invest the necessary funds or
energies in <u>rehabilitation</u> of its poor so long as Vietnam continued to
draw men and skills and money like some demonic, destructive suction
tube. So I was increasingly compelled to see the war as an enemy of the
poor and to attack it as such.

    Perhaps the more tragic recognition of reality took place when it
became clear to me that the war was doing far more than devastating the
hopes of the poor at home. It was sending their sons and their brothers
and their husbands to fight and to die in extraordinarily high proportions
relative to the rest of the population. We were taking the young black
20 men who had been crippled by our society and sending them eight
thousand miles away to guarantee liberties in Southeast Asia which they
had not found in southwest Georgia and East Harlem. So we have been
repeatedly faced with the cruel irony of watching Negro and white boys
on TV screens as they kill and die together for a nation that has been
unable to seat them together in the same schools. So we watch them in
brutal solidarity[3] burning the huts of a poor village, but we realize that
they would never live on the same block in Detroit. I could not be silent
in the face of such cruel <u>manipulation</u> of the poor.

    My third reason grows out of my experience in the ghettos of the
30 North over the last three years—especially the last three summers. As I
have walked among the desperate, rejected, and angry young men, I
have told them that Molotov cocktails[4] and rifles would not solve their
problems. I have tried to offer them my deepest <u>compassion</u> while
maintaining my conviction that social change comes most meaningfully
through nonviolent action. But, they asked, what about Vietnam? They
asked if our own nation wasn't using massive doses of violence to solve
its problems, to bring about the changes it wanted. Their questions hit
home, and I knew that I could never again raise my voice against the
violence of the oppressed in the ghettos without having first spoken
40 clearly to the greatest purveyor[5] of violence in the world today—my own
government. . . .

    Somehow this madness must cease. I speak as a child of God and a
brother to the suffering poor of Vietnam and the poor of America who
are paying the double price of smashed hopes at home and death and
corruption in Vietnam. I speak as a citizen of the world, for the world as
it stands <u>aghast</u> at the path we have taken. I speak as an American to
the leaders of my own nation. The great <u>initiative</u> in this war is ours.
The initiative to stop must be ours . . . .

---

2. **eviscerated** (ē·vis′ər·āt′id) *v.* used as *adj.:* gutted; having its force or significance taken
  away.
3. **solidarity** *n.:* complete unity.
4. **Molotov cocktails:** makeshift explosives.
5. **purveyor** (pər·vā′ər) *n.:* provider; supplier.

IDENTIFY

Rhetorical questions are questions that do not require an answer. Underline the rhetorical questions in lines 57–62.

_____

_____

_____

_____

EVALUATE

How convincing do you find King's speech? Why?

_____

_____

_____

_____

_____

_____

_____

_____

_____

_____

_____

_____

_____

_____

_____

_____

_____

_____

50 We must move past indecision to action. We must find new ways to speak for peace in Vietnam and justice throughout the developing world—a world that borders on our doors. If we do not act, we shall surely be dragged down the long dark and shameful corridors of time reserved for those who possess power without compassion, might without morality, and strength without sight.

Now let us begin. Now let us rededicate ourselves to the long and bitter—but beautiful—struggle for a new world. This is the calling of the sons of God, and our brothers wait eagerly for our response. Shall we say the odds are too great? Shall we tell them the struggle is too hard? Will our message be that the forces of American life militate[6] against their
60 arrival as full men, and we send our deepest regrets? Or will there be another message, of longing, of hope, of solidarity with their yearnings, of commitment to their cause, whatever the cost? The choice is ours, and though we might prefer it otherwise, we *must* choose in this crucial moment of human history.

April 4, 1967

---

6. **militate** *v.* (used with *against*): work to prohibit.

Analyze and Evaluate Chart

Part 1

Complete the chart below to help you analyze and evaluate the two selections you just read.

Features	The War Escalates	Declaration of Independence from the War in Vietnam
Purpose	To inform students about history of U.S. involvement in Vietnam War. Especially, to shed light on causes of that involvement.	
Tone	Informative, often concerned. Deeply critical of Johnson's actions and U.S. draft policies.	
Audience	probably high school students	
Credibility of source • writer's qualifications? • does writer have a bias?	• Writer is unknown. Generally one can assume that textbook writers are well-qualified. • Writer seems to have a bias against U.S. policy in Vietnam.	

Part 2

In a notebook, write a short paragraph in which you draw **conclusions** about the American involvement in Vietnam based on the sources you have read in this lesson.

Analyzing Informational Materials

Reading Check

1. What power did the Tonkin Gulf Resolution give to the president?

_____

_____

2. How many American troops served in the Vietnam War? How many women served in the armed forces?

_____

_____

3. According to King, why was the Vietnam War an enemy of poor Americans?

_____

_____

Test Practice

Circle the letter of the correct answer.

1. Both of the sources concern —

A the history of Vietnam
B the causes of the Vietnam War
C the U.S. armed forces in Vietnam
D the U.S. Congress and president

2. From what you've read in "The War Escalates," you can infer that the Tonkin Gulf Resolution —

F was a turning point in U.S. involvement in the war
G was an unimportant piece of legislation
H gave unusual powers to Congress
J confirmed the president's constitutional powers

3. The primary **purpose** of the excerpt from "Declaration of Independence from the War in Vietnam" is to —

A give information about the war
B give information about the Viet Cong
C persuade listeners of King's point of view about the war
D describe specific events in the war

4. The value of the excerpt from the "Declaration of Independence from the War in Vietnam" as a research source is that it —

F is objective and factual
G relates a firsthand experience of combat in the war
H expresses the feelings of an influential person of that time on the relevant topic
J is written by an expert

Vocabulary: How to Own a Word

Clarifying Word Meanings

Word Bank
facile
rehabilitation
manipulation
compassion
aghast
initiative

You reinforce your understanding of an unfamiliar word's meaning each time you use it in a sentence or think about how it should be used. Briefly answer the following questions about each of the words from the Word Bank. Make sure to use the Word Bank word in your answer.

1. Identify a local, national, or world problem for which you think there is no facile solution.

   _____

   _____

2. What should be done for the rehabilitation of a person who has broken a leg?

   _____

   _____

3. How did Lyndon Johnson's actions demonstrate a manipulation of events during the Tonkin Gulf crisis?

   _____

   _____

4. How would you show your compassion for someone who has suffered a great loss?

   _____

   _____

5. What might someone do or say that would leave you aghast?

   _____

   _____

6. If you could take the initiative for a new project or organization at your school, what would you do?

   _____

   _____

Coming of Age, Latino Style; Vision Quest

Make the Connection

Synthesizing Different Sources

When you research a topic, you often need to get a balanced view by looking at different sources. Then you can **synthesize** what you've read—pull it all together so that you can better understand the subject. The following guidelines will help:

- **Determine the message.** Look for the **main ideas** and **supporting details**.
- **Paraphrase ideas.** To help you understand a source better, try paraphrasing its ideas, which means restating them *in your own words*.
- **Evaluate each source.** Determine if the kinds and amount of support the writer gives is enough to make his or her ideas **credible**.
- **Determine the author's purpose and audience.** Identify why the piece was written (for example, to tell a personal story, to change your opinion, or to provide background information). Establish whether the source is **objective** (based solely on facts) or **subjective** (expressing the writer's opinions and feelings).
- **Compare and contrast.** Compare the type of information in each source. Think about what the sources have in common and how they relate to each other.
- **Connect to other sources.** Connect the ideas to related topics and to stories and other articles you've read.
- **Synthesize.** Now, consider all your sources as a group. Draw **conclusions** from the sources and form connections with other sources you have read.

The following selections describe how different cultures mark a child's passage to adulthood. On the index card provided below, name two ceremonies, or rites, that you are familiar with (through personal experience, prior reading, films, or television) that mark a passage from one stage of life to another. Include some details about the ceremonies—such as their purpose and where and when the ceremony takes place.

Rite-of-Passage Ceremonies

1. _____
   _____

2. _____
   _____

COMING OF AGE, LATINO STYLE

Special Rite Ushers Girls into Adulthood

FROM *Boston Globe*, January 5, 1997

Cindy Rodriguez, Globe Staff

Vision Quest

FROM *Encyclopædia Britannica*, 1995

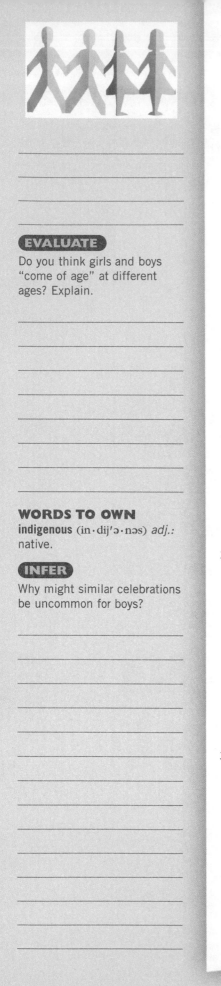

Coming of Age, Latino Style
Special Rite Ushers Girls into Adulthood
from *Boston Globe*; January 5, 1997;
Cindy Rodriguez, Globe Staff

EVALUATE

Do you think girls and boys "come of age" at different ages? Explain.

WORDS TO OWN

indigenous (in·dij′ə·nəs) *adj.:* native.

INFER

Why might similar celebrations be uncommon for boys?

LOWELL—Iris Cancel's eyes filled with pride, not tears, as she watched her daughter Glenda glide down the church aisle, her tiny frame covered by a white satin and lace dress that flared at the hips and trailed behind her. Small white flowers speckled the bodice,[1] and her long, dark hair, wrapped in baby's breath,[2] was encircled by a shimmery crown.

"I think it's an exciting day for her and everyone involved," Iris Cancel said. "Her father's a nervous wreck. I keep telling him, 'She's not getting married.'"

Glenda, a sophomore at Greater Lowell Vocational Technical School,
10 did not celebrate her wedding a week ago Saturday, although the ceremony did resemble one. She celebrated a special birthday. She turned 15 on Dec. 26 and toasted it two days later with a *quinceañera*,[3] a custom in Hispanic communities that marks a girl's entrance into adulthood.

Experts of Hispanic culture disagree on the origin of the quinceañera. The word literally means "15-year-old girl" but is also used to describe the entire celebration. Some say coming-of-age traditions in general, though not the quinceañera in particular, can be traced back to indigenous cultures. Then, it was a recognition that boys were ready
20 to be warriors and girls were ready to bear children.

Some experts believe that for years the quinceañera was most often celebrated by upper-class Hispanics, who wrapped the social custom in religious symbolism and personal wealth. Elaborate celebrations similar to debutante balls[4] showed off a family's social status and daughter to possible suitors. A similar celebration for boys is uncommon among Hispanics.

Today the quinceañera is celebrated in the United States and abroad by Latinos of varied cultural backgrounds and economic classes. Glenda, one of six children, was born in Lowell to Puerto Rican parents. Iris, a
30 mail handler at Holland Mark Martin in Burlington, and Marcos, a school bus driver in Lowell, have lived in Massachusetts for 29 years.

The celebration can be religious or secular,[5] inexpensive or costly. Some Hispanic families still host debutante-style balls that can cost up to $10,000, while others plan simple birthday parties.

---

1. **bodice** *n.:* upper part of a woman's dress.
2. **baby's breath** *n.:* a type of flower.
3. **quinceañera** (kēns′ə·nye′·rə).
4. **debutante balls** *n.:* formal dances held to introduce a group of young women into society.
5. **secular** (sek′yə·lər) *adj.:* worldly, as distinguished from religious.

Still, the quinceañera in any form remains an important rite of passage for many Hispanic girls. For girls like Glenda, the purpose is not so much to find a future mate at the reception as to celebrate themselves.

"I feel like I deserve it," said Glenda, who gets good grades, has
40 near-perfect school attendance and attends church regularly. She plans to attend college to be a pediatrician[6] or a professional basketball player.

And, of course, it's fun to get dressed up for a celebration that in Glenda's case took a year to plan.

Vision Quest

from *Encyclopædia Britannica*, 1995

Vision quest, among the American Indian hunters of the eastern woodlands and the Great Plains, an essential part of a young boy's (or, more rarely, a girl's) initiation into adulthood. The youth was sent out from the camp on a solitary vigil involving fasting[1] and prayer in order to gain some sign of the presence and nature of his guardian spirit (*q.v.*).[2] The specific techniques varied from tribe to tribe, as did the age at which the quest was to be undertaken, its length and intensity, and the nature of the sign.

In some traditions the youth would watch for an animal who
10 behaved in a significant way; in others he discovered an object (usually a stone), which resembled some animal. In the predominant form, he had a dream in which his guardian appeared (usually in animal form), instructed him, took him on a visionary journey, and taught him songs. Upon receiving these signs and visions he returned to his home, indicated his success, and sought out a religious specialist for help in interpreting his visions.

The techniques of the vision quest are not confined only to those at puberty. They underlie every visionary experience of the Indian, from those of the ordinary man who seeks to gain contact with and advice
20 from his guardian to the visions of the great prophets and shamans (religious personages with healing and psychic transformation powers). Among the South American Indians, the vision quest, like the guardian spirit, is confined exclusively to the shaman.

---

6. **pediatrician** (pē′dē·ə·trish′ən) *n.:* doctor who specializes in the care of children.

1. **fasting** *v.* used as *n.:* not eating.
2. ***q.v.:*** abbreviation for Latin *quod vide,* "which see." This abbreviation indicates that the encyclopedia from which this entry was taken contains a separate entry for "guardian spirit."

WORDS TO OWN
solitary (säl′ə·ter′ē) *adj.:* without others.
vigil (vij′əl) *n.:* watchful staying awake during the usual hours of sleep.

WORDS TO OWN
predominant (prē·däm′ə·nənt) *adj.:* most frequent or noticeable.

EVALUATE
Which do you think is more important to the successful vision quest: the quester's desire to fulfill the rite or the techniques of the rite? Explain.

Compare, Contrast, and Synthesize Chart

Answer the three questions below for each of four life-passage ceremonies. Use the two examples you provided earlier in the lesson and the two presented in the selections to answer each question. Compare and contrast your answers. In the last column, state what the similarities or differences among the ceremonies indicate about a person's passage from one stage of life to another.

	Ceremony 1	Ceremony 2	Quinceañera	Vision Quest	Conclusions
Who is the focus of the ritual?					
Who else participates?					
What stage of life does the ritual focus on?					

Analyzing Informational Materials

Reading Check

1. What special occasion does a quinceañera celebrate?

_____

_____

2. For certain American Indian tribes, what is the purpose of a vision quest?

_____

_____

Test Practice

Circle the letter of the correct answer to each question.

1. What is the **purpose** of *each* of the two selections?

  A To discuss one kind of initiation into adulthood

  B To persuade readers of the importance of initiation ceremonies

  C To provide eyewitness accounts of coming of age rituals

  D To compare initiation rites across cultures

2. From these two selections, you can infer that in most societies, the passage into adulthood is marked by some kind of —

  F vision quest

  G ceremony or ritual

  H large party or dance

  J painful ordeal

3. Which article is **subjective**—that is, the writer expresses mostly personal thoughts and feelings?

  A "Coming of Age, Latino Style"

  B "Vision Quest"

  C Both articles

  D None of the articles

4. The experiences described in these two articles —

  F follow a particular cultural tradition

  G are dangerous and life-threatening

  H take place indoors, surrounded by people

  J take place when the individual is alone

Vocabulary: How to Own a Word

Word Maps: Pinning Down Meaning

Creating a **word map**, or **semantic map**, will help you pin down the precise meaning of any unfamiliar word. When you create a word map, you don't just memorize the new word's definition. Rather, you make up questions about the word and then answer them. Here's a word map for *indigenous*:

Word Bank
indigenous
solitary
vigil
predominant

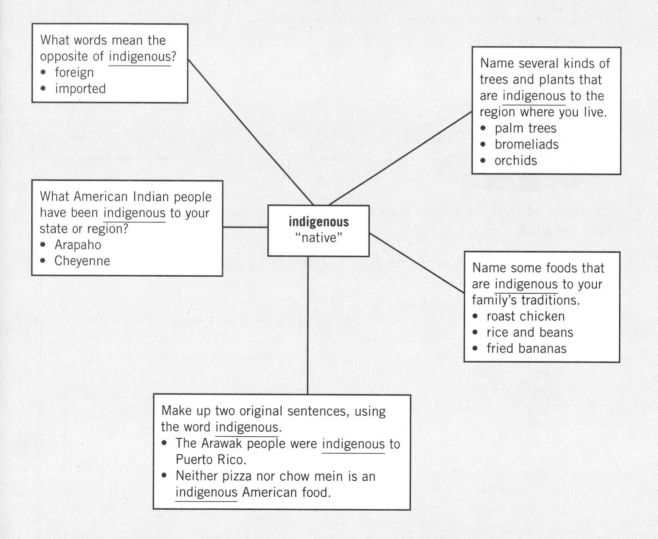

What words mean the opposite of <u>indigenous</u>?
• foreign
• imported

Name several kinds of trees and plants that are <u>indigenous</u> to the region where you live.
• palm trees
• bromeliads
• orchids

What American Indian people have been <u>indigenous</u> to your state or region?
• Arapaho
• Cheyenne

indigenous
"native"

Name some foods that are <u>indigenous</u> to your family's traditions.
• roast chicken
• rice and beans
• fried bananas

Make up two original sentences, using the word <u>indigenous</u>.
• The Arawak people were <u>indigenous</u> to Puerto Rico.
• Neither pizza nor chow mein is an <u>indigenous</u> American food.

Practice

Make a word map for each of the remaining words in the Word Bank. The questions you ask will vary for each map, but try to include two original sentences and examples of when you would use the word.

Selection: _____

Comparison and Contrast

Issues/Characteristics	Topic / Item 1	Topic / Item 2

Summary Statements: _____

_____

_____

Epidemic! On the Trail of Killer Diseases

Make the Connection

Researching Information on the Internet

After you have come up with research questions, you'll need to search for answers. The Internet is an invaluable source of up-to-date information. However, navigating the Web requires recognizing the features of a Web site:

- **The table of contents**, usually near the top or at the side of a page, lists the site's other pages.
- Click on highlighted or underlined **links** to jump to other sources of information on your topic. **Internal links** take you to other pages in the same Web site. **External links** lead you to different Web sites.
- **Multimedia and interactive features** link you to sound and video components and allow you to interact with other users of the Web site.

Look for information that is recent, reliable, and relevant. Learn to **evaluate** each Web source. Ask yourself: are you reading someone's opinion on a bulletin board, a home page by a high school student, or data from a government agency's Web site? Is its creator reliable, expert, and objective? Is the site updated frequently?

Below is a list of Web sites you might encounter while researching "chicken pox." Evaluate each site for its timeliness, reliability, and relevance to the topic.

1. Jenny's home page. Lists facts about chicken pox, along with pictures of her and her brother covered with chicken pox.

   _____

   _____

2. Web site for World Health Organization. Guidelines for effective treatment of chicken pox (last updated 1998).

   _____

   _____

3. Web site for a company that manufactures an anti-itch lotion. Guidelines for treatment of chicken pox.

   _____

   _____

Epidemic!
On the Trail
of Killer
Diseases

Karen Watson

IDENTIFY

In the Biblical story of David and Goliath, David was a small shepherd boy who defeated the mighty giant Goliath. In what ways is the bacterium that causes TB similar to David?

INTERPRET

Look up the word *consumption*. Why is this an appropriate term for TB?

- TB
- Flu
- Polio
- Dengue
- Hanta

EPIDEMIC! ON THE TRAIL OF KILLER DISEASES

The struggle between critters that cause disease and humans is a long one, and it's unlikely to end any time soon.

An Ancient Enemy Gets Tougher
Karen Watson

It's easy to think of David and Goliath when faced with the size of the creature that kills more people through disease than any other in the world. It's so small that it's invisible to the eye. Even viewed under a souped-up microscope it doesn't look like much—a tiny, capsule-like thing that could be a sprinkle on a frosted cake.

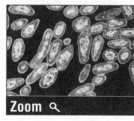

Zoom

10

Yet the microorganism that causes tuberculosis has felled millions through a terrible wasting of the body— it takes just one bacterium to start what ultimately could become a fatal infection. For thousands of years, this invisible David has been knocking down human Goliaths in shocking numbers.

Stone Age skeletons unearthed in Britain and Germany show tell-tale TB damage. Egyptian tomb portraits include images of hunchbacks curled by spinal TB. Scribes from ancient Hindu, Babylonian, Assyrian, Chinese, Greek and Roman cultures all describe the signs and symptoms of what in more modern times came to be called "consumption."

20

Follow TB's trail through time.
RealVideo 28.8 (RealPlayer required)
RealVideo 56.6 | Quicktime

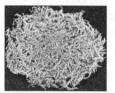

Fight the Invaders

Hidden Enemies

Ask the Experts

Name That Creature

Go Inside a Virus

Tales of a Survivor

Views from Space

Disease Alert!

In 1908, when the <u>American Museum of Natural History in New York</u> opened its international exhibition on TB, people stood in lines that wrapped around the block to find out more about the disease that devastated families. Nearly 100 years later, as the museum launches a major new exhibition, "Epidemic!
30 The World of Infectious Disease," TB remains a killer. These days, 2 to 3 million people a year die from tuberculosis worldwide, according to the World Health Organization. Someone is infected every second.

Is the little guy that packs a TB wallop out to get us? Do any of the microscopic critters that cause infectious diseases—the oddball zoo of viruses, bacteria, and protozoa—really want to see us dead?

No, say scientists. These inhabitants of a vast micro-world are just out to make a living. It just so
40 happens that the living is on us.

Take the TB "bug." It likes us for some reason, along with a startling collection of other animals. Lions, tigers, sheep, cows, guinea pigs, dogs, and cats are a few. Name it, and it likely gets the disease. Why? For some reason, the TB bacterium

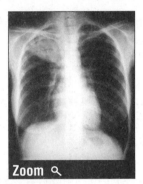

Zoom

50 actually prefers life inside one of the body's defenders. It makes a living from an immune system cell that normally munches up such invaders.

<u>Ask the experts</u> about TB and our struggles with it.

Breathe in an airborne TB bacterium and it typically lands in the lungs. There, immune system cells quickly surround it and wall it off, forming a firm white ball the size of a pinhead. Inside this ball, the bug persists, perhaps for years. Exactly what happens there remains unclear, and most people with the TB bug inside them never experience the disease or become
60 infectious themselves. Their body successfully keeps the invader in check.

INTERPRET

Re-read lines 38–40. Explain how the writer uses the phrase "makes a living" in regard to TB.

IDENTIFY

So far, what questions about TB would you like to "ask the experts"?

But if there's a glitch in the body's defense system, and if it doesn't work quite right, these once tiny balls can grow, some to the size of a baseball, as the bacteria inside them reproduce. These balls can erupt, spreading bacteria to other parts of the body through the blood. More balls, or "tubercles," grow, eventually clogging up the way the body does its daily business.

70 Every time someone sick with TB sneezes or coughs or exhales, they help the bacterium out. "Spreading is survival for the bug," says Dr. Ann Ginsberg, a TB scientist with the National Institute of Allergy and Infectious Diseases.

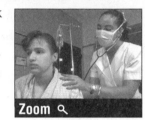

Hear about how tough TB is to tackle.
(RealPlayer required)

So why haven't we figured out a way to knock TB off the planet? The bug that scientists now call
80 *Mycobacterium tuberculosis*, which long ago made a successful jump from living in dirt to living off animals, has turned out to be quite a survivor.

It hides well in humans— nearly 2 billion people are thought to carry the bacterium these days, though they show no signs. When symptoms do pop up, they are easily confused with those of other
90 illnesses. The bug lives off lots of other animals besides humans, and it has so far proved to be a tricky adversary when it comes to the creation of an effective vaccine, says Dr. Rick O'Brien, chief of research and development of TB elimination at the Centers for Disease Control and Prevention.

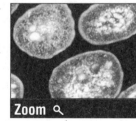

For more about TB:

Centers for Disease Control and Prevention

World Health Organization

National Tuberculosis Center, NJ

National Tuberculosis Center, NY

National Tuberculosis Center, CA

National Institute of Allergy and Infectious Diseases

INFER

In lines 87–90, the writer tells us that TB's symptoms are similar to those of other diseases. Why would this fact make TB more difficult to fight?

In cities worldwide, though mostly in Africa and East Asia where the disease is most prevalent, TB now has a new ally of sorts in the virus that causes AIDS. It weakens the immune 100 system, giving TB a kick-start.

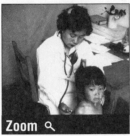
Zoom

This has doctors and researchers worried, since it creates a double disease-whammy in places where people were just getting a handle on TB. Moreover, those who have the disease must take a special combination of antibiotics for at least six months. If they don't complete their 110 treatment, they risk nurturing new strains of drug-resistant TB.

Expedition Live!

The deceptively tiny David carries a big bag of survival tricks.

Got a question about TB? Ask the experts.

Find out what happens when a microbe invades your body: Fight the Invaders.

Turn to Disease Alert! for the latest on outbreaks.

EPIDEMIC!

TB   Flu   Polio   Dengue   Hanta   At the Museum
Disease Alert   Tune In

EXPEDITIONS
Pictures: A.B. Dowsett/CAMR/Photo Researchers |
Mireille Vautier/Woodfin Camp/PNI | Courtesy of the American
Museum of Natural History | Daniel Morel/Associated Press |
P.A. Pittet/World Health Organization |
Audio: Courtesy of the American Museum of Natural History |
Video: Pan American Health Organization |
Copyright © 1999 Discovery Communications, Inc.

http://www.discovery.com/exp/epidemic/tb/tb.html

INFER
Why would a disease that weakens the immune system help spread TB?

_____

_____

_____

_____

_____

_____

_____

_____

EVALUATE
Do you think the story of David and Goliath provides a good analogy for TB's relationship to humans? Explain.

_____

_____

_____

_____

_____

_____

_____

_____

_____

_____

_____

_____

Generating Relevant Questions: Practice Activities

Below is a list of questions someone might have after reading "Epidemic! On the Trail of Killer Diseases." Next to each question, write the letter of the Web page link that might lead you to some answers. There can be more than one answer to each question.

Part 1

Questions

1. How do other diseases' survival rates compare with that of TB? _____

2. Do people respond to treatment for TB differently? If so, how? _____

3. How do microbes, or germs, reproduce? _____

4. How does it feel to have TB? _____

Web Links

A. Ask the experts

B. Polio

C. Hear about the secret world of microbes

D. Go inside a virus

E. Tales of a Survivor

F. Centers for Disease Control

Part 2

What questions popped into your mind as you were reading about TB? What Internet sources would you turn to for answers? Make some notes below.

_____
_____
_____
_____
_____
_____
_____
_____
_____
_____

Analyzing Informational Materials

Reading Check

1. What evidence do scientists have that tuberculosis is an ancient disease?

   _____

   _____

2. How widespread is tuberculosis today?

   _____

   _____

Test Practice

Circle the letter of the best answer to each question.

1. If you want to do research on why TB is still deadly, which of the following questions would be most relevant?

   A What have Stone Age skeletons revealed about TB?

   B How many species of animals can contract TB?

   C Why is TB currently most common in Africa and East Asia?

   D How does the human immune system function?

2. If you are using a **search engine** to learn about treating TB in domestic cats, which search term would probably yield the best results?

   F Tuberculosis

   G Tuberculosis in cats

   H Pet care

   J Curing and preventing tuberculosis

3. Which source would provide the most reliable information about the latest methods of treating tuberculosis?

   A An interview with an emergency room doctor

   B The online National Library of Medicine of the U.S. National Institutes of Health

   C A research paper by a high school senior

   D An article on tuberculosis in an encyclopedia for young readers

4. If you want to find out about the life cycle of a virus, which link on this Web page would probably be most helpful?

   F Tales of a Survivor

   G Views from Space

   H National Tuberculosis Center

   J Go Inside a Virus

From Into Thin Air

Make the Connection

Identifying Causes, Effects, Ironies, and Contradictions

A **cause** is the reason why something happens; an **effect** is the result of some event. A single effect may have several causes, and a single cause may lead to many effects. Everything that happens in the following excerpt is connected by a complex pattern of causes and effects, many of which are filled with **irony.** As you read, look for examples of **situational irony**—when what occurs is the opposite of what's expected. Look also for the real-life **contradictions** and **incongruities** that lead to disaster—instances where people don't do what they say they will do or when things don't come together as they are expected to. Also note the causes that led to the disasters on Mount Everest, and note the effects of decisions made by the climbers.

The journalist who wrote this story barely escaped with his life. The day he reached the summit, eight other climbers (including Krakauer's tour leader) died on the mountain. Krakauer practices the riskiest form of journalism—**participatory journalism,** in which a reporter actually takes part in events.

Imagine that you are a participatory journalist. What story would you write? Why?

_____

_____

_____

_____

What risks might there be?

_____

_____

_____

_____

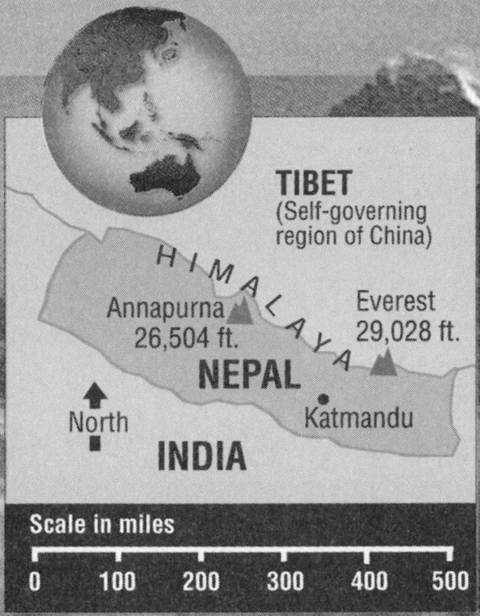

TIBET
(Self-governing
region of China)

HIMALAYA

Annapurna
26,504 ft.

Everest
29,028 ft.

NEPAL

North

Katmandu

INDIA

Scale in miles

0   100   200   300   400   500

From

Into Thin Air

Jon Krakauer

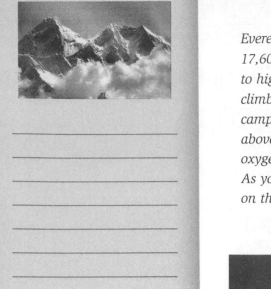

Everest expeditions ascend the mountain in stages. From Base Camp at 17,600 feet, they make short trips up and down to acclimatize, or get used to higher elevations. This process may last several weeks before the final climb to the top, which is also done in stages. Krakauer's group made camp at 19,500 feet, 21,300 feet, 24,000 feet, and 26,000 feet. The area above 25,000 feet is known as the Death Zone. Here the air is so poor in oxygen that it's almost impossible for climbers to make rational decisions. As you read, refer to the map on this page to chart the climbers' progress on their descents.

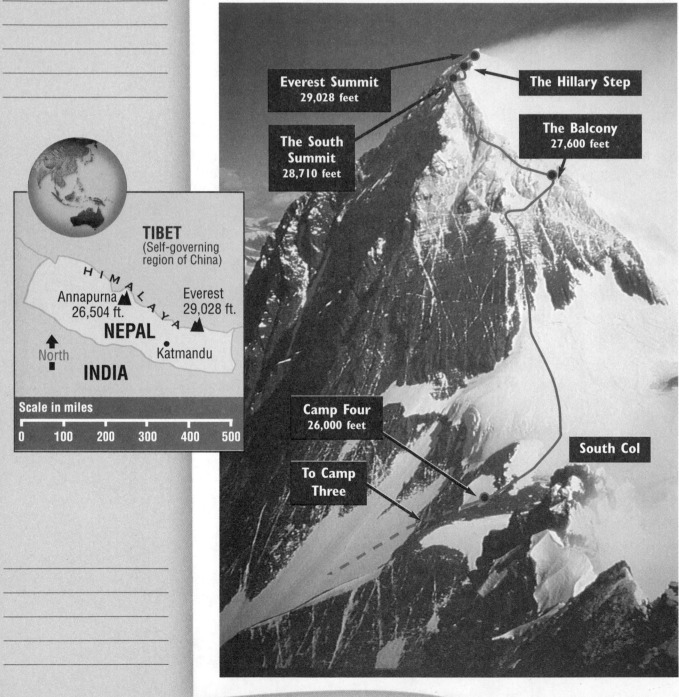

TIBET
(Self-governing region of China)

HIMALAYA

Annapurna
26,504 ft.

Everest
29,028 ft.

NEPAL

North

Katmandu

INDIA

Scale in miles

0   100   200   300   400   500

Everest Summit
29,028 feet

The Hillary Step

The South Summit
28,710 feet

The Balcony
27,600 feet

Camp Four
26,000 feet

South Col

To Camp Three

Straddling the top of the world, one foot in Tibet and the other in Nepal, I cleared the ice from my oxygen mask, hunched a shoulder against the wind, and stared absently at the vast sweep of earth below. I understood on some dim, detached level that it was a spectacular sight. I'd been fantasizing about this moment, and the release of emotion that would accompany it, for many months. But now that I was finally here, standing on the summit of Mount Everest, I just couldn't summon the energy to care.

10 It was the afternoon of May 10. I hadn't slept in 57 hours. The only food I'd been able to force down over the preceding three days was a bowl of Ramen soup and a handful of peanut M&M's. Weeks of violent coughing had left me with two separated ribs, making it excruciatingly painful to breathe. Twenty-nine thousand twenty-eight feet up in the troposphere, there was so little oxygen reaching my brain that my mental capacity was that of a slow child. Under the circumstances, I was incapable of feeling much of anything except cold and tired.

I'd arrived on the summit a few minutes after Anatoli Boukreev,[1] a Russian guide with an American expedition, and just ahead of Andy Harris, a guide with the New Zealand–based commercial team that 20 I was a part of and someone with whom I'd grown to be friends during the last six weeks. I snapped four quick photos of Harris and Boukreev striking summit poses, and then turned and started down. My watch read 1:17 p.m. All told, I'd spent less than five minutes on the roof of the world.

After a few steps, I paused to take another photo, this one looking down the Southeast Ridge, the route we had ascended. Training my lens on a pair of climbers approaching the summit, I saw something that until that moment had escaped my attention. To the south, where the sky had been perfectly clear just an hour earlier, a blanket of clouds 30 now hid Pumori, Ama Dablam, and the other lesser peaks surrounding Everest.

Days later—after six bodies had been found, after a search for two others had been abandoned, after surgeons had amputated the gangrenous right hand of my teammate Beck Weathers—people would ask why, if the weather had begun to deteriorate, had climbers on the upper mountain not heeded the signs? Why did veteran Himalayan guides keep moving upward, leading a gaggle of amateurs, each of whom had paid as much as $65,000 to be ushered safely up Everest, into an apparent death trap?

40 Nobody can speak for the leaders of the two guided groups involved, for both men are now dead. But I can attest that nothing I saw early on

---

1. **Anatoli Boukreev:** Boukreev was killed about a year and a half later, on December 26, 1997. He was trapped in an avalanche while climbing Annapurna, a mountain peak in the Himalayas.

WORDS TO OWN

innocuous (i·näk′yōō·əs) *adj.:*
harmless.

PREDICT

What do you think will happen
if Krakauer runs out of oxygen?

_____

_____

_____

_____

_____

VISUALIZE

Re-read lines 51–59.
Underline the words that help
you create a mental image of
the terrain Krakauer is crossing.

WORDS TO OWN

notorious (nō·tôr′ē·əs) *adj.:*
famous, usually in an
unfavorable sense.

INFER

How does this "traffic jam"
intensify Krakauer's problem?

_____

_____

_____

_____

_____

_____

_____

_____

_____

_____

_____

_____

_____

the afternoon of May 10 suggested that a murderous storm was about to
bear down on us. To my oxygen-depleted mind, the clouds drifting up
the grand valley of ice known as the Western Cwm looked <u>innocuous</u>,
wispy, insubstantial. Gleaming in the brilliant midday sun, they appeared
no different from the harmless puffs of convection condensation that rose
from the valley almost daily. As I began my descent, I was indeed
anxious, but my concern had little to do with the weather. A check of
the gauge on my oxygen tank had revealed that it was almost empty. I
50 needed to get down, fast.

The uppermost shank of the Southeast Ridge is a slender, heavily
corniced fin of rock and wind-scoured snow that snakes for a quarter-
mile toward a secondary pinnacle known as the South Summit.
Negotiating the serrated ridge presents few great technical hurdles,
but the route is dreadfully exposed. After 15 minutes of cautious
shuffling over a 7,000-foot abyss, I arrived at the <u>notorious</u> Hillary Step,
a pronounced notch in the ridge named after Sir Edmund Hillary, the
first Westerner to climb the mountain, and a spot that does require a
fair amount of technical maneuvering. As I clipped into a fixed rope and
60 prepared to rappel[2] over the lip, I was greeted by an alarming sight.

Thirty feet below, some 20 people were queued up[3] at the base of
the Step, and three climbers were hauling themselves up the rope that I
was attempting to descend. I had no choice but to unclip from the line
and step aside.

The traffic jam comprised climbers from three separate expeditions:
the team I belonged to, a group of paying clients under the leadership of
the celebrated New Zealand guide Rob Hall; another guided party headed
by American Scott Fischer; and a nonguided team from Taiwan. Moving
at the snail's pace that is the norm above 8,000 meters, the throng
70 labored up the Hillary Step one by one, while I nervously bided my time.

Harris, who left the summit shortly after I did, soon pulled up
behind me. Wanting to conserve whatever oxygen remained in my tank,
I asked him to reach inside my backpack and turn off the valve on my
regulator, which he did. For the next ten minutes I felt surprisingly
good. My head cleared. I actually seemed less tired than with the gas
turned on. Then, abruptly, I felt like I was suffocating. My vision
dimmed and my head began to spin. I was on the brink of losing
consciousness.

Instead of turning my oxygen off, Harris, in his hypoxically[4] impaired
80 state, had mistakenly cranked the valve open to full flow, draining the
tank. I'd just squandered the last of my gas going nowhere. There was

---

2. **rappel** (ra·pel′): descend a mountain by means of a double rope arranged around the
climber's body so that he or she can control the slide downward.
3. **queued** (kyōōd) **up:** lined up.
4. **hypoxically:** characterized by hypoxia, a condition resulting from a decrease in the oxygen
reaching body tissues. Hypoxia is a common condition at very high altitudes.

another tank waiting for me at the South Summit, 250 feet below, but to get there I would have to descend the most exposed terrain on the entire route without benefit of supplemental oxygen.

But first I had to wait for the crowd to thin. I removed my now useless mask, planted my ice ax into the mountain's frozen hide, and hunkered on the ridge crest. As I exchanged banal congratulations with the climbers filing past, inwardly I was frantic: "Hurry it up, hurry it up!" I silently pleaded. "While you guys are messing around here, I'm losing brain cells by the millions!"

Most of the passing crowd belonged to Fischer's group, but near the back of the parade two of my teammates eventually appeared: Hall and Yasuko Namba. Girlish and reserved, the 47-year-old Namba was 40 minutes away from becoming the oldest woman to climb Everest and the second Japanese woman to reach the highest point on each continent, the so-called Seven Summits.

Later still, Doug Hansen—another member of our expedition, a postal worker from Seattle who had become my closest friend on the mountain—arrived atop the Step. "It's in the bag!" I yelled over the wind, trying to sound more upbeat than I felt. Plainly exhausted, Doug mumbled something from behind his oxygen mask that I didn't catch, shook my hand weakly, and continued plodding upward.

The last climber up the rope was Fischer, whom I knew casually from Seattle, where we both lived. His strength and drive were legendary—in 1994 he'd climbed Everest without using bottled oxygen— so I was surprised at how slowly he was moving and how hammered he looked when he pulled his mask aside to say hello. "Bruuuuuuce!" he wheezed with forced cheer, employing his trademark, fratboyish greeting. When I asked how he was doing, Fischer insisted he was feeling fine: "Just dragging a little today for some reason. No big deal." With the Hillary Step finally clear, I clipped into the strand of orange rope, swung quickly around Fischer as he slumped over his ice ax, and rappelled over the edge.

It was after 2:30 when I made it down to the South Summit. By now tendrils of mist were wrapping across the top of 27,890-foot Lhotse and lapping at Everest's summit pyramid. No longer did the weather look so benign. I grabbed a fresh oxygen cylinder, jammed it onto my regulator, and hurried down into the gathering cloud.

Four hundred vertical feet above, where the summit was still washed in bright sunlight under an immaculate cobalt sky, my compadres were dallying, memorializing their arrival at the apex of the planet with photos and high-fives—and using up precious ticks of the clock. None of them imagined that a horrible ordeal was drawing nigh. None of them suspected that by the end of that long day, every minute would matter. . . .

90

100

110

120

IDENTIFY

Underline the phrase in which the writer compares Everest to an animal.

_____

_____

_____

_____

_____

_____

INFER

What **inference** can you make about Fischer's character from lines 104–110?

_____

_____

_____

_____

_____

_____

_____

_____

WORDS TO OWN

benign (bi·nīn′) adj.: here, favorable or harmless.

BUILD FLUENCY

As you read this paragraph aloud, try to convey a sense of the rising drama. Now read the passage again, paying special attention to the sentence rhythm and punctuation. Did you read more effectively the second time?

WORDS TO OWN

apex (ā′peks′) n.: highest point; top.

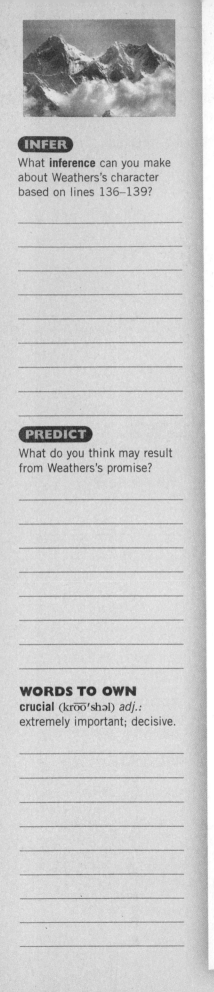

INFER

What **inference** can you make about Weathers's character based on lines 136–139?

_____

_____

_____

_____

_____

_____

_____

PREDICT

What do you think may result from Weathers's promise?

_____

_____

_____

_____

_____

_____

WORDS TO OWN
crucial (kroo′shəl) *adj.:* extremely important; decisive.

_____

_____

_____

_____

_____

_____

_____

At 3 P.M., within minutes of leaving the South Summit, I descended into clouds ahead of the others. Snow started to fall. In the flat, diminishing light, it became hard to tell where the mountain ended and where the sky began. It would have been very easy to blunder off the edge of the

130 ridge and never be heard from again. The lower I went, the worse the weather became.

When I reached the Balcony again, about 4 P.M., I encountered Beck Weathers standing alone, shivering violently. Years earlier, Weathers had undergone radial keratotomy to correct his vision. A side effect, which he discovered on Everest and consequently hid from Hall, was that in the low barometric pressure at high altitude, his eyesight failed. Nearly blind when he'd left Camp Four in the middle of the night but hopeful that his vision would improve at daybreak, he stuck close to the person in front of him and kept climbing.

140 Upon reaching the Southeast Ridge shortly after sunrise, Weathers had confessed to Hall that he was having trouble seeing, at which point Hall declared, "Sorry, pal, you're going down. I'll send one of the Sherpas[5] with you." Weathers countered that his vision was likely to improve as soon as the sun crept higher in the sky; Hall said he'd give Weathers 30 minutes to find out—after that, he'd have to wait there at 27,500 feet for Hall and the rest of the group to come back down. Hall didn't want Weathers descending alone. "I'm dead serious about this," Hall admonished his client. "Promise me that you'll sit right here until I return."

150 "I crossed my heart and hoped to die," Weathers recalls now, "and promised I wouldn't go anywhere." Shortly after noon, Hutchison, Taske, and Kasischke[6] passed by with their Sherpa escorts, but Weathers elected not to accompany them. "The weather was still good," he explains, "and I saw no reason to break my promise to Rob."

By the time I encountered Weathers, however, conditions were turning ugly. "Come down with me," I implored, "I'll get you down, no problem." He was nearly convinced, until I made the mistake of mentioning that Groom was on his way down, too. In a day of many mistakes, this would turn out to be a <u>crucial</u> one. "Thanks anyway,"

160 Weathers said. "I'll just wait for Mike. He's got a rope; he'll be able to short-rope[7] me." Secretly relieved, I hurried toward the South Col, 1,500 feet below.

These lower slopes proved to be the most difficult part of the descent. Six inches of powder snow blanketed outcroppings of loose

---

5. **Sherpas:** a Tibetan people living on the southern slopes of the Himalayas. As experienced mountain climbers, the Sherpas are hired by expeditions to haul loads and set up camps and ropes.
6. Stuart Hutchison, Dr. John Taske, and Lou Kasischke were three clients on Rob Hall's team.
7. **short-rope:** assist a weak or injured climber by hauling him or her.

shale. Climbing down them demanded unceasing concentration, an all but impossible feat in my current state. By 5:30, however, I was finally within 200 vertical feet of Camp Four, and only one obstacle stood between me and safety: a steep bulge of rock-hard ice that I'd have to descend without a rope. But the weather had deteriorated into a full-scale blizzard. Snow pellets borne on 70-mph winds stung my face; any exposed skin was instantly frozen. The tents, no more than 200 horizontal yards away, were only intermittently visible through the whiteout. There was zero margin for error. Worried about making a critical blunder, I sat down to marshal my energy.

Suddenly, Harris[8] appeared out of the gloom and sat beside me. At this point there was no mistaking that he was in appalling shape. His cheeks were coated with an armor of frost, one eye was frozen shut, and his speech was slurred. He was frantic to reach the tents. After briefly discussing the best way to negotiate the ice, Harris started scooting down on his butt, facing forward. "Andy," I yelled after him, "it's crazy to try it like that!" He yelled something back, but the words were carried off by the screaming wind. A second later he lost his purchase[9] and was rocketing down on his back.

Two hundred feet below, I could make out Harris's motionless form. I was sure he'd broken at least a leg, maybe his neck. But then he stood up, waved that he was OK, and started stumbling toward camp, which was for the moment in plain sight, 150 yards beyond.

I could see three or four people shining lights outside the tents. I watched Harris walk across the flats to the edge of camp, a distance he covered in less than ten minutes. When the clouds closed in a moment later, cutting off my view, he was within 30 yards of the tents. I didn't see him again after that, but I was certain that he'd reached the security of camp, where Sherpas would be waiting with hot tea. Sitting out in the storm, with the ice bulge still standing between me and the tents, I felt a pang of envy. I was angry that my guide hadn't waited for me.

Twenty minutes later I was in camp. I fell into my tent with my crampons still on, zipped the door tight, and sprawled across the frost-covered floor. I was drained, more exhausted than I'd ever been in my life. But I was safe. Andy was safe. The others would be coming into camp soon. We'd done it. We'd climbed Mount Everest.

It would be many hours before I learned that everyone had in fact not made it back to camp—that one teammate was already dead and that 23 other men and women were caught in a desperate struggle for their lives. . . .

---

8. After writing this article, Krakauer discovered through conversations with Martin Adams (a client from Scott Fischer's team) that the person he thought was Harris was, in fact, Martin Adams.
9. **purchase:** firm hold.

VISUALIZE

On the map on page 266, draw a line tracing Krakauer's descent down the mountain. Put an "x" where Krakauer is now.

RETELL

Use your own words to describe the challenge that Krakauer faces.

_____
_____
_____
_____
_____
_____
_____
_____
_____
_____
_____
_____

INTERPRET

Re-read lines 199–200. How is Krakauer's thought process **ironic** in light of what we know of later events?

_____
_____
_____
_____
_____
_____

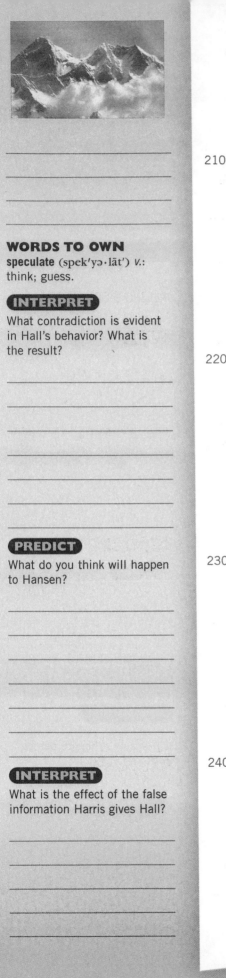

WORDS TO OWN

speculate (spek′yə·lāt′) *v.*: think; guess.

INTERPRET

What contradiction is evident in Hall's behavior? What is the result?

_____

_____

_____

_____

_____

_____

_____

PREDICT

What do you think will happen to Hansen?

_____

_____

_____

_____

_____

_____

_____

INTERPRET

What is the effect of the false information Harris gives Hall?

_____

_____

_____

_____

_____

Meanwhile, Hall and Hansen were still on the frightfully exposed summit ridge, engaged in a grim struggle of their own. The 46-year-old Hansen, whom Hall had turned back just below this spot exactly a year ago, had been determined to bag the summit this time around. "I want to get this thing done and out of my life," he'd told me a couple of days
210 earlier. "I don't want to have to come back here."

Indeed Hansen had reached the top this time, though not until after 3 P.M., well after Hall's predetermined turnaround time. Given Hall's conservative, systematic nature, many people wonder why he didn't turn Hansen around when it became obvious that he was running late. It's not far-fetched to speculate that because Hall had talked Hansen into coming back to Everest this year, it would have been especially hard for him to deny Hansen the summit a second time—especially when all of Fischer's clients were still marching blithely toward the top.

"It's very difficult to turn someone around high on the mountain,"
220 cautions Guy Cotter, a New Zealand guide who summited Everest with Hall in 1992 and was guiding the peak for him in 1995 when Hansen made his first attempt. "If a client sees that the summit is close and they're dead set on getting there, they're going to laugh in your face and keep going up."

In any case, for whatever reason, Hall did not turn Hansen around. Instead, after reaching the summit at 2:10 P.M., Hall waited for more than an hour for Hansen to arrive and then headed down with him. Soon after they began their descent, just below the top, Hansen apparently ran out of oxygen and collapsed. "Pretty much the same thing happened to
230 Doug in '95," says Ed Viesturs, an American who guided the peak for Hall that year. "He was fine during the ascent, but as soon as he started down he lost it mentally and physically. He turned into a real zombie, like he'd used everything up."

At 4:31 P.M., Hall radioed Base Camp to say that he and Hansen were above the Hillary Step and urgently needed oxygen. Two full bottles were waiting for them at the South Summit; if Hall had known this he could have retrieved the gas fairly quickly and then climbed back up to give Hansen a fresh tank. But Harris, in the throes of his oxygen-starved dementia,[10] overheard the 4:31 radio call while descending the Southeast
240 Ridge and broke in to tell Hall that all the bottles at the South Summit were empty. So Hall stayed with Hansen and tried to bring the helpless client down without oxygen, but could get him no farther than the top of the Hillary Step.

Cotter, a very close friend of both Hall and Harris, happened to be a few miles from Everest Base Camp at the time, guiding an expedition on Pumori. Overhearing the radio conversations between Hall and Base Camp, he called Hall at 5:36 and again at 5:57, urging his mate to leave

---

10. **dementia** (di·men′shə): mental impairment; madness.

Hansen and come down alone. . . . Hall, however, wouldn't consider going down without Hansen.

250　　　There was no further word from Hall until the middle of the night. At 2:46 A.M. on May 11, Cotter woke up to hear a long, broken transmission, probably unintended: Hall was wearing a remote microphone clipped to the shoulder strap of his backpack, which was occasionally keyed on by mistake. In this instance, says Cotter, "I suspect Rob didn't even know he was transmitting. I could hear someone yelling—it might have been Rob, but I couldn't be sure because the wind was so loud in the background. He was saying something like 'Keep moving! Keep going!' presumably to Doug, urging him on."

　　　If that was indeed the case, it meant that in the wee hours of the
260　morning Hall and Hansen were still struggling from the Hillary Step toward the South Summit, taking more than 12 hours to <u>traverse</u> a stretch of ridge typically covered by descending climbers in half an hour.

　　　Hall's next call to Base Camp was at 4:43 A.M. He'd finally reached the South Summit but was unable to descend farther, and in a series of transmissions over the next two hours he sounded confused and irrational. "Harold[11] was with me last night," Hall insisted, when in fact Harris had reached the South Col at sunset. "But he doesn't seem to be with me now. He was very weak."

　　　Mackenzie[12] asked him how Hansen was doing. "Doug," Hall
270　replied, "is gone." That was all he said, and it was the last mention he ever made of Hansen.

　　　On May 23, when Breashears and Viesturs, of the IMAX team,[13] reached the summit, they found no sign of Hansen's body but they did find an ice ax planted about 50 feet below the Hillary Step, along a highly exposed section of ridge where the fixed ropes came to an end. It is quite possible that Hall managed to get Hansen down the ropes to this point, only to have him lose his footing and fall 7,000 feet down the sheer Southwest Face, leaving his ice ax jammed into the ridge crest where he slipped.

280　　　During the radio calls to Base Camp early on May 11, Hall revealed that something was wrong with his legs, that he was no longer able to walk and was shaking uncontrollably. This was very disturbing news to the people down below, but it was amazing that Hall was even alive after spending a night without shelter or oxygen at 28,700 feet in hurricane-force wind and minus-100-degree windchill.

　　　At 5 A.M., Base Camp patched through a call on the satellite telephone to Jan Arnold, Hall's wife, seven months pregnant with their first child in Christchurch, New Zealand. Arnold, a respected physician,

---

11. **Harold:** Andy Harris's nickname.
12. **Mackenzie:** Dr. Caroline Mackenzie was Base Camp doctor for Rob Hall's team.
13. **IMAX team:** Another team of climbers, who were shooting a $5.5 million giant-screen movie about Mount Everest. The movie was released in 1998.

WORDS TO OWN
traverse (trə·vʉrs′) v.: cross.

INFER
Why does it take them so long to traverse the ridge?

IDENTIFY
How many days passed between Krakauer's ordeal and the IMAX team's ascent?

IDENTIFY
Underline the sentence that suggests Hall possesses unusual physical endurance.

INTERPRET

Explain what Hall had meant
by comparing Everest to the
moon.

INFER

What **inferences** about Hall's
character can you make from
lines 309–312?

had summited Everest with Hall in 1993 and entertained no illusions
290 about the gravity of her husband's predicament. "My heart really sank
when I heard his voice," she recalls. "He was slurring his words
markedly. He sounded like Major Tom[14] or something, like he was just
floating away. I'd been up there; I knew what it could be like in bad
weather. Rob and I had talked about the impossibility of being rescued
from the summit ridge. As he himself had put it, 'You might as well be
on the moon.' "

By that time, Hall had located two full oxygen bottles, and after
struggling for four hours trying to de-ice his mask, around 8:30 A.M.
he finally started breathing the life-sustaining gas. Several times he
300 announced that he was preparing to descend, only to change his mind
and remain at the South Summit. The day had started out sunny and
clear, but the wind remained fierce, and by late morning the upper
mountain was wrapped with thick clouds. Climbers at Camp Two
reported that the wind over the summit sounded like a squadron of
747s, even from 8,000 feet below. . . .

Throughout that day, Hall's friends begged him to make an effort
to descend from the South Summit under his own power. At 3:20 P.M.,
after one such transmission from Cotter, Hall began to sound annoyed.
"Look," he said, "if I thought I could manage the knots on the fixed
310 ropes with me frostbitten hands, I would have gone down six hours ago,
pal. Just send a couple of the boys up with a big thermos of something
hot—then I'll be fine."

At 6:20 P.M., Hall was patched through a second time to Arnold in
Christchurch. "Hi, my sweetheart," he said in a slow, painfully distorted
voice. "I hope you're tucked up in a nice warm bed. How are you doing?"

"I can't tell you how much I'm thinking about you!" Arnold replied.
"You sound so much better than I expected. . . . Are you warm, my
darling?"

"In the context of the altitude, the setting, I'm reasonably
320 comfortable," Hall answered, doing his best not to alarm her.

"How are your feet?"

"I haven't taken me boots off to check, but I think I may have a bit
of frostbite."

"I'm looking forward to making you completely better when you
come home," said Arnold. "I just know you're going to be rescued. Don't
feel that you're alone. I'm sending all my positive energy your way!"
Before signing off, Hall told his wife, "I love you. Sleep well, my
sweetheart. Please don't worry too much."

These would be the last words anyone would hear him utter.
330 Attempts to make radio contact with Hall later that night and the next

---

14. **Major Tom:** refers to the song "Space Oddity" by David Bowie about an astronaut, Major
Tom, who is lost and floating in space.

day went unanswered. Twelve days later, when Breashears and Viesturs climbed over the South Summit on their way to the top, they found Hall lying on his right side in a shallow ice-hollow, his upper body buried beneath a drift of snow.

Early on the morning of May 11, when I returned to Camp Four, Hutchison, standing in for Groom, who was unconscious in his tent, organized a team of four Sherpas to locate the bodies of our teammates Weathers and Namba. The Sherpa search party, headed by Lhakpa Chhiri, departed ahead of Hutchison, who was so exhausted and
340 befuddled that he forgot to put his boots on and left camp in his light, smooth-soled liners. Only when Lhakpa Chhiri pointed out the blunder did Hutchison return for his boots. Following Boukreev's directions, the Sherpas had no trouble locating the two bodies at the edge of the Kangshung Face.

IDENTIFY
Who is Boukreev? Why would he be able to give the Sherpas directions?

The first body turned out to be Namba, but Hutchison couldn't tell who it was until he knelt in the howling wind and chipped a three-inch-thick carapace of ice from her face. To his shock, he discovered that she was still breathing. Both her gloves were gone, and her bare hands appeared to be frozen solid. Her eyes were dilated. The skin on her face
350 was the color of porcelain. "It was terrible," Hutchison recalls. "I was overwhelmed. She was very near death. I didn't know what to do."

He turned his attention to Weathers, who lay 20 feet away. His face was also caked with a thick armor of frost. Balls of ice the size of grapes were matted to his hair and eyelids. After cleaning the frozen detritus from his face, Hutchison discovered that he, too, was still alive: "Beck was mumbling something, I think, but I couldn't tell what he was trying to say. His right glove was missing and he had terrible frostbite. He was as close to death as a person can be and still be breathing."

Badly shaken, Hutchison went over to the Sherpas and asked Lhakpa
360 Chhiri's advice. Lhakpa Chhiri, an Everest veteran respected by Sherpas and sahibs[15] alike for his mountain savvy, urged Hutchison to leave Weathers and Namba where they lay. Even if they survived long enough to be dragged back to Camp Four, they would certainly die before they could be carried down to Base Camp, and attempting a rescue would needlessly jeopardize the lives of the other climbers on the Col, most of whom were going to have enough trouble getting themselves down safely.

IDENTIFY
Underline the reasons Chhiri gives for leaving Namba and Weathers.

WORDS TO OWN
jeopardize (jep′ər·dīz′) v.: endanger.

Hutchison decided that Chhiri was right. There was only one choice, however difficult: Let nature take its inevitable course with Weathers and
370 Namba, and save the group's resources for those who could actually be helped. It was a classic act of triage.[16] When Hutchison returned to camp

---

15. **sahibs** (sä′ibz′): term used by Sherpas to refer to the paying members of the expeditions.
16. **triage** (trē·äzh′): assigning of priorities of medical care based on chances for survival.

EVALUATE

Do you think Hutchison made the right decision? Explain.

_____

_____

_____

_____

_____

_____

_____

_____

_____

INFER

Why would Weathers think the tents were rocks?

_____

_____

_____

_____

_____

_____

WORDS TO OWN

tenuous (ten′yoo·əs) *adj.*: weak; slight.

_____

_____

_____

_____

_____

_____

at 8:30 A.M. and told the rest of us of his decision, nobody doubted that it was the correct thing to do.

Later that day a rescue team headed by two of Everest's most experienced guides, Pete Athans and Todd Burleson, who were on the mountain with their own clients, arrived at Camp Four. Burleson was standing outside the tents about 4:30 P.M. when he noticed someone lurching slowly toward camp. The person's bare right hand, naked to the wind and horribly frostbitten, was outstretched in a weird, frozen salute.
380 Whoever it was reminded Athans of a mummy in a low-budget horror film. The mummy turned out to be none other than Beck Weathers, somehow risen from the dead.

A couple of hours earlier, a light must have gone on in the reptilian core of Weathers' comatose brain, and he regained consciousness. "Initially I thought I was in a dream," he recalls. "Then I saw how badly frozen my right hand was, and that helped bring me around to reality. Finally I woke up enough to recognize that the cavalry wasn't coming so I better do something about it myself."

Although Weathers was blind in his right eye and able to focus his
390 left eye within a radius of only three or four feet, he started walking into the teeth of the wind, deducing correctly that camp lay in that direction. If he'd been wrong he would have stumbled immediately down the Kangshung Face, the edge of which was a few yards in the opposite direction. Ninety minutes later he encountered "some unnaturally smooth, bluish-looking rocks," which turned out to be the tents of Camp Four.

The next morning, May 12, Athans, Burleson, and climbers from the IMAX team short-roped Weathers down to Camp Two. On the morning of May 13, in a hazardous helicopter rescue, Weathers and Gau[17] were
400 evacuated from the top of the icefall by Lieutenant Colonel Madan Khatri Chhetri of the Nepalese army. A month later, a team of Dallas surgeons would amputate Weather's dead right hand just below the wrist and use skin grafts to reconstruct his left hand.

After helping to load Weathers and Gau into the rescue chopper, I sat in the snow for a long while, staring at my boots, trying to get some grip, however <u>tenuous</u>, on what had happened over the preceding 72 hours. Then, nervous as a cat, I headed down into the icefall for one last trip through the maze of decaying seracs.[18]

I'd always known, in the abstract, that climbing mountains was a
410 dangerous pursuit. But until I climbed in the Himalayas this spring, I'd never actually seen death at close range. And there was so much of it: Including three members of an Indo-Tibetan team who died on the north

---

17. **Gau:** "Makalu" Gau Ming-Ho, leader of the Taiwanese National Expedition, another team climbing on Everest.
18. **seracs:** pointed masses of ice.

side just below the summit in the same May 10 storm and an Austrian killed some days later, 11 men and women lost their lives on Everest in May 1996, a tie with 1982 for the worst single-season death toll in the peak's history. . . .[19]

420   Climbing mountains will never be a safe, predictable, rule-bound enterprise. It is an activity that idealizes risk-taking; its most celebrated figures have always been those who stuck their necks out the farthest and managed to get away with it. Climbers, as a species, are simply not distinguished by an excess of common sense. And that holds especially true for Everest climbers: When presented with a chance to reach the planet's highest summit, people are surprisingly quick to abandon prudence altogether. "Eventually," warns Tom Hornbein, 33 years after his ascent of the West Ridge, "what happened on Everest this season is certain to happen again."

EVALUATE

Is this quotation an effective way to end the article? Explain.

---

19. It actually was the worst death toll on record. After Krakauer wrote this article, a twelfth death was discovered.

Cause-and-Effect Chart

Choose one tragedy that resulted from the expedition—for example, the death of Doug Hansen or the loss of Beck Weathers's right hand. Write this event in the center box of the **cause-and-effect chart** below. Look back through the story to identify as many **causes** as you can for why this happened. Then, complete the rest of the diagram.

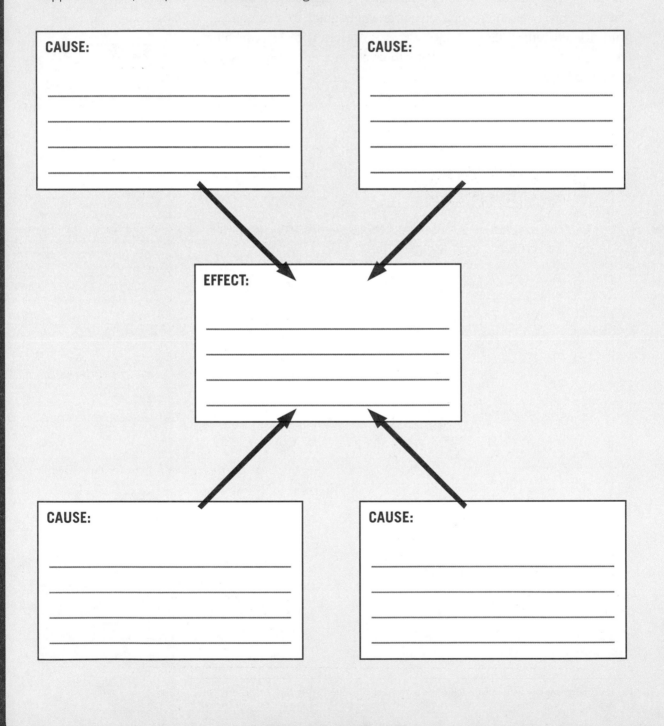

CAUSE:

_____

_____

_____

CAUSE:

_____

_____

_____

EFFECT:

_____

_____

_____

_____

CAUSE:

_____

_____

_____

CAUSE:

_____

_____

_____

Analyzing Informational Materials

Reading Check

1. Why does Krakauer feel better after Harris turns the valve on his oxygen regulator?

   _____

   _____

2. How did Weathers save his own life?

   _____

   _____

Test Practice

Circle the letter of the best answer to each of the following items.

1. What is Jon Krakauer's main emotion as he stands at the top of Mount Everest?

   A Regret
   B Happiness
   C Detachment
   D Nostalgia

2. Which of the following items is an example of **foreshadowing**?

   F Krakauer's eating noodle soup and candy
   G Krakauer's early mention of the number of people who died
   H The blanket of clouds Krakauer sees when he turns to take photographs
   J Krakauer's references to money people paid to be guided on the climb

3. Most tragic events on the mountain are caused by —

   A decisions made in anger
   B understandable mistakes
   C excessive fear
   D inexperienced guides

4. Beck Weathers becomes stranded alone because of all the following conditions *except* —

   F he had difficulty seeing
   G the guide asks him to wait
   H he loses one of his gloves
   J he chooses not to follow Krakauer down

5. All of the following phrases use metaphor to describe setting *except* —

   A fin of rock
   B wind-scoured snow
   C mountain's frozen hide
   D full-scale blizzard

Vocabulary: How to Own a Word

Analogies: Parallel Word Pairs

In an **analogy,** the words in one pair relate to each other in the same way as the words in a second pair. Fill in each blank below with the word from the Word Bank that best completes the analogy. (Two words on the list are synonyms and may be used interchangeably.)

Word Bank
deteriorate
innocuous
notorious
benign
apex
crucial
speculate
traverse
jeopardize
tenuous

1. base : bottom : : _____ : top.

2. safe : dangerous : : _____ : harmful.

3. mislead : deceive : : _____ : endanger.

4. trivial : minor : : _____ : important.

5. try : attempt : : _____ : guess.

6. minor : major : : _____ : malignant.

7. famous : star : : _____ : criminal.

8. weaken : strengthen : : _____ : improve.

9. climb : stairs : : _____ : bridge.

10. strong : powerful : : _____ : weak.

Selection: _____

The Writer's Purpose

Type of Writing	Definition	Example from Selection
Exposition	Writing that informs or explains.	
Narration	Writing that tells about a sequence of events.	
Description	Writing that creates a mood using images that appeal to our senses.	
Persuasion	Writing that tries to make the reader think or feel a certain way about something.	

Main Purpose of Selection

Julius Caesar in an Absorbing Production

Make the Connection

Evaluating an Argument

The article you are about to read is a **critical review** of a 1937 stage production of Shakespeare's *Julius Caesar*. As in all such reviews (book reviews, movie reviews, restaurant reviews), the writer states an opinion and then tries to convince you that the opinion is right. The author's **purpose** is persuasive.

In reading a review, follow the **argument,** which may consist of an opinion or claim. Pay careful attention to the **evidence** used to support the writer's opinion. Infer the reviewer's **criteria,** or standards of excellence. Identify the writer's experience and qualifications, if you can, to determine how **credible** his or her opinion is.

Comparing Persuasive Writing

Different types of persuasive writing require different kinds of evidence. The following chart lists some kinds of evidence that can effectively support a writer's argument. For each type of evidence, decide whether it would be more useful in a critical review or a political speech and place a check in the box under the appropriate column. If you think a specific type of evidence equally important to both kinds of persuasive writing, place a check in both boxes.

Kinds of Evidence	Critical Review	Political Speech
Facts		
Statistics		
Examples		
Anecdotes		
Quotations		
Comparisons		
Opinions		

Julius Caesar in an Absorbing Production

John Mason Brown

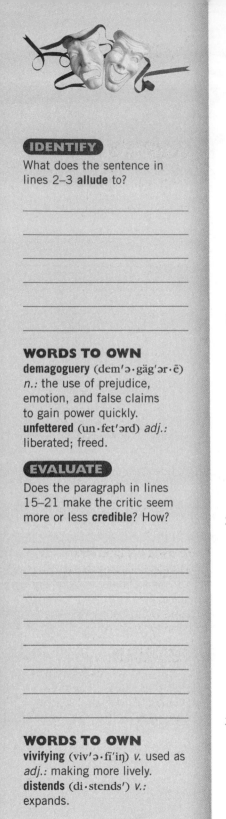

IDENTIFY

What does the sentence in lines 2–3 **allude** to?

_____

_____

_____

_____

_____

_____

WORDS TO OWN

demagoguery (dem′ə·gäg′ər·ē)
n.: the use of prejudice,
emotion, and false claims
to gain power quickly.
unfettered (un·fet′ərd) *adj.:*
liberated; freed.

EVALUATE

Does the paragraph in lines
15–21 make the critic seem
more or less **credible**? How?

_____

_____

_____

_____

_____

_____

_____

_____

WORDS TO OWN

vivifying (viv′ə·fī′iŋ) *v.* used as
adj.: making more lively.
distends (di·stends′) *v.:*
expands.

_____

_____

_____

_____

_____

*On November 11, 1937, when Hitler and Mussolini were in power, the
American director Orson Welles staged a modern-dress* Julius Caesar *at
the Mercury Theater in New York City.*

This is no funeral oration such as Miss Bankhead and Mr. Tearle forced
me to deliver yesterday when they interred *Antony and Cleopatra.*[1] I
come to praise *Caesar* at the Mercury, not to bury it. Of all the many
new plays and productions the season has so far revealed, this modern-
dress version of the mob mischief and demagoguery which can follow
the assassination of a dictator is by all odds the most exciting, the
most imaginative, the most topical, the most awesome, and the most
absorbing.

The touch of genius is upon it. It liberates Shakespeare from the
10 straitjacket of tradition. Gone are the togas and all the schoolroom
recollections of a plaster Julius. Blown away is the dust of antiquity.
Banished are the costumed Equity members,[2] so ill-at-ease in a painted
forum, spouting speeches which have tortured the memory of each
member of the audience.

Due to Orson Welles's inspirational concept and the sheer brilliance
of his staging, Shakespeare ceases at the Mercury to be the darling of the
College Board of Examiners.[3] Unfettered and with all the vigor that was
his when he spoke to the groundlings[4] of his own day, he becomes the
contemporary of us who are Undergroundlings. What he wrote with
20 Plutarch[5] in his mind, we are privileged to hear with today's headlines
screaming in our eyes.

New York has already enjoyed its successful Shakespearean revivals
in modern dress. There was *Hamlet.* There was *The Taming of the
Shrew.* Then, under this same Mr. Welles's direction, Harlem flirted
with a tantalizing, if unrealized, idea in its voodoo *Macbeth.* But these
productions, vivifying as they have proven, have at their best been
no more than quickening experiences *in* the theater.

The astonishing, all-impressive virtue of Mr. Welles's *Julius Caesar*
is that, magnificent as it is as theater, it is far larger than its medium.
30 Something deathless and dangerous in the world sweeps past you down
the darkened aisles at the Mercury and takes possession of the proud,
gaunt stage. It is something fearful and ominous, something turbulent
and to be dreaded, which distends the drama to include the life of

---

1. The actress Tallulah Bankhead opened in *Antony and Cleopatra* on November 10, 1937. Mr.
   Brown gave the production an unfavorable review.
2. **Equity members:** members of the professional actors union.
3. A group of college professors who set standards for college-entrance exams and for
   evaluating theses for advanced degrees.
4. **groundlings:** in the Elizabethan theater, the people who watched performances standing at
   ground level for the lowest entrance fee.
5. **Plutarch** (c. A.D. 46–c. 120): ancient Greek historian and biographer.

nations as well as of men. It is an ageless warning, made in such arresting terms that it not only gives a new vitality to an ancient story but unrolls in your mind's eye a map of the world which is increasingly splotched with sickening colors.

Mr. Welles does not dress his conspirators and his Storm Troopers in Black Shirts or in Brown.[6] He does not have to. The antique Rome,
40 which we had thought was securely Roman in Shakespeare's tragedy, he shows us to be a dateless state of mind. Of all the conspirators at work in the text, Mr. Welles is the most artful. He is not content to leave Shakespeare a great dramatist. He also turns him into a great anticipator. At his disposal Mr. Welles places a Time-Machine which carries him away from the past at which he had aimed and down through the centuries to the present. To an extent no other director in our day and country has equaled, Mr. Welles proves in his production that Shakespeare was indeed not of an age but for all time. After this surly modern Caesar, dressed in a green uniform and scowling behind the
50 mask-like face of a contemporary dictator, has fallen at the Mercury and new mischief is afoot, we cannot but shudder before the prophet's wisdom of those lines which read:

"How many ages hence
Shall this our lofty scene be acted over
In states unborn and accents yet unknown!"[7]

To fit the play into modern dress and give it its fullest implication, Mr. Welles has not hesitated to take his liberties with the script. Unlike Professor Strunk, however, who attempted to improve upon *Antony and Cleopatra*, he has not stabbed it through the heart. He has only chopped
60 away at its body. You may miss a few fingers, even an arm and leg in the *Julius Caesar* you thought you knew. But the heart of the drama beats more vigorously in this production than it has in years. If the play ceases to be Shakespeare's tragedy, it does manage to become ours. That is the whole point and glory of Mr. Welles's <u>unorthodox</u>, but welcome, restatement of it.

He places it upon a bare stage, the brick walls of which are crimson and naked. A few steps and a platform and an <u>abyss</u> beyond are the setting. A few steps—and the miracle of enveloping shadows, knife-like rays, and superbly changing lights. That is all. And it is all that is
70 needed. In its streamlined simplicity this setting achieves the glorious, <u>unimpeded</u> freedom of an Elizabethan stage. Yet no backgrounds of

---

6. Storm troopers, members of Hitler's Nazi militia, wore brown shirts. In Italy, Mussolini's Fascist party members wore uniforms with black shirts.
7. Lines spoken by Cassius, Act III, Scene 1, lines 111–113.

EVALUATE

How is a director's interpretation of a play as crucial to a production as the text of the play itself?

WORDS TO OWN
unorthodox (un·ôr′thə·däks′) *adj.:* unusual; not conforming to usual norms.
abyss (ə·bis′) *n.:* deep chasm or pit.

IDENTIFY
What kinds of evidence does the writer use to support his approval of Welles's "liberties with the script"?

WORDS TO OWN
unimpeded (un′im·pēd′əd) *adj.:* not obstructed or hindered.

INFER

From his praise of Welles's performance (lines 91–99), infer the critic's standard for judging an actor's delivery of Shakespeare's language.

WORDS TO OWN
reticent (ret′ə·sənt) *adj.*: habitually silent; reserved.
harangue (hə·raŋ′) *n.*: noisy, scolding speech.
imperious (im·pir′ē·əs) *adj.*: arrogant; domineering.

the winter have been as eloquent or contributive as is this frankly presentational set. It is a setting spacious enough for both the winds and victims of demagoguery to sweep across it like a hurricane. And sweep across it they do, in precisely this fashion.

Mr. Welles's direction is as heightening as is his use of an almost empty stage. His groupings are of that fluid, stressful, virtuoso sort one usually has to journey to Russia to see. He proves himself a brilliant innovator in his deployment of his principals and his movement of his
80 crowds. His direction, which is constantly creative, is never more so than in its first revelation of Caesar hearing the warning of the soothsayer, or in the fine scene in which Cinna, the poet, is engulfed by a sinister crowd of ruffians. Even when one misses Shakespeare's lines, Mr. Welles keeps drumming the meaning of his play into our minds by the scuffling of his mobs when they prowl in the shadows, or the herd-like thunder of their feet when they run as one threatening body. It is a memorable device. Like the setting in which it is used, it is pure theater: vibrant, unashamed, and enormously effective.

The theatrical virtues of this modern-dress *Julius Caesar* do not stop
90 with its excitements as a stunt in showmanship. They extend to the performances. As Brutus Mr. Welles shows once again how uncommon is his gift for speaking great words simply. His tones are conversational. His manner is quiet. The deliberation of his speech is the mark of the honesty which flames within him. His <u>reticent</u> Brutus is at once a foil[8] to the staginess of the production as a whole and to the oratory of Caesar and Antony. He is a perplexed liberal, this Brutus; an idealist who is swept by bad events into actions which have no less dangerous consequences for the state. His simple reading of the funeral oration is in happy contrast to what is usually done with the speech.

100 George Coulouris is an admirable Antony. So fresh is his characterization, so intelligent his performance that even "Friends, Romans, countrymen" sounds on his tongue as if it were a rabble-rousing <u>harangue</u> which he is uttering for the first time. Joseph Holland's Caesar is an <u>imperious</u> dictator who could be found frowning at you in this week's newsreels. He is excellently conceived and excellently projected. Some mention, however inadequate, must also be made of Martin Gabel's capable Cassius, of John Hoysradt's Decius Brutus, of the conspirators whose black hats are pluck'd about their ears, and Norman Lloyd's humorous yet deeply affecting Cinna.

110 It would be easy to find faults here and there: to wonder about the wisdom of some of the textual changes even in terms of the present production's aims; to complain that the whole tragedy does not fit with equal ease into its modern treatment; and to wish this or that scene had

---

8. **foil**: character that sets off or enhances another by contrast.

been played a little differently. But such fault-findings strike me in the case of this *Julius Caesar* as being as picayune[9] as they are ungrateful. What Mr. Welles and his associates at the Mercury have achieved is a triumph that is exceptional from almost every point of view.

—from the *New York Post*,
November 12, 1937

---

9. picayune (pĭk′ə·yo͞on′): trivial; unimportant.

Developing an Argument

Use the following graphic to construct a review of a movie you have seen recently. First, consider how you would evaluate the movie as a whole and write an opinion statement. Then, judge each of the four main parts that go into a film: the script, the direction, the acting, and the cinematography (camera work). Establish your criteria, or standards of excellence, by describing what you look for in a good film or by offering examples of other films that have fulfilled or failed to meet your expectations. Pass judgment on the film being reviewed and support your opinion with specific evidence.

Opinion of the Film:	
Script	
Criteria	
Judgment	
Support (evidence)	
Direction	
Criteria	
Judgment	
Support (evidence)	
Acting	
Criteria	
Judgment	
Support (evidence)	
Cinematography (camera work)	
Criteria	
Judgment	
Support (evidence)	

Analyzing Informational Materials

Reading Check

1. What is the purpose of the article?

_____

_____

2. Who is the writer's audience?

_____

_____

3. What is the writer's opinion of Orson Welles's production of *Julius Caesar*?

_____

_____

4. How is Mr. Welles's production different from a traditional production of the play?

_____

_____

Test Practice

Circle the letter of the correct answer to each question.

1. The writer's **opinion statement,** or **claim** about the play appears in —

    A the first sentence of paragraph 1

    B the last sentence of paragraph 1

    C the last sentence of paragraph 2

    D the last sentence in the article

2. To support his opinion, Brown discusses —

    F the staging of the production

    G the history of the play

    H Shakespeare's biography

    J none of the above

3. One aspect of the production that Brown does not discuss in this review is the —

    A actors' performances

    B set

    C costumes

    D price of tickets

4. When Brown claims that Welles's production "distends the drama to include the life of nations as well as of men," he means that Welles has —

    F made the play relevant to world politics of 1937

    G changed the script to focus on nations instead of characters

    H made each character stand for a nation

    J none of the above

Test Practice

5. Which of the following statements can you make about this review?

  A The writer is biased against the play.

  B The writer is biased against modern-dress productions of Shakespeare.

  C The writer presents a great deal of evidence to support his opinion.

  D The writer does not give enough evidence to be convincing.

6. Which of these statements is an **opinion**?

  F "Mr. Welles does not dress his conspirators and his Storm Troopers in Black Shirts or in Brown."

  G "But the heart of the drama beats more vigorously in this production than it has in years."

  H "New York has already enjoyed its successful Shakespearean revivals in modern dress."

  J "He places it upon a bare stage, the brick walls of which are crimson and naked."

7. If you outline the **argument** of this review, you discover that the writer supports his opinion statement with —

  A opinions—critical judgments about various aspects of the production

  B many facts about Shakespeare's original version of *Julius Caesar*

  C many facts about world politics during Caesar's day

  D many facts about world politics during Shakespeare's day

8. The **tone** of this article is best described as —

  F humorous

  G sarcastic

  H informal

  J admiring

9. Brown tailors his argument to fit his **audience,** who are —

  A high school students

  B professional actors and directors

  C readers of a New York newspaper

  D listeners of a radio program

10. Before you decide whether you find Brown's critical review convincing, you'd want to know more about —

  F Orson Welles's movies

  G William Shakespeare's tragedies

  H Julius Caesar's life and death

  J Brown's qualifications

11. When Brown says that "George Coulouris is an admirable Antony," he is stating —

  A his opinion of Coulouris's acting

  B his opinion of Antony's character

  C a fact that can be proved

  D a quotation from the director

Vocabulary: How to Own a Word

Analogies

Complete the following analogies. Word Bank words are boldfaced.

unfettered : **unimpeded** : : bound : _____

imperious : **arrogant** : : _____ : **reticent**

dictator : **demagoguery** : : _____ : **harangue**

unorthodox : _____ : : **vivifying** : vitalizing

abyss : deepens : : _____ : **distends**

Installing a Computer Sound Card

Make the Connection

Following Directions

The directions for computers and other electronic, mechanical, and scientific products and activities are called **technical directions.** You follow technical directions when you perform an experiment in the biology lab, program a friend's number into a cell phone, or install a dish on your roof for TV reception. When you first look at them, technical directions may seem complex. However, all you have to do is to pay attention and follow the steps carefully, and they will teach you what you need to know.

Technical directions are a type of **functional document.** Other examples include product reviews, contracts, and warranties. Functional documents come in many guises, but they all share one basic goal: to help get things done. Successful functional documents meet two criteria:

1. They are clearly organized and easily understood.
2. They follow a logical sequence of information or procedures.

There are many types of **logical sequences.** Some examples of logical sequences and the types of functional documents that use them are:

- **step-by-step sequence**—recipes and other instructions
- **point-by-point sequence**—legal documents and informational articles
- **highest-to-lowest sequence,** or vice versa—often used to structure product reviews and may be based on price or quality.

The failure to be clear and follow a logical sequence in functional documents can cause reader misunderstandings, which increase user dissatisfaction with the product. After all, no matter how good a product is, what good is it to you if you can't make it work?

As you read the technical directions that follow, ask yourself:

- Is each section clear and easy to understand?
- Is the sequence of information logical?

Installing a Computer Sound Card

Flo Ota De Lange and Sheri Henderson

PREDICT

What will happen if you fail to follow step 2?

_____

_____

_____

_____

_____

INFER

Why are the steps on lines 8–18 labeled "5a" and "5b," rather than "5" and "6"?

_____

_____

_____

_____

_____

EVALUATE

Step 8 describes two different ways in which the slot may be covered. Why?

_____

_____

_____

_____

_____

VISUALIZE

Re–read these directions and try to imagine each step. Are the directions clear enough for you to picture each step in your mind? Explain.

_____

_____

_____

_____

_____

_____

1. Be sure your computer is powered down and that it is unplugged.

2. Touch your fingers against something metal (*not* your computer) to discharge static electricity.

3. Open your computer's case.

4. Locate the slot you want on your computer's motherboard. See your owner's manual for more specific instructions about the location and types of slots on your computer.

5a. If the slot is empty, remove the screw that holds the metal slot cover in place, slide the cover out, and set both screw and cover aside for

10   later.

5b. If the slot is currently in use by the old sound card, remove the screw that holds the card in place and gently pull the card from the slot. You may need to give it a firm tug; however, remember that the card is brittle. Be careful not to rock it against the sides of the slot; it could snap off in the slot, or worse, pry the slot from the motherboard. You will see an audio cable attached at one end to the sound card and at the other end to the CD- or DVD-ROM drive. Disconnect this cable from the drive by pulling gently.

6. Plug the new sound card into the slot you have prepared by pressing

20   down firmly until the connector is fully inserted. It should be a tight fit, but you should not use undue force. If you encounter unexpected resistance, take the card out, check for alignment and possible obstructions, and try again.

7. To be sure the card is in place, give it a gentle tug. It should resist and stay in place. The connector strip's metal conductors should also be just barely visible when viewed at eye level.

8. Find the screw and slot cover you removed in step 5. You may need to replace both, or you may only have to replace the screw to hold the new card in place if it is built with an integrated slot cover.

30   Either way, be sure the slot is covered, and then tighten the screw to hold the new sound card in place.

9. Connect the included audio cable from the sound card to the CD- or DVD-ROM drive. You will find connector pins on the sound card and on the back of the disk drive that correspond to the plugs on each end of the audio cable. Be sure to line these pins up very carefully and press gently. As in step 6, if you encounter resistance, check to see that all pins are straight and that there are no other obstructions, then try again.

10. Close your computer case.

40 11. Connect the external speakers to their appropriate jacks.

12. Plug in the power cord, and turn on your computer and monitor. Once your computer is up and running, insert the CD that accompanies the sound card and complete the driver installation by following the on-screen instructions.

Functional Documents: The Recipe

Would you categorize recipes as a kind of functional document? Well, they are. Like all successful functional documents, recipes must be clearly organized, be easily understood, and present a logical sequence of information.

In the following graphic, write out your favorite recipe. Be sure to follow a logical sequence and construct clearly organized directions that anyone can understand.

Name of Dish: _____

Ingredients _____

_____

_____

_____

Steps 1. _____

2. _____

3. _____

4. _____

5. _____

6. _____

7. _____

Number of people served by this dish: _____

Analyzing Informational Materials

Reading Check

1. Why should you touch something metal before touching your computer?

_____

_____

2. Describe the dangers in removing or installing a sound card. What precautions must be taken with the card, and what things could go wrong?

_____

_____

3. How does the sound card connect to the CD- or DVD-ROM drive?

_____

_____

4. How will you know when the sound card is properly in place?

_____

_____

5. What information will you need to look up in your user manual? At what point in the project should you get this information?

_____

_____

Test Practice

Circle the letter of the correct answer for each question.

1. Which of the following steps can be broken into several steps for clarity of organization?

   A 3
   B 4
   C 5a
   D 5b

2. Which step can be skipped without causing the computer's sound *not* to work?

   F 3
   G 6
   H 7
   J 9

3. How can you find where to install the new sound card?

   A Consult your owner's manual.
   B Locate the old sound card, if one is present.
   C Follow the audio cable from the CD- or DVD-ROM drive.
   D All of the above

4. Users whose computers already have a sound card installed will complete which step *first*?

   F Turn computer on.
   G Remove the old card.
   H Install the new card.
   J Install the new software driver.

5. If your expansion slot is currently in use by the old sound card, which step will you *not* have to do?

   A Remove slot cover.
   B Disconnect audio cable.
   C Connect audio cable.
   D Install the new software driver.

PART 3   STANDARDIZED TEST PRACTICE

Literature

Informational Materials

DIRECTIONS

Read the short story. Then, read each multiple-choice question, and circle the letter of the best response.

Powder

Tobias Wolff

Just before Christmas my father took me skiing at Mount Baker. He'd had to fight for the privilege of my company, because my mother was still angry with him for sneaking me into a nightclub during our last visit, to see Thelonious Monk.[1]

He wouldn't give up. He promised, hand on heart, to take good care of me and have me home for dinner on Christmas Eve, and she relented. But as we were checking out of the lodge that morning it began to snow, and in this snow he observed some quality that made it necessary for us to get in one last run. We got in several last runs. He was indifferent to my fretting.[2] Snow whirled around us in bitter, blinding squalls, hissing like sand, and still we skied. As the lift bore us to the peak yet again, my father looked at his watch and said, "Criminey. This'll have to be a fast one."

By now I couldn't see the trail. There was no point in trying. I stuck to him like white on rice and did what he did and somehow made it to the bottom without sailing off a cliff. We returned our skis and my father put chains on the Austin-Healy while I swayed from foot to foot, clapping my mittens and wishing I were home. I could see everything. The green tablecloth, the plates with the holly pattern, the red candles waiting to be lit.

We passed a diner on our way out. "You want some soup?" my father asked. I shook my head. "Buck up," he said. "I'll get you there. Right, doctor?"

I was supposed to say, "Right, doctor," but I didn't say anything.

A state trooper waved us down outside the resort. A pair of sawhorses were blocking the road. The trooper came up to our car and bent down to my father's window. His face was bleached by the cold. Snowflakes clung to his eyebrows and to the fur trim of his jacket and cap.

"Don't tell me," my father said

The trooper told him. The road was closed. It might get cleared, it might not. Storm took everyone by surprise. So much, so fast. Hard to get people moving. Christmas Eve. What can you do?

My father said, "Look. We're talking about four, five inches. I've taken this car through worse than that."

The trooper straightened up, boots creaking. His face was out of sight but I could hear him. "The road is closed."

My father sat with both hands on the wheel, rubbing the wood with his thumbs. He looked at the barricade for a long time. He seemed to be trying to master the idea of it. Then he thanked the trooper, and with a weird, old-maidy show of caution turned the car around. "Your mother will never forgive me for this," he said.

"We should have left before," I said. "Doctor."

---

1. **Thelonious Monk** (1917–1982): American jazz musician, famed as a pianist and composer; one of the creators of the bop style of jazz.
2. **fretting:** *v. used as n.:* worrying.

He didn't speak to me again until we were both in a booth at the diner, waiting for our burgers. "She won't forgive me," he said. "Do you understand? Never."

"I guess," I said, but no guesswork was required; she wouldn't forgive him.

"I can't let that happen." He bent toward me. "I'll tell you what I want. I want us to be together again. Is that what you want?"

I wasn't sure, but I said, "Yes, sir."

He bumped my chin with his knuckles. "That's all I needed to hear."

When we finished eating he went to the pay phone in the back of the diner, then joined me in the booth again. I figured he'd called my mother, but he didn't give a report. He sipped at his coffee and stared out the window at the empty road. "Come on!" When the trooper's car went past, lights flashing, he got up and dropped some money on the check. "Okay. *Vámonos.*"[3]

The wind had died. The snow was falling straight down, less of it now; lighter. We drove away from the resort, right up to the barricade. "Move it," my father told me. When I looked at him he said, "What are you waiting for?" I got out and dragged one of the sawhorses aside, then pushed it back after he drove through. When I got inside the car, he said, "Now you're an accomplice.[4] We go down together." He put the car in gear and looked at me. "Joke, doctor."

"Funny, doctor."

Down the first long stretch I watched the road behind us, to see if the trooper was on our tail. The barricade vanished. Then there was nothing but snow: snow on the road, snow kicking up from the chains, snow on the trees, snow in the sky; and our trail in the snow. I

faced around and had a shock. The lie of the road behind us had been marked by our own tracks, but there were no tracks ahead of us. My father was breaking virgin snow between a line of tall trees. He was humming "Stars Fell on Alabama." I felt snow brush along the floorboards under my feet. To keep my hands from shaking I clamped them between my knees.

My father grunted in a thoughtful way and said, "Don't ever try this yourself."

"I won't."

"That's what you say now, but someday you'll get your license and then you'll think you can do anything. Only you won't be able to do this. You need, I don't know—a certain instinct."

"Maybe I have it."

"You don't. You have your strong points, but not . . . you know. I only mention it because I don't want you to get the idea this is something just anybody can do. I'm a great driver. That's not a virtue, okay? It's just a fact, and one you should be aware of. Of course you have to give the old heap some credit, too—there aren't many cars I'd try this with. Listen!"

I listened. I heard the slap of the chains, the stiff, jerky rasp of the wipers, the purr of the engine. It really did purr. The car was almost new. My father couldn't afford it, and kept promising to sell it, but here it was.

I said, "Where do you think that policeman went to?"

"Are you warm enough?" He reached over and cranked up the blower. Then he turned off the wipers. We didn't need them. The clouds had brightened. A few sparse, feathery flakes drifted into our slipstream and were swept away. We left the trees and entered a broad field of

---

3. *Vamonos* (vä′mō·nōs): Spanish for "Let's go."
4. **accomplice** (ə·käm′plis) *n.*: partner in crime.

snow that ran level for a while and then tilted sharply downward. Orange stakes had been planted at intervals in two parallel lines and my father ran a course between them, though they were far enough apart to leave considerable doubt in my mind as to where exactly the road lay. He was humming again, doing little scat riffs[5] around the melody.

"Okay then. What are my strong points?"

"Don't get me started," he said. "It'd take all day."

"Oh, right. Name one."

"Easy. You always think ahead."

True. I always thought ahead. I was a boy who kept his clothes on numbered hangers to ensure proper rotation. I bothered my teachers for homework assignments far ahead of their due dates so I could make up schedules. I thought ahead, and that was why I knew that there would be other troopers waiting for us at the end of our ride, if we got there. What I did not know was that my father would wheedle and plead his way past them—he didn't sing "O Tannenbaum"[6] but just about—and get me home for dinner, buying a little more time before my mother decided to make the split final. I knew we'd get caught; I was resigned to it. And maybe for this reason I stopped moping and began to enjoy myself.

Why not? This was one for the books. Like being in a speedboat, only better. You can't go downhill in a boat. And it was all ours. And it kept coming, the laden trees, the unbroken surface of snow, the sudden white vistas. Here and there I saw hints of the road, ditches, fences, stakes, but not so many that I could have found my way. But then I didn't have to. My father in his forty-eighth year, rumpled, kind, bankrupt of honor, flushed with certainty. He was a great driver. All persuasion, no coercion.[7] Such subtlety at the wheel, such tactful pedalwork. I actually trusted him. And the best was yet to come— switchbacks and hairpins impossible to describe. Except maybe to say this: If you haven't driven fresh powder,[8] you haven't driven.

---

5. **scat riffs:** short, improvised musical phrases in the style of scat, a kind of jazz singing.
6. **"O Tannenbaum":** title of a German Christmas carol, known in English as "O Christmas Tree."
7. **coercion** (kō·ur′shən) *n.*: use of force.
8. **powder** *n.*: light, dry snow, considered to be best for skiing.

---

1. Two adjectives that can be used to describe the father's **character traits** are —

   A daring, humorous
   B dull, hesitant
   C mean, responsible
   D fearful, serious

2. The father's drive down the mountain is **motivated** by his desire to —

   F seek thrills no matter how great the danger
   G prove his skill as a driver
   H prove his concern for his son's safety
   J keep his promise to his wife

3. The boy's mother, whom we never meet, influences the events of the **plot** since we infer that she might —

   A punish the son for being late
   B send out a search party
   C celebrate Christmas without him
   D prevent the father from seeing his son again

4. The relationship between which of the following characters in the story does *not* involve **conflict**?

   F The father and the state trooper
   G The father and the mother
   H The son and his mother
   J The father and his son

5. From what the **narrator** says about himself, which of the following statements can we infer?

    A He misses his mother.

    B He is very self-confident.

    C He is a bully.

    D He is a worrier.

6. From what the narrator says about his habits, we learn that he is —

    F sloppy and reckless

    G cautious and organized

    H carefree and fun loving

    J angry and depressed

7. When the son calls his father "rumpled, kind, bankrupt of honor, flushed with certainty," we can infer that the son —

    A fears his father

    B loves his father

    C despises his father

    D doesn't know his father well

8. The **dialogue** in the story between the father and son reveals the father's —

    F love for his son

    G need to be serious

    H lack of self-confidence

    J lack of humor

9. At the story's end the son feels —

    A respect for his mother's judgment

    B admiration for his father's skills

    C an increase in self-confidence

    D disappointment in his father

DIRECTIONS

Read the essay. Then, read each question that follows, and circle the letter of the best response.

from Another Writer's Beginnings

by R. A. Sasaki

I was an ugly child. I had a long horse face, not much of a nose, and two front teeth that got in the way no matter what I tried to do and made my expressions for surprise, friendliness, confusion, and anger all look the same. On top of that, my hair, lopped straight across the front above the eyebrows and straight around from side to side just above the earlobes, looked like a lumberjack had taken a buzz saw to it. Actually, my father was not a lumberjack. Neither was he a barber; but for some reason, it always fell to him to do the job. As if that weren't enough, I had glasses that winged up like the back fins of a Cadillac—white, speckled with silver.

I was sheltered from the crushing reality of my own plainness by the reassurances of a loving family. I was no different from other little girls in that I spent long hours before my mother's looking glass trying out different expressions, poses, angles, looking for that glimmer of beauty that could make me a Mouseketeer. My sister had a much better sense of reality. She knew, at the age of eight, that there was no such thing as a Japanese Mouseketeer. Reality never stopped *me* from hoping. Had I been aware of it, it might have. But I was oblivious. That was the source of my confidence.

My first inkling of ugliness was when I brought home my fifth-grade school picture. There I was in a pink dress with a white collar, bangs cut straight across my face, their line

marred only by the Cad fins winging up to each corner. It looked like I had a mouth full of marbles. (It was just my teeth.) I dutifully delivered the picture over to my mother, without pride, without apology, in the same way I'd hand over a report card—impersonally, dissociating myself from it so that whatever the reaction, I would not be culpable. Then I retired to the stairway as my mother studied the picture.

There was a rather long silence, followed by a sigh.

You have to know my mother in order to understand just how devastating this reaction was, even in my dissociated state. My mother believes in being positive. One summer when we went to Yosemite, the waterfalls were dry. My sister expressed her disappointment in a postcard to a friend: "There's no water in Yosemite Falls." My mother was horrified. "You shouldn't write a thing like that," she chided. "You should say Yosemite is beautiful and you're having a wonderful time."

Well, when my mother saw my fifth-grade picture, I knew there was no water in Yosemite Falls; but I expected some encouraging remark. I realized the extent of my plainness when even my mother could find absolutely nothing to say. I was sorry for her and thought she deserved better: a daughter like my friend Marilyn, for example, who was cute and sweet and always took Shirley Temple pictures full of personality. Instead, she had this horse-faced daughter, whose picture was full of teeth. Teeth and wings.

So for the first time I considered the possibility that I might not make it as a Mouseketeer after all. Looks would never be my meal ticket. I would have to develop other talents.

1. To what does the author compare her glasses?

   A A bird's wings

   B Goggles

   C Shark fins

   D A car's fins

2. What does the author dream of becoming?

   F A lumberjack

   G A Mouseketeer

   H A famous author

   J A Japanese Shirley Temple

3. The author implies that she developed her writing talent because —

   A she was naturally good with words

   B beauty is a drawback for a writer

   C her sister suggested she write

   D she couldn't rely on her beauty for recognition

4. How does the author act when she shows her mother her school picture?

   F She pretends she is unconcerned about her mother's reaction.

   G She tries to show pride in her looks.

   H She tries to keep her mother from getting a good look at the picture.

   J She laughs and makes a joke about the picture.

5. What does the author realize as a result of her mother's reaction to her school picture?

   A Her mother wanted to change the subject.

   B Her mother could think of no way to soften the truth of the author's plainness.

   C Her mother was once again offering reassurances.

   D Her mother distracted herself with thoughts of summer in Yosemite Falls.

DIRECTIONS

Read the folk tale. Then, read each question that follows, and circle the letter of the best response.

Green Willow

retold by Paul Jordan-Smith

In the era of Bummei there lived a young samurai, Tomotada, in the service of the daimyo of Noto. He was a native of Echizen, but had been accepted at a young age into the palace of the Lord of Noto, where he proved himself a good soldier and a good scholar as well, and enjoyed the favor of his prince. Handsome and amiable, he was admired also by his fellow samurai.

One day, the Lord of Noto called for Tomotada and sent him on a special quest to the Lord of Kyoto. Being ordered to pass through Echizen, Tomotada asked and was granted permission to visit his widowed mother. And so he set out on his mission.

Winter had already come; the countryside was covered with snow, and though his horse was among the most powerful in the Lord of Noto's stable, the young man was forced to proceed slowly. On the second day of his journey, he found himself in mountain districts where settlements were few and far between. His anxiety was increased by the onslaught of a heavy snowstorm, and his horse was showing signs of extreme fatigue. In the very moment of his despair, however, Tomotada caught sight of a cottage among the willows on a nearby hill. Reaching the dwelling, he knocked loudly on the storm doors which had been closed against the wind. Presently the doors opened, and an old woman appeared, who cried out with compassion at the sight of the noble Tomotada.

"Ah, how pitiful! Traveling in such weather, and alone! Come in, young sir, come in!"

"What a relief to find a welcome in these lonely passes," thought Tomotada, as he led his horse to a shed behind the cottage. After seeing that his horse was well sheltered and fed, Tomotada entered the cottage, where he beheld the old woman and her husband, and a young girl as well, warming themselves by a fire of bamboo splints. The old couple respectfully requested that he be seated, and proceeded to warm some rice wine and prepare food for the warrior. The young girl, in the meantime, disappeared behind a screen, but not before Tomotada had observed with astonishment that she was extremely beautiful, though dressed in the meanest attire. He wondered how such a beautiful creature could be living in such a lonely and humble place. His thoughts, however, were interrupted by the old man, who had begun to speak.

"Honored Sir," he began. "The next village is far from here and the road is unfit for travel. Unless your quest is of such importance that it cannot be delayed, I would advise you not to force yourself and your horse beyond your powers of endurance. Our hovel is perhaps unworthy of your presence, and we have no comforts to offer; nevertheless, please honor us by staying under this miserable roof."

Tomotada was touched by the old man's words—and secretly, he was glad of the chance afforded him to see more of the young girl. Before long, a simple meal was set before him, and the girl herself came from behind the screen to serve the wine. She had changed her dress, and though her clothes were still of homespun, her long loose hair was neatly combed and smoothed. As she bent to fill his cup, Tomotada was amazed to see that she was even more beautiful than he had at first thought: she was the most beautiful creature he had ever seen. She moved with a grace that captivated him, and he could not take his eyes from her. The old man spoke apologetically, saying, "Please forgive the clumsy service of our daughter, Green Willow. She has been raised alone in these mountains and is only a poor, ignorant girl." But Tomotada protested that he considered himself lucky indeed to be served by so lovely a maiden. He saw that his admiring gaze made her blush, and he left his wine and food untasted before him. Suddenly struck by inspiration, he addressed her in a poem.

> As I rode through the winter
> I found a flower and thought,
> "Here I shall spend the day."
> But why does the blush of dawn appear
> When the dark of night is still around us?

Without a moment's hesitation, the girl replied:

> If my sleeve hides the faint color of dawn,
> Perhaps when morning has truly come
> My lord will remain.

Then Tomotada knew that the girl had accepted his admiration, and he was all the more taken by the art of her verse and the feelings it expressed. "Seize the luck that has brought you here!" he thought to himself, and he resolved to ask the old couple to give him the hand of their daughter in marriage. Alas for the Lord of Noto's quest!

The old couple were astonished by the request of Tomotada, and they bowed themselves low in gratitude. After some moments of hesitation, the father spoke: "Honored master, you are a person of too high a degree for us to consider refusing the honor your request brings. Indeed our gratitude is immeasurable. But this daughter of ours is merely a country girl, of no breeding and manners, certainly not fit to become the wife of a noble samurai such as yourself. But since you find the girl to your liking, and have condescended to overlook her peasant origins, please accept her as a gift, a humble handmaid. Deign, O Lord, to regard her henceforth as yours, and act toward her as you will."

Now, a samurai was not allowed to marry without the consent of his lord, and Tomotada could not expect permission until his quest was finished. When morning came, Tomotada resumed his journey, but his heart grew more apprehensive with every footfall of his horse. Green Willow rode behind her lord, saying not a word, and gradually the progress of the young man slowed to a halt. He could not tear his thoughts from the girl, and did not know whether he should bring her to Kyoto. He was afraid, moreover, that the Lord of Noto would not give him permission to marry a peasant girl, and afraid also that his daimyo might be likewise captivated by her beauty and take her for himself. And so he resolved to hide with her in the mountains, to settle there and become himself a simple farmer. Alas for the Lord of Noto's quest!

For five happy years, Tomotada and Green Willow dwelt together in the mountains, and not a day passed that did not bring them both joy and delight in each other and their life together. Forgotten was the time before Green Willow had come into his life. But one day, while talking with her husband about some household matter, Green Willow uttered a loud cry of pain, and became very white and still. "What is it, my wife?" cried Tomotada as he took her in his arms. "Forgive me, my lord, for crying out so rudely, but the pain was so sudden . . . My dear husband, hold me to you and listen—do not let me go! Our union has been filled with great joy, and I have known with you a happiness that cannot bear description. But now it is at an end: I must beg of you to accept it."

"Ah!" cried Tomotada, "It cannot be so. What wild fancies are these? You are only a little unwell, my darling. Lie down and rest, and the pain shall pass."

"No, my dearest, it cannot be. I am dying— I do not imagine it. It is needless to hide from you the truth any longer, my husband. I am not a human being. The soul of a tree is my soul, the heart of a tree my heart, the sap of a willow is my life. And someone, at this most cruel of moments, has cut down my tree—even now its branches have fallen to the ground. And this is

---

1. **itinerant:** traveling from place to place.
2. **mendicant:** a monk or priest who lives mostly on charitable contributions.

why I must die! I have not even the strength left to weep, nor the time . . . "

With another cry of pain, Green Willow turned her head and tried to hide her face behind her sleeve. In the same moment, her form seemed to fold in upon itself, and before Tomotada's astonished and grief-stricken eyes, her robes crumpled in the air and fell empty to the ground.

Many years after this, an itinerant[1] monk came through the mountain passes on his way to Echizen. He stopped for water beside a stream, on the banks of which stood the stumps of three willow trees—two old and one young. Nearby, a rude stone memorial had been set up, which showed evidence of regular care unusual in such a remote place. He inquired about it from an old priest who lived in the neighborhood and was told the story of Green Willow.

"And what of Tomotada?" asked the mendicant[2], when the priest had finished his tale. But the old man had fallen into a reverie and gazed at the shrine, oblivious of his guest.

"Alas for the Lord of Noto's quest!" the old man sighed to himself and fell silent. The air grew chill as the evening drew on. At length, the old priest shook himself from his dreams.

"Forgive me!" he told his guest. "As age creeps upon me, I sometimes find myself lost in the memories of a young samurai."

---

1. Why does Tomotada stop at the cottage among the willows?

   A   To find a bride
   B   To begin his quest
   C   To rest himself and his horse
   D   To beg for money

2. What is the old couple's attitude toward Tomotada?

   F   Fear
   G   Respect
   H   Love
   J   Pity

3. Why does Tomotada recite a poem to the girl?

    A To intimidate her

    B To confuse her

    C To show her how educated he is

    D To show his admiration for her

4. Which is **not** a reason that Tomotada decides against returning with the girl to Kyoto?

    F He fears that his lord would argue that she could not adapt to the city.

    G He fears that his lord would disapprove of her peasant status.

    H He fears that his lord would want her for himself.

    J He fears that his lord would deny him permission to marry her.

5. What has happened to Tomotada at the end of the story?

    A He has returned to Kyoto.

    B He has become a willow.

    C He has become a priest.

    D He has become a samurai again.

DIRECTIONS

Read the following short story and poem. Then, read each multiple-choice question, and circle the letter of the best response.

What Happened During the Ice Storm

Jim Heynen

One winter there was a freezing rain. "How beautiful!" people said when things outside started to shine with ice. But the freezing rain kept coming. Tree branches glistened like glass. Then broke like glass. Ice thickened on the windows until everything outside blurred. Farmers moved their livestock into the barns, and most animals were safe. But not the pheasants. Their eyes froze shut.

Some farmers went ice-skating down the gravel roads with clubs to harvest pheasants that sat helplessly in the roadside ditches. The boys went out into the freezing rain to find pheasants too. They saw dark spots along a fence. Pheasants, all right. Five or six of them. The boys slid their feet along slowly, trying not to break the ice that covered the snow. They slid up close to the pheasants. The pheasants pulled their heads down between their wings. They couldn't tell how easy it was to see them huddled there.

The boys stood still in the icy rain. Their breath came out in slow puffs of steam. The pheasants' breath came out in quick little white puffs. Some of them lifted their heads and turned them from side to side, but they were blindfolded with ice and didn't flush. The boys had not brought clubs, or sacks, or anything but themselves. They stood over the pheasants, turning their own heads, looking at each other, each expecting the other to do something. To pounce on a pheasant, or to yell "Bang!" Things around them were shining and dripping with icy rain. The barbed-wire fence. The fence posts. The broken stems of grass. Even the grass seeds. The grass seeds looked like little yolks inside gelatin whites. And the pheasants looked like unborn birds glazed in egg white. Ice was hardening on the boys' caps and coats. Soon they would be covered with ice too.

Then one of the boys said, "Shh." He was taking off his coat, the thin layer of ice splintering in flakes as he pulled his arms from the sleeves. But the inside of the coat was dry and warm. He covered two of the crouching pheasants with his coat, rounding the back of it over them like a shell. The other boys did the same. They covered all the helpless pheasants. The small gray hens and the larger brown cocks. Now the boys felt the rain soaking through their shirts and freezing. They ran across the slippery fields, unsure of their footing, the ice clinging to their skin as they made their way toward the blurry lights of the house.

Gracious Goodness

Marge Piercy

On the beach where we had been idly
telling the shell coins
cat's paw, crossbarred Venus, china cockle,
we both saw at once
5   the sea bird fall to the sand
and flap grotesquesly.
He had taken a great barbed hook
out through the cheek and fixed
in the big wing.
10   He was pinned to himself to die,
a royal tern with a black crest blown back
as if he flew in his own private wind.
He felt good in my hands, not fragile
but muscular and glossy and strong,
15   the beak that could have split my hand
opening only to cry
as we yanked on the barbs.
We borrowed a clippers, cut and drew out the hook.
Then the royal tern took off, wavering,
20   lurched twice,
then acrobat returned to his element, dipped,
zoomed, and sailed out to dive for a fish.
Virtue: what a sunrise in the belly.
Why is there nothing
25   I have ever done with anybody
that seems to me so obviously right?

1. In "What Happened During the Ice Storm," which element is important in establishing the **theme**?

   A Setting
   B Dialogue
   C Point of view
   D Tone

2. Which of the following influences provides the main source of **conflict** in the short story?

   F The boys' sympathy for the birds
   G The farmers' actions
   H The pretty landscape
   J The boys' fear of the birds

3. In "Gracious Goodness" the narrator seems to experience —

   A conflict
   B boredom
   C satisfaction
   D regret

4. One way the story differs from the poem is in the story's —

   F unexpected ending
   G humorous tone
   H first-person narration
   J outdoor setting

5. Which word *best* describes the **tone** of the poem?

   A Angry
   B Ironic
   C Sad
   D Reflective

6. Which statement *best* describes the common **theme** of both selections?

   F Helping others can be a rewarding experience.
   G Nature is both inspiring and terrifying.
   H No matter what we do, death comes to all living things.
   J Life is full of unexpected turns.

7. Despite their different genres, these two selections share a basically similar —

   A setting and plot
   B plot and cast of characters
   C point of view and theme
   D theme and subject matter

8. How does the genre of each selection affect the way the **theme** is developed?

   F Since the poem is shorter, its theme is not as rich.
   G Since the poem is shorter, it expresses its theme and subject matter more compactly.
   H The story can reveal characters' thoughts, but the poem cannot.
   J Since the poem has no plot, its theme must be inferred from imagery.

DIRECTIONS

Read the title and the selection. Then, read each question, and circle the letter of the best answer.

Two Sides of the Brain: Both Have Something to Offer

Physically, the two hemispheres, or sides, of the brain seem to be mirror duplicates of each other. Despite this apparent symmetry, however, scientific research has shown that the brain's two hemispheres are functionally different. The left hemisphere controls the right half of the body, and the right hemisphere controls the left half. Nerves connect the opposing sides in the spinal column and in the corpus callosum, where the two sides of the brain meet.

Split-brain research is a fairly recent area of study. It began with discoveries made while observing patients who had lost either left-side or right-side brain function. For example, it was noted that left-hemisphere damage adversely affected speech and language competence. This led to the conclusion that these skills are located in the left side of the brain. Such discoveries have supplied a foundation for further study. Advances in research tools and techniques are allowing scientists to pinpoint which parts of the brain are responsible for certain activities and responses. By recording brain waves and monitoring blood flow in each hemisphere of the brain, researchers can correlate these aspects of brain activity with various kinds of mental performance. These observations have enhanced our understanding of the complexities of human intelligence.

Generally speaking, creativity and intuition are associated with the right side of the brain; abilities of a more analytical or logical nature are located in the left hemisphere. Functions of the right side also include spatial perception and pattern recognition. As mentioned, the left side is the primary center of language.

It is important, however, not to oversimplify these distinctions. Such thinking can lead to stereotyping. A "left-brained" person might thus be classified as a whiz at math but dull and unimaginative; a "right-brained" thinker might be considered creative but unfocused and illogical. Such classifications do not accurately represent the whole picture.

A more wholistic view tells us that while the hemispheres' specific functions may differ, these functions interrelate in such a way as to enhance each other's effectiveness. For instance, the left side of the brain uses an analytical, focused approach to find a specific answer to a problem. Simultaneously, the right brain uses a broader approach to examine the problem, seeking out complexities and subtleties that the left brain might miss. These combined functions enlighten the thinker, allowing recognition of the solution. Even within a particular skill area, both sides have something to offer. Music is a good example of this. While the ability known as perfect pitch is located in the left side of the brain, the activity of listening to music seems to take place on the right side.

Numerous theories about intelligence have been proposed, many of which have been based primarily on analysis of mental performance.

Advances in biological testing of the brain are playing an important role as intelligence theories continue to evolve. The biological differences between the left and right sides of the brain are distinct, but neither hemisphere is at its best without the help of the other.

1. In paragraph 1, which word provides a clue that this is a comparison-contrast article?

   A Scientific
   B However
   C Controls
   D Sides

2. The first discoveries in the field of split-brain research were made studying —

   F adults with interesting brain-wave patterns
   G young children who were learning language
   H musicians who played instruments
   J patients who had suffered brain damage

3. In this article, the subjects are grouped —

   A haphazardly
   B together
   C separately
   D in sequence

4. According to this passage, right-brain and left-brain functions are —

   F exactly identical
   G unconnected
   H insignificant
   J distinct but related

5. What is the **main idea** of paragraph 3?

   A Human intelligence can be measured in split-brain studies.
   B Each side of the brain is associated with unique functions.
   C Using the left side of the brain allows you to function creatively.
   D Brain research is advancing because of recent technological developments.

6. Characterizing someone as "left-brained" probably is —

   F an oversimplification
   G sympathetic concern
   H an accurate classification
   J a wholistic concept

7. The focus of paragraph 5 is on —

   A a single point
   B a single subject
   C paired points
   D multiple subjects

8. Identifying left- and right-brain functions provides a foundation for the study of —

   F emotional illness
   G mathematical concepts
   H human intelligence
   J athletic training

9. Which method is used to compare and contrast in this article?

   A Context clues

   B Block

   C Point-by-point

   D Repeated points

10. What is the **main idea** of this passage?

   F Scientists are finally discovering ways to study human experience.

   G The brain's two sides perform different functions but operate together for mental effectiveness.

   H Musicians use one side of the brain to appreciate music and the other side to sing.

   J In the human brain, the left and right sides are duplicates with exactly the same functions.

DIRECTIONS

Read the passage. Then, read each question that follows the passage. Decide which is the best answer to each question. Circle the letter for that answer.

Opportunity

In ancient Greece, girls participated in sports only in limited ways and were not even permitted to watch the Olympic games. In several cultures throughout history, females have been discouraged from becoming athletes. They often had few opportunities to compete in sports while they were young.

Many United States' high schools had sports programs for females, but funding to develop well-run and interesting competitions was limited. Even if a high school female showed athletic ability, she had little opportunity to win an athletic scholarship or have a professional sports career. Athletic opportunities for females were so few that many did not dare dream of pursuing their interest in sports.

In spite of limited opportunities, some female athletes excelled. During the 1930s and 40s, "Babe" Didrikson impressed the public with her superstar athletic abilities in multiple sports, especially track and golf. The All-American Girls Professional Baseball League attracted nearly ten million baseball fans during the 1940s and 50s. In 1967, Kathryn Switzer became the first woman to enter the Boston Marathon.

In 1972, the sports picture for females finally changed in the United States when Congress passed the Federal Educational Amendments, including Title IX. Title IX opened up new possibilities by stating that "no person in the United States shall, on the basis of sex, be excluded from participation in, be denied the benefits of, or be subjected to discrimination under any education program or activity receiving Federal financial assistance." The stage was set for females to develop their athletic potential.

When Title IX became law in 1972, about 800,000 females participated in high school sports. By 1984, nearly twice as many were involved in school sports. In 1996, almost 2.5 million females participated in school athletic events. Clearly, once athletic opportunities were offered, females were eager to play.

It was not always easy for school administrators to implement Title IX. It took many lawsuits and many determined females to open up such sports as volleyball, soccer, tennis, basketball, golf, and softball to widespread participation. Their determination paid off.

Basketball has become a particular favorite of high school females, and women's professional basketball has benefited from those who excelled on school courts. One outstanding example is Lynette Woodard. A few short years after Congress passed Title IX, Woodard played on the championship basketball team of Wichita North High School. In 1985, she signed with the Harlem Globetrotters.

For many people, Title IX has become synonymous with opportunity. As females' participation in school sports has evolved, so have the numbers of athletic scholarships. As females have continued to participate and compete throughout their high school and college years, professional opportunities for them have also increased.

Perhaps some of the females who are playing high school softball and basketball will play in a professional league—maybe even in the majors. Title IX holds out the promise of success in sports to all athletically inclined females.

1. From this article, you can infer that opportunities for females in sports —

   A will continue to expand
   B have peaked
   C were unwarranted
   D have followed an easy progression

2. Prior to 1972, a female who showed athletic promise could expect —

   F a great deal of recognition
   G few or no chances to play
   H an athletic scholarship
   J a professional career

3. Why did female participation in sports increase?

   A Greater public interest in basketball
   B Establishment of more baseball leagues
   C The Boston Marathon
   D Title IX

4. Before 1972, athletic opportunities for females were limited because —

   F there had been no successful women athletes
   G females did not want to participate in sports
   H sports for females were not a major part of school athletic programs
   J only certain sports were acceptable to females

5. Which of these is the **thesis** of this passage?

   A Opening professional sports to women has been an easy transition.
   B Babe Didrikson led the campaign for more participation in female sports.
   C Sports opportunities for females increased because of the Educational Amendments.
   D Funding for high school female sports programs was too low before the 1950s.

6. In this article, the structural focus is mostly —

   F causal chain
   G composite
   H effects
   J causes

7. Which of these is a causative verb in the passage?

   A Impressed
   B Benefited
   C Signed
   D Holds

8. The next to the last paragraph demonstrates a pattern that —

   F traces a causal chain
   G emphasizes causes
   H emphasizes effects
   J shows no cause-and-effect relationship

9. From this article, you can tell that the increase in professional female sports —

    A causes increased funding for school programs for female athletes

    B contributes to a decline in scholarships

    C is an effect of more basketball facilities

    D is a result of increased participation in school athletic programs for females

10. What does the title of this article represent?

    F A cause

    G An effect

    H Neither a cause nor an effect

    J Both a cause and an effect

DIRECTIONS

Read the following passage. Then, read each question about the passage. Decide which is the best answer to the question. Circle the letter of the answer you have chosen.

Changing Weather and Climate

In a 1961 television episode, a young woman suffers from 120-degree heat. The reason for her discomfort is a change in the earth's orbit, which is moving closer to the sun. At the end of the television episode, the woman wakes from a dream to discover that, in fact, the earth is moving *away* from the sun. This is a science fiction example of climatic change. In reality, scientific evidence suggests that there is a global warming trend, and the indisputable geologic record of ice ages indicates that the earth's climate does change. The results of such changes can have a tremendous impact on human life, disrupting people's food supplies, personal comfort, and choices of places to live.

The long-term state of the atmosphere in a particular location is called climate; the short-term state is called weather. Life and climate interact and alter each other, and this has occurred throughout history. Growing evidence indicates that the great societies of the Bronze Age collapsed because a severe dust storm brought on an extended drought, with resulting changes in climate. The Sahara Desert was once fertile and green. In the last century, the surface temperature of the earth has warmed about one degree, and a pattern of increased weather variability has been noted in recent years.

Significant weather changes are occurring throughout the world. For instance, La Niña, a cool trough of water in the Pacific Ocean, shifted the jet stream and funneled storms with heavy rainfall and snow to the Northwest and upper Midwest of the United States. At the same time, it left the Southwest much drier than usual. As weather patterns shift, the increase in floods, droughts, hurricanes, tornadoes, and extreme differences in temperature may alter people's lives drastically. An intense hurricane season in the Caribbean or dry summers in the wheat belt may result in economic hardships or personal tragedy.

Intense concern and debate revolves around global climate, especially global warming. Some scientists think the warming is a natural process with inherent cycles, while others claim that human action, such as burning fossil fuels and deforestation, is the major cause. The problem of global warming affects everyone, whether in urban areas with the aggravation of increased temperatures and smog or in agricultural environments with the uncertainty of harvests and destructive storms. Both public policies and individual efforts may lessen the effects of global warming.

Facing crop failure, property damage, or health issues, people are always concerned about the changeable nature of weather. This has led some scientists to study weather phenomena and develop models to project the long-term effects of weather and climate.

An increased ability to predict weather conditions before they occur has helped prevent many communication and transportation disasters. Meteorologists still seek methods with which to make more accurate and timely forecasts in order to preserve human life and resources.

The impact of rapidly changing weather patterns on human life may be overwhelming as living conditions, scarce resources, and economic conditions are altered. Because life and climate can transform each other, all people, not only scientists, must be vigilant and active to mollify the consequences of weather and climatic changes.

---

1. Which of these sources of information would the author use to make a hasty generalization?

   A Historical facts
   B An example from a television program
   C Observations of weather disasters
   D A body of scientific evidence

2. Which fact supports the writer's generalization about weather patterns?

   F A television character suffers from extreme heat.
   G Ice ages show that the earth's climate changes.
   H La Niña affects weather in widespread regions.
   J Scientists study weather and its effects on people.

3. Which of these sentences states the problem addressed in the article?

   A Droughts are a weather phenomenon.
   B Extreme weather events are unpredictable.
   C Unexpected downpours occur.
   D Weather and climate changes impact people.

4. Which evidence of climatic change is given in the article?

   F The earth's orbit
   G Communication problems
   H The end of the Bronze Age
   J Damaged property

5. According to the article, which may be a contributing factor to climatic change?

   A Computer models
   B Ravaging floods
   C The Sahara
   D Burning fossil fuels

6. The statement that the surface temperature of the earth has warmed about one degree in the last century is relevant because —

   F temperature is a weather condition
   G it demonstrates a weather change
   H it indicates rising food supplies
   J it shows a particular measurement

7. The statement "the Sahara Desert was once fertile and green" is —

   A a fictional instance
   B a real-world example
   C a statistic
   D a guess

8. In this article, the author focuses on —

   F the problem
   G the solutions
   H both problems and solutions
   J an analysis of causes

9. In the statement "people are always concerned about the changeable nature of weather," which word may make the generalization too broad?

A Nature

B Concerned

C Changeable

D Always

10. Which of the following is a suggested solution in the article?

F Better agricultural methods

G Attention to climatic changes

H Continued deforestation

J More energy supplies

DIRECTIONS

Read the following article. Then, read each multiple-choice question, and circle the letter of the best response.

Local Hands on a New Space Project

Seema Mehta

Crystal capsules prepared by UC Irvine[1] scientist Alexander McPherson and schoolchildren across the United States are scheduled to be launched into space this morning on the shuttle Atlantis, destined for the International Space Station, a gigantic laboratory taking shape about 200 miles above earth.

The station is a 16-nation effort led by the U.S. that should be completed in 2005. The finished lab, which will house scientists, should be as big as a football field and would weigh 1 million pounds on the ground.

The growing of protein crystals is the first experiment aboard the massive lab. Protein crystals, used for new HIV inhibitors, cancer drugs, nonpolluting laundry detergent, and more, grow better in the low-gravity environment of space.

About 150 of the 500 crystal samples being sent up were made by students in California, Alabama, Florida, and Tennessee. A total of 87 California students and teachers participated, most in Los Angeles and Orange counties.

"Our intention is not just to use the space station as a lab, but as a scientific classroom for the United States," McPherson said.

McPherson said student participation is a key element, because today's students are tomorrow's scientists. He traces his own interest in science to his youth.

A Mission to Excite Kids About Space

"Since I grew up in Orlando, I saw all the early missions. I've been following the space program since Alan Shepard went up in the early 1960s," he said.

But today, "the students are simply not going into science and mathematics—they think it's too hard or intimidating or not interesting," he said. "We're trying to turn that around. Science is the most interesting thing in the world."

Researchers and the students, working under McPherson's direction, sealed chemicals into small tubes that were then frozen to minus 320 degrees Fahrenheit. Scientists placed the samples into thermos-like containers that are kept cool with liquid nitrogen. Once in orbit, the nitrogen naturally boils off, thawing the samples and allowing the protein crystals to begin growing, according to the National Aeronautics and Space Administration.

The crystals will remain in orbit until October, when they will be retrieved by another manned space shuttle.

Once the crystals are brought back to Earth, scientists will use X-rays to deduce the detailed atomic structure of the molecules.

Such studies have significant implications for humans because information gathered from the crystals can ultimately be used for manufacturing pharmaceuticals[2] and to learn more about human ailments such as genetic defects.[3]

---

1. **UC Irvine:** University of California campus at Irvine.
2. **pharmaceuticals** (fär'mə·sŏot'i·kəlz) *n.*: medicines.
3. **genetic defects:** disorders carried in the body's genes that can be passed from parent to child.

"Those protein molecules are extremely important because they are the major biochemical element of all living tissue," said McPherson, who has been involved with NASA protein crystal projects since 1984. He received the agency's Exceptional Scientific Achievement Medal in 1999. "We can use our knowledge of those to design new drugs."

The information also has applications in the manufacturing of insecticides,[4] herbicides,[5] and industrial products, such as laundry detergents that use enzymes.[6]

—from *The Los Angeles Times,* Sept. 8, 2000

---

4. **insecticide** (in·sek′tə·sīd′) *n.:* any substance used to kill insects.
5. **herbicide** (hɜrb′ ə·sīd′) *n.:* any chemical used to destroy plants, especially weeds.
6. **enzymes** (en′ zīmz′) *n.:* here, synthetic proteins used to create kinds of chemical reactions.

---

1. Which research question would probably yield the most relevant information about future experiments planned for the International Space Station (ISS)?

    A What is the likelihood of future experimentation in space?

    B How profitable is experimentation on the ISS?

    C What do scientists hope to learn from space experiments?

    D What are the research plans for the ISS for the next two years?

2. Which of the following research questions about protein crystals is the most narrow and focused?

    F Why are protein crystals important?

    G What are the results of some recent experiments in space?

    H How will the information gained from protein-crystal research be applied for practical uses?

    J What are the different types of crystals, and how does each grow?

3. If you were using a search engine on the Internet to try to find out more about the experiment described in this article, which search term would probably be most helpful?

    A UC Irvine

    B space science

    C International Space Station

    D Exceptional Scientific Achievement Medal

4. Which research question is most relevant to the information in the article?

    F What have scientists deduced about the atomic structure of the molecules of a protein crystal?

    G What techniques do master teachers use to make science and math more appealing to high school students?

    H What is the history of the U.S. space program?

    J Who is Alan Shepard?

5. To find out the design of the ISS (what it looks like), which resource would be the most helpful?

    A A recent magazine article about experiments aboard the ISS

    B The ISS NASA-sponsored Web site

    C An encyclopedia article about Alexander McPherson

    D A book about the history of the U.S. space program, published in 1997

DIRECTIONS

Read the following two articles. Then, read each multiple-choice question, and circle the letter of the best response.

What Price Glory?

Len Lewis

Your flight is delayed for the third time this week, you have 22 e-mails and 10 voice messages since you checked one hour ago, and another late night will turn into another lost weekend of just trying to catch up—let alone getting ahead of the power curve.

If this seems like a familiar scenario,[1] it's one being played out every day in the industry by a cast of thousands. When playwright Arthur Miller created the character of Willy Loman,[2] the quintessential[3] road warrior, one character uttered the now famous line: "Attention must be paid." But attention to business and career at what price?

Clearly, success in an increasingly competitive and complex industry carries a stiff price. The question is, how much is too much?

Will the legacy of the late twentieth century be a generation of managers whose commitment and passion for career and company lead to emotional distress or boardroom burnout? When does an executive's total attention to business become his or her downfall? How many boards, committees, synergy or share groups can you sit on? And what is the point of diminishing returns when building a career makes you a better candidate for antidepressants, psychotherapy, and family counseling than a promotion?

An overstatement? Perhaps! But the road to success for a new generation of managers is a bumpy one in terms of personal growth. Adding richness to daily life by striking a balance between home and office is the essence of a successful businessperson. Yet emotional connections to home and family and even oneself can be easily lost in a maze of meetings, workshops, committee work, or just the frustrating business of clearing the morning's e-mails.

Life outside the office is not a weakness. It's what makes people stronger. Taking the time to attend a school function or have dinner with a spouse or friend will not burst the new economic bubble. A child's hug after a bad day won't suffocate, but invigorate. And taking the time to decompress alone or with family—even if it means missing a conference or another meeting—won't derail years of hard work and dedication.

The solution to this dilemma won't be found in the hallowed halls of academia[4] or in the next workshop. It lies in a self-analysis of what we want to be. Maybe it is this self-analysis that has led so many food executives to walk away from 30-year careers into the arms of the new economy—for better or worse.

—from *Progressive Grocer*, May 2000

---

1. **scenario** (sə·ner′ē·ō′) *n.:* outline of a play of movie or of any planned series of events.
2. **Willy Loman:** traveling salesman and the main character in Arthur Miller's 1949 play *Death of a Salesman.*
3. **quintessential** (kwin′te·sen′shəl) *adj.:* serving as a perfect example.
4. **academia** (ak′ə·dē′mē·ə) *n:* academic world; colleges and universities.

Deprived of Parent Time?

Kim Campbell

Houses may be messier and parents may be sleepier, but that's a good sign for kids.

Across America, time spent in the company of children has become the holy grail[1] of working parents—and it appears to be well within their grasp. By curtailing everything from shut-eye to volunteer work to vacuuming, most moms and dads today are finding ways to put kids first, perhaps more consciously than in earlier eras.

"Anytime I'm not working, I'm with my kids," says Pamela Alexander, a manager at Ford Motor Company in Deerborn, Mich. To have more hours with their two girls, she and her husband hire out the housecleaning, and instead of giving time to charities, "I write big checks," she says.

With dual-income families now the norm, spending time with children requires more creativity than it did during the days of *Ozzie and Harriet*.[2] Solutions vary—from staggered job schedules, to one parent quitting work for a time, to dads picking up more of the child-rearing responsibility.

"We're in the midst of an evolution, not a revolution," says James Levine, director of the Fatherhood Project at the Families and Work Institute in New York.

Changes in technology and lifestyle patterns have certainly helped parents eke out more family time. Fast food and microwaves, for example, offer shortcuts for meal preparation. Children are also home less often than they used to be, being pulled out for activities like preschool, summer camp, and swimming lessons. Couples today also have fewer children than did their counterparts of recent decades, allowing for more parental "face time" per child.

Thanks to such changes, mothers today spend about the same amount of time with their children as mothers did in the 1960s, according to new findings by Suzanne Bianchi, a sociologist at the University of Maryland in College Park. In 1998, women spent 5.8 waking hours with their children each day, versus 5.6 hours for mothers in l965. Fathers did even better—increasing their time from 2.7 hours per day in 1965 to 4 hours in 1998.

Indeed, dads are the resource parents are drawing on most often to make up for the time women are spending at the office. Perhaps as a result, attitudes about men's role in the family are gradually changing.

"When fathers define success today, it's no longer just in terms of being a breadwinner. It means being involved with the kids as well," says Dr. Levine, author of *Working Fathers*.

Many mothers say their husbands help with everything from folding laundry to picking up kids after school. Fathers' share of housework has increased in recent years, too, with men taking over some of the duties (although not half of them) from moms—both working and nonworking.

Luvie Myers, a stay-at-home mom in Winnetka, Illinois, says that her husband can more easily leave work for a family event than a father could have in her parents' era. "Spending time with family is an excuse at work that people are willing to accept," she says.

—from *The Christian Science Monitor*, April 5, 2000

---

1. **holy grail** (grāl): ultimate, hard-to-attain goal. According to medieval legend, the grail was a magical cup that Jesus drank from at the Last Supper.
2. ***Ozzie and Harriet***: *The Adventures of Ozzie and Harriet* was a very popular TV show from the early 1950s to the mid-1960s.

1. The **main idea** of "What Price Glory?" is that busy executives —

   A need more time to do their jobs well
   B need to work more efficiently
   C need to balance their home and office lives
   D should change careers

2. In "What Price Glory?" the author's **attitude** toward the topic can *best* be described as —

   F hesitant
   G impassioned
   H bitter
   J indifferent

3. One of the **main ideas** of "Deprived of Parent Time?" is that fathers today —

   A spend less time with their children than in the past
   B spend more time with their children than in the past
   C cannot juggle jobs and family life
   D are conflicted over family roles

4. "Deprived of Parent Time?" includes all of the following types of **supporting evidence** *except* —

   F quotations
   G examples
   H statistics
   J opinion polls

5. Which article would you cite in a research report on boardroom burnout?

   A "Deprived of Parent Time?"
   B "What Price Glory?"
   C Both articles
   D Neither article

6. "What Price Glory?" differs from "Deprived of Parent Time?" because it is based on —

   F the author's opinion
   G statistical research
   H extensive interviews
   J opinion polls

7. *Both* articles discuss the importance of —

   A more efficient work schedules
   B better child care programs
   C a shorter work week
   D more quality time for families

8. Which of the following ideas is *not* discussed in *both* articles?

   F Many working people are redefining the meaning of success.
   G Spending time with children brings parents many rewards.
   H Modern technology can help solve our time-crunch problems.
   J Career success alone is not enough for a rich life.

ACKNOWLEDGMENTS

PHOTO CREDITS

AUTHOR AND TITLE INDEX